MW01010942

APPLIED SURVEY SAMPLING

In memory of Seymour Sudman

APPLIED SURVEY SAMPLING

Edward Blair
University of Houston

Johnny Blair
Independent Consultant

Los Angeles | London | New Delhi
Singapore | Washington DC | Boston

Los Angeles | London | New Delhi
Singapore | Washington DC | Boston

FOR INFORMATION:

SAGE Publications, Inc.
2455 Teller Road
Thousand Oaks, California 91320
E-mail: order@sagepub.com

SAGE Publications Ltd.
1 Oliver's Yard
55 City Road
London EC1Y 1SP
United Kingdom

SAGE Publications India Pvt. Ltd.
B 1/I 1 Mohan Cooperative Industrial Area
Mathura Road, New Delhi 110 044
India

SAGE Publications Asia-Pacific Pte. Ltd.
3 Church Street
#10-04 Samsung Hub
Singapore 049483

Copyright © 2015 by SAGE Publications, Inc.

All rights reserved. No part of this book may be reproduced or utilized in any form or by any means, electronic or mechanical, including photocopying, recording, or by any information storage and retrieval system, without permission in writing from the publisher.

Printed in the United States of America

Cataloging-in-publication data is available for this title from the Library of Congress

ISBN 978-1-4833-3433-2

Acquisitions Editor: Vicky Knight
Associate Editor: Katie Bierach
Editorial Assistant: Yvonne Mcduffee
Production Editor: Laura Barrett
Copy Editor: Gillian Dickens
Typesetter: C&M Digitals (P) Ltd.
Proofreader: Jennifer Grubba
Indexer: Molly Hall
Cover Designer: Candice Harman
Marketing Manager: Nicole Elliott

This book is printed on acid-free paper.

SFI label applies to text stock

14 15 16 17 18 10 9 8 7 6 5 4 3 2 1

BRIEF CONTENTS

SAGE was founded in 1965 by Sara Miller McCune to support the dissemination of usable knowledge by publishing innovative and high-quality research and teaching content. Today, we publish more than 750 journals, including those of more than 300 learned societies, more than 800 new books per year, and a growing range of library products including archives, data, case studies, reports, conference highlights, and video. SAGE remains majority-owned by our founder, and after Sara's lifetime will become owned by a charitable trust that secures our continued independence.

Los Angeles | London | Washington DC | New Delhi | Singapore | Boston

DETAILED CONTENTS

PREFACE

The goal of this book is to provide you with knowledge about survey sampling in an accessible and useful way. Throughout the book, we discuss practical issues related to sample quality and sample efficiency, and we demonstrate procedures that may be useful in your research.

The book has three key features. The first and most important of these is usability. Our discussion is designed to be accessible without requiring advanced statistical training. We present sampling concepts in clear language and illustrate them with real-world examples. We don't just describe techniques; we tell you when and how to use them. Early reviewers have praised the book's clarity, accessibility, and practicality.

The second feature of this book is broad topic coverage. The book covers a wide range of topics, from the basics of sampling to special topics such as sampling rare populations, sampling organizational or institutional populations, and sampling visitors to a place.

The third feature of this book is currency. The technological and social changes of recent years have brought corresponding changes to the survey research environment, such as declining response rates, the rise of Internet surveys, the need to accommodate cellphones in telephone surveys, and emerging uses of social media and big data. We address sampling issues related to all of these developments.

This book is inspired by the book *Applied Sampling* by Seymour Sudman (1976). Both of the authors began our careers working for Seymour, who was a great teacher and mentor as well as a seminal figure in modern survey methods. *Applied Sampling* was his effort to make survey sampling accessible to students and working researchers who were not professional sampling statisticians, on the premise that everyone can do better research if they understand the conceptual and practical aspects of sampling and how samples go wrong. *Applied Survey Sampling* is our effort to pay tribute to Seymour and carry his inspiration forward. In fact, as you go through this book, you will find places where we have incorporated examples or materials from *Applied Sampling* to keep them alive.

Apart from our intellectual debt to Seymour, we wish to acknowledge the guidance of our editor, Vicki Knight, and other members of the SAGE Publications team. We would also like to recognize the following reviewers for their contributions to the manuscript:

Patrick Miller, Albertus Magnus College

Ludmila Anderson, University of New Hampshire–Durham

Dawn Gilpin, Arizona State University College of Law–Temple

Neal Jesse, Bowling Green State University

Bruce Keith, United Military Academy–West Point

Lindsay A. Phillips, Albright College

ABOUT THE AUTHORS

Edward Blair is the Michael J. Cemo professor of marketing and entrepreneurship and chair of the Department of Marketing and Entrepreneurship in the Bauer College of Business at the University of Houston. He has been chair of the American Statistical Association Committee on Energy Statistics, which advises the U.S. Energy Information Administration on statistical matters, and previously served on the U.S. Census Bureau Advisory Committee. He has been a National Science Foundation panelist; national conference chair for the American Marketing Association; editorial board member for *Journal of Marketing Research, Journal of the Academy of Marketing Science,* and *Journal of Business Research;* and instructor in sampling and survey methods for the American Marketing Association School of Marketing Research. His research interests include survey sampling and cognitive aspects of survey methodology.

Johnny Blair is an independent consultant. Previously, he was a principal scientist and senior survey methodologist at Abt Associates, Inc., where he directed the Cognitive Testing Laboratory. He has conducted research on sampling rare populations, measurement error in proxy reporting, and cognitive interviewing for pretesting survey instruments. He is a member of the Design and Analysis Committee, which provides statistical advice for the National Assessment of Educational Progress (NAEP), often referred to as The Nation's Report Card. He has served on National Research Council panels to assess major government-sponsored surveys. His research publications include many book chapters and over 50 articles in academic journals and in the *Proceedings of the Joint Statistical Meetings of the American Statistical Association Section on Survey Methods.* He served two terms on the editorial board of *Public Opinion Quarterly* and is a frequent peer reviewer for several other research journals. He coauthored, with Edward Blair and Ronald Czaja, *Designing Surveys* (3rd edition). He is a Fellow of the American Statistical Association.

SECTION I

Sampling Basics

Welcome to *Applied Survey Sampling*. This first section of the book provides a start-to-finish overview of issues and procedures associated with the general sampling process. When you finish this section, you should know (a) how bias and other kinds of error arise in samples, such that a sample does not accurately represent the population from which it is drawn; (b) how to control sample bias; and (c) how to draw a sample.

1

Introduction to Sampling

Imagine the following situation. A friend of yours is running for a place on the local school board. You agree to help her by surveying local voters to learn which issues are most important to them and what they would like the school board to do.

In this situation, will you interview every single person in town? The answer almost certainly is no. It would cost too much money and take too much time to gather data from everyone. Instead, you will rely on a sample of the population. But how will you obtain this sample? Should you just interview people that you know? Should you stand on a busy street and ask passers-by for their opinions? Should you call telephone numbers at random in local area codes? Should you do some kind of online survey? However you initially select people, should you limit the interviews to adults? To people with children in school? To registered voters? If you call telephone numbers and a household has two adults, should both be interviewed? If nobody answers when you call, should you call back?

The answers to these questions will affect your results. In some cases, it is easy to see why this might happen: For example, if interviews are limited to people with children in school, we might expect the study to show higher support for school programs even if higher taxes are needed to support those programs. In other cases, the implications are not so obvious. Can you see whether it is likely to make a difference in the results to use an online versus a telephone survey? Whether it will make a difference to call back telephone numbers that don't answer? Whether it will make a difference to interview every adult in a household? (See Footnote 1 for answers.[1])

Obvious or not, these issues are important to your results, and you should know something about them. Such situations are typical throughout the social sciences, including business fields such as marketing and management. Few research projects gather data from an entire population of interest. Rather, most projects are done with samples, and the decisions that are made in drawing and obtaining these samples underlie the usefulness of the results. Samples can be better or worse, biased or unbiased, efficient or inefficient, and a poor sample may lead to incorrect conclusions. The issues can be subtle, and you should know what you are doing.

The goal of this book is to provide you with knowledge about sampling in an accessible and useful way. Throughout the book, we discuss practical issues related to sample quality and sample efficiency, and we demonstrate procedures that may be useful in your own research. Since our focus is on practical applications, our general approach is to introduce a sampling idea and then illustrate it with real-world examples. We hope that the book will enable you to approach research projects or secondary data with a better understanding of how your results may be affected by the nature of the sample and how to make good decisions about sampling.

The book will proceed as follows. In the remainder of this chapter, we provide a general introduction to sampling in social research. After giving a brief history to show how sampling has evolved over time, we introduce basic ideas about sampling and sample quality. Subsequently, in Chapters 2 and 3, we consider issues that arise at each step in the process of obtaining a sample. These chapters, with Chapter 1, provide a start-to-finish overview of issues and procedures associated with the general sampling process. In Chapters 4 to 6, we turn to how large the sample should be and how to improve the cost-effectiveness of a research project. Given this foundation, in Chapters 7 to 9, we address issues related to (a) estimating population characteristics from samples, (b) sampling in special contexts, and (c) evaluating samples.

---

1. If you use an online survey, you will tend to underrepresent people with lower incomes and/or lower education because these people are less likely to be online, so the resulting sample may overrepresent better educated, higher income people who are more sympathetic to educational initiatives. In a telephone survey, if you don't call back numbers where you don't get an answer, you will tend to miss young, active, employed people, so the resulting sample may overrepresent older people, homemakers, and people without jobs. If you take all adults in selected landline telephone households, your observations will not be entirely independent, but if you take one adult at each selected landline number, you will tend to underrepresent married people relative to single people, because the married people must split their household's chance of selection. All of these issues (and many more) are discussed later in the book.

In this chapter, you will learn the following:

- How modern survey sampling has evolved
- Definitions of basic sampling concepts
- The sources of research error: nonsampling error, sampling error, and sample bias
- The sources of sample bias: coverage bias, selection bias, and nonresponse bias
- The distinction between probability and nonprobability samples
- Different types of probability and nonprobability samples
- How to calculate sampling probabilities

1.2 A BRIEF HISTORY OF SAMPLING[2]

Sampling issues are relevant to all forms of social research, but most of the developments in sampling theory and practice have come in the context of survey research. In particular, political preference surveys have provided the history of sampling with its most spectacular events. Political preference surveys provide a highly visible "acid test" of research procedures, in that the predicted candidate either does or doesn't win the election.

Although there are mentions of censuses and surveys dating back to biblical times, survey research is primarily a 20th-century phenomenon that developed rapidly after the establishment of the Gallup and Roper polls in the mid-1930s. Surveys provided mass opinions to guide the new mass marketing that had arisen with national radio networks and magazines. They also provided political preference data and other forms of public opinion as a source of news.

Perhaps the best-known political poll of the era was operated by the *Literary Digest* magazine. This was a large mail survey that used telephone records and automobile registrations for its mailing list. At that time, the proportion of households with telephones was low and heavily skewed toward upper-income households, so the poll was similarly biased. This bias was revealed in the 1936 presidential election, when the *Literary Digest* predicted that Republican Alf Landon would defeat Democrat Franklin Delano Roosevelt, but Roosevelt won in a crushing landslide. It became the most famous debacle in the history of public opinion research. Since Gallup and Roper had correctly predicted the Roosevelt

---

2. This history was originally drafted by Seymour Sudman for Sudman and Blair (1999). For additional information, see Bethelhem (2009), *The Rise of Survey Sampling.*

victory, the sampling methods used by Gallup and Roper were seen as clearly superior to very large but biased mail surveys. It became evident that *what kinds* of people were selected was more important than *how many*.

The sampling methods used by Gallup and Roper were what became known as *quota sampling*. The method involved selection of geographic locations such as cities, towns, and rural areas with probabilities proportionate to their populations. Larger cities would be divided into subparts and assigned to interviewers. Within her assigned geographic area, an interviewer was free to go anywhere to collect interviews but was given quotas on the number of men and women as well as the number of high-, medium-, and low-income respondents to interview. Although interviewing door-to-door was one way of filling the quotas, most interviews were conducted in public places such as parks or on the street. This became the widely accepted method used in both public opinion polling and marketing research.

At roughly the same time, just before the start of World War II, U.S. federal statisticians led by Morris Hansen were devising sampling methods for use in government surveys that did not leave the ultimate choice of respondents to the interviewers' judgment (Hansen, Dalenius, & Tepping, 1985). These procedures, which came to be called *area probability sampling*, selected geographic areas down to the city block or small rural segment level with probabilities proportionate to the size of estimated populations and then randomly selected specific households from these blocks or segments (cf. Hansen, Hurwitz, & Madow, 1953; Kish, 1965). The sampling process was centrally controlled all the way through the selection of individual households. Area probability sampling eliminated interviewer influences on the sample and made it possible to specify explicitly the probability of selection for any household in the population.

Gallup, Roper, and market research companies were reluctant to adopt area probability sampling because it was significantly more expensive than quota sampling. From a sampling perspective, area probability samples required mapping and developing address lists for the city blocks or rural areas where respondents were to be drawn. From an interviewing perspective, area probability samples were costlier because the process selected specific households, requiring callbacks if the respondent was not at home. Quota sample users claimed that the results they obtained were as good as those from the more expensive methods, and usually when comparisons were made, no major differences were detected.

The major shift to area probability samples occurred after the 1948 presidential elections when all major polls incorrectly predicted a victory by

Republican challenger Thomas Dewey over Democrat Harry Truman. The polls were criticized for their quota sampling procedures, although later analysis showed that their major error was stopping their surveys too soon, so the last-minute changes in voter preference that led to Truman's victory were not detected. Since that time, probability sampling procedures that control selection all the way down to the individual household or respondent have been seen as a "gold standard" of research practice.

In subsequent decades, research practice in the United States moved away from the in-home interviews for which area probability sampling was developed. The most widely used method for conducting surveys on the general population from the late 1960s into the 1990s was telephone. There were two major reasons for the switch from in-home surveys to telephone surveys. First, telephone sampling became much more attractive as the percentage of Americans with telephones rose from less than half before World War II to more than 90% by the 1960s. Bias caused by omission of people without telephones became much less of a concern.

Exhibit 1.1   Pollsters weren't the only ones who got it wrong in the 1948 U.S. presidential election.

Source: Library of Congress, Prints & Photographs Division, NYWT&S Collection, LC-DIG-ppmsca-33570

The second major reason for the shift to telephone interviewing was a steep cost increase for door-to-door surveys. The major factor in this cost increase was the reduced availability of respondents. A rapid rise in the percentage of American women with jobs outside the home made it time-consuming and costly to find people at home, even if interviewing was done on evenings and weekends. For door-to-door interviews, this translated into a larger proportion of interviewer travel expenditures that yielded no results. Telephone interviewing eliminated travel expenditures and cut interviewing costs dramatically.

Currently, other shifts in survey methods are under way in the United States. Telephone surveys have become increasingly difficult because of complications with cellphones versus landlines, call blocking, caller ID, answering machines, and declining response rates. Meanwhile, the percentage of people who have home access to the Internet has been rising, and the cost of online surveys compares favorably with other forms of administration. As a result, online surveys have become far more common, especially for special populations that have high levels of Internet access. In fact, the *New York Times* recently marked a transition in political polling methods when, for the first time, it reported and implicitly placed its reputation behind poll results drawn entirely from online data collection (Cillizza, 2014; Cohn, 2014). Researchers also are grappling with how to incorporate developments such as smartphones and social media into survey methods. This continues the pattern of earlier developments in that "statistical theory was not in the vanguard of the changes [e.g., the shift to telephone data collection]; rather, statistical theory was developed to support existing practices" (Brick, 2011).

As the research environment evolves, sampling problems likewise evolve. While the specific problems change over time, the broad principles that came out of the *Literary Digest* fiasco and the Truman/Dewey election remain; to wit: (a) the *who* of sampling is more important than the *how many*, and (b) the best sampling procedures are those in which the researcher gives a fair chance of selection to every member of the population and maintains control throughout the research process.

1.3 SAMPLING CONCEPTS

Given this historical background, let us begin to formally define sampling concepts. First, let's define a sample. A *sample* is a subset of a larger population. The *population*, or *universe*, is the set of elements about which you would like to draw conclusions. If a sample captures the entire population, it is called a *census*.

1.3.1 Sources of Research Error

When you work with sample data, you typically want your sample to provide an accurate representation of the broader population. For example, if you do a survey to support your friend's school board campaign, and your data show that 64% of the respondents want the school district to place more emphasis on reading skills, you want this 64% figure to be an accurate reflection of feelings in the total population. There are three reasons why it might not be:

- Nonsampling error
- Sampling error, also known as *sampling variance*
- Sample bias

Nonsampling error consists of all error sources unrelated to the sampling of respondents. General sources of nonsampling error include *interviewer error* related to the administration of the survey, *response error* related to the accuracy of responses as given, and *coding error* related to the accuracy of responses as recorded. For a discussion of specific sources of nonsampling error and how to control each source, see Blair, Czaja, and Blair (2013).

Sampling error refers to the fact that samples don't always reflect a population's true characteristics because of random variation in sample composition, even if the samples are drawn using fair procedures. For example, if you flip a coin 10 times, then 10 more times, then 10 more times, and so on, you won't always get five "heads" out of 10 flips. The percentage of "heads" in any given sample will be affected by chance variation. In the same way, if you ask 100 people whether the school district should cut other programs to place more emphasis on reading, the percentage that say yes will be affected by chance variation in the composition of the sample, and a second sample of 100 people is likely to produce somewhat different results.

The level of sampling error is controlled by sample size. As samples get larger and larger, the distribution of possible sample outcomes gets tighter and tighter around the true population figure. To put it another way, larger samples have less chance of producing results that are uncharacteristic of the population as a whole. We will expand upon this point in Chapter 4 and show how to set sample size based on acceptable levels of sampling error.

Sample bias refers to the possibility that members of a sample differ from the larger population in some systematic fashion. For example, if you limit interviews about a school board election to people with schoolchildren, then your results may not reflect opinions among voters at large. Similarly, if your sample contains a disproportionately large percentage of older people because you didn't make the callbacks needed to find younger people, or if your sampling procedure underrepresents married people, then you are likely to have sample bias.

Sample bias can arise in three general ways:

- *Coverage bias* will occur if some segment of the population is improperly excluded from consideration in the sample or is not available through the data collection method employed in the research. Limiting research about a school board election to people with schoolchildren is an example of potential coverage bias (if the population of interest is the broader electorate), as is limiting the research to people with online access.

- *Selection bias* will occur if some population groups are given disproportionately high or low chances of selection (e.g., if the sampling procedure gives a higher chance of selection to single people over married people).

- Finally, even if the sample is fairly drawn, *nonresponse bias* will occur if failure to respond is disproportionate across groups (e.g., if younger people are less likely to respond because they are less likely to be available when called).

Unlike sampling error, sample bias is *not* controlled by sample size. Increasing the sample size does nothing to remove systematic biases; in fact, a larger sample could increase bias if fixed resources are spread over a larger sample, permitting less follow-up effort to minimize nonresponse. Rather, sample bias is controlled by defining the population of interest prior to drawing the sample, attempting to maximize population coverage, selecting a sample that fairly represents the entire population, and obtaining data from as much of the selected sample as possible.

People who are unsophisticated about sampling usually think that sample size is the most important consideration in sampling. In presenting research results, you'll be asked about sample size more often than you'll be asked about sampling procedures. This focus on sample size probably occurs because, in addition to its effect on sampling error, size is the most visible aspect of the sample. Whatever the reason, the focus on sample size is misplaced. Sample bias is normally a bigger threat to the accuracy of survey results than sample size. If you don't get the right information from the right people, then it doesn't really matter how much information you get or how many people you get it from.

We cannot emphasize this point strongly enough. People often ask, "What percentage of the population is required to have a valid sample?" or "How many observations are needed to have a valid sample?" as if the key question in sampling is *how many.* Or people will defend a large but biased sample by arguing that "bias may be a problem in small samples, but as a sample gets larger and larger, it becomes more credible." This just isn't the way it works. Remember the *Literary Digest* fiasco: The key issue is not *how many,* but *who.*

Sample size is meaningful because of its relationship with (random) sampling error, and we saw an illustration of its importance during election night coverage of the 2000 U.S. presidential race, when television networks went back and forth between saying that the crucial state of Florida had been won by Democrat Al Gore versus Republican George W. Bush, at least partly because their "exit poll" samples were not large enough to be reliable in the razor-thin contest. However, while sample size is meaningful, a sophisticated researcher will almost always prefer a smaller, better sample over a larger, worse sample.

1.3.2 Probability Versus Nonprobability Samples

There are two general types of samples: probability samples and nonprobability samples. *Probability samples,* also called *random samples,* use some random process to select population elements for the sample and give every population element a known, nonzero chance of selection. *Nonprobability samples* do not use a random process; instead, elements are typically selected by judgment, quotas, or convenience.

The two types of samples rely on different mechanisms to control selection bias. Probability samples rely on chance. The idea is that if selections are made purely by chance, then a large sample will naturally contain a representative cross section of the population. Nonprobability samples, in contrast, rely on some form of judgment or assumptions. The idea is that samples can be judgmentally controlled to produce a representative cross section of the population or that a representative cross section is not needed to make usable estimates.[3]

Types of Probability Samples

There are three broad types of probability samples. *Simple random sampling* is the basic version of probability sampling. *Stratified sampling* and *cluster sampling* are special forms of probability sampling that can improve the cost-effectiveness of research under certain circumstances.

---

3. We will return to this topic in Chapter 7, when we discuss model-based sampling, and Chapter 9, when we discuss how good the sample must be.

In simple random sampling, population members are selected directly at random (like drawing names from a hat). This type of sample usually gives equal probabilities of selection to all population members. We will refer to simple random samples as *srs* samples, and we will refer to samples that give equal probabilities of selection for every member of the population as *EPSEM* (equal probability selection method) samples. A variation on simple random sampling is *systematic sampling*, where every *i*th member of the population is chosen after a random start. We will discuss how to draw simple random samples and systematic samples in Chapter 3.

In stratified sampling, the population is separated into subgroups, which are called strata, and separate samples are drawn for each subgroup. For example, in drawing a sample of students from a university, we might separate graduate and undergraduate students and sample each group separately. A stratified sample can be EPSEM if desired, but the usual reason for stratified sampling is that we want to sample different groups at different rates; for example, the university has more undergraduate than graduate students, but we want the sample to contain an equal number of each to facilitate comparisons between the two groups. We will discuss stratified samples in Chapter 5.

In cluster sampling, the population is separated into subgroups called *clusters*, and a sample of clusters is drawn. Cluster sampling often uses groups that have already been defined for some other purpose, such as classrooms of students, or geographic entities such as states or counties. It is common to subsample within selected clusters, but clusters also may be used in their entirety. For example, in planning a national assessment of educational progress, we might draw a sample of schools, then classrooms within selected schools, after which we might administer the assessment to all students in selected classrooms. Cluster samples usually are designed as EPSEM samples, because the purpose of cluster sampling is not to sample subgroups at different rates but simply to draw the sample in clusters for reasons of convenience or cost. For example, it is cheaper and less disruptive to gather data from entire classrooms in selected locations than from a national sample of individual students. We will discuss cluster samples in Chapter 6.

Calculating Sampling Probabilities

A defining characteristic of probability sampling is that every member of the population has a known, nonzero chance of being selected for the sample. It is important to be able to calculate these probabilities of selection, to know whether they are equal across different members of the population, and, if not, what to do about it. The calculation of these probabilities follows some simple rules.

If the selection procedure is random, each population member has a chance of $1/N$ of being selected for the sample on any given draw, where N is the population size, or the number of population members in the particular sampling pool. If there are n such draws, then each population member has n such chances, and the total probability of selection is n/N. For example, if we randomly draw one card from a deck of 52 cards, the chance of selection for any given card, such as the queen of hearts, is 1/52. If we randomly draw 26 cards, the chance of selection for any given card is 26/52, or 1/2. Likewise, if we randomly draw one student from a school with 500 pupils, the probability of selection for any given student is 1/500. If we draw 100 students, the probability of selection is 100/500, or 1/5, or 0.20.[4]

The probability of selection also can be expressed as the *sampling rate*. For example, saying that we will draw 100 of 500 students is equivalent to saying that we will draw at a rate of 1 in 5.

As our examples illustrate, if we know the sample size and the population size, we can calculate the probability of selection and the sampling rate in numerical terms; for example, if sample size equals 100 and population size equals 500, and selection is random, then the probability of selection, n/N, equals 100/500, and the sampling rate equals 1 in 5. However, even if we lack some of this information, we can still define the probability of selection in symbolic terms (n/N) or in a mixture of numbers and symbols. For example, assume that we want a sample of 25 females from a school that has 500 students of both sexes. We will simply ignore males if they are selected, and we will draw females until we get 25 of them. Here, the probability of selection for any given female is $25/N_{female}$, where N_{female} is the number of females in the school. The fact that we don't know the exact number does not stop us from expressing the probability. (Note that we can estimate the number of females in the school from our sampling experience—for example, if we have to draw 50 names to get 25 females, we can infer that half the school's 500 students are female—but this is only an estimate.)

_____

4. Here, and throughout this book, we will assume sampling *without* replacement. In sampling *with* replacement, the selected population member is returned to the sampling pool after each draw and may be drawn again. In sampling *without* replacement, a population member may be selected only once: so, for example, if we draw Student 33 in a sample of students and then draw the number 33 again, the second selection is ignored, because the student is already in the sample. Almost all sampling in the social sciences is done without replacement, which is why we will assume it. In calculating sampling probabilities, sampling with replacement is a little more complicated, because the population member's total chance of selection is composed of the probability of being selected once, the probability of being selected twice, and so on.

Sometimes, it is necessary to supplement a sample, and probabilities of selection in this situation are additive. Say, for example, that we draw an initial sample of 50 students with a goal of getting 25 females, but the sample only yields 20 females, so we draw additional names to get 5 more females. The combined sample can be treated as a single entity—a random sample plus a random sample is a random sample—and the overall probability of selection is $(n_1 + n_2)/N$, where n_1 is the size of the first sample, n_2 is the size of the second sample, and N is the size of the population or sampling pool. In our example, the probability of selecting any given female in the school is $(20 + 5)/N_{female}$, or $25/N_{female}$.

Similarly, we sometimes trim samples, and probabilities of selection in this situation are subtractive. Say, for example, that we draw an initial sample of 50 students with a goal of getting 25 females, but the sample yields 30 females, so we randomly select 5 to drop. The resulting sample can be treated as a single entity—a random sample minus a random sample is a random sample—and the overall probability of selection is $(n_1 - n_2)/N$. In our example, the probability of selecting any given female in the school is $(30 - 5)/N_{female}$, or $25/N_{female}$.

We also might subsample from an initial sample, or draw a sample in stages, and probabilities of selection in this situation are multiplicative; that is, the probability of being selected in the first stage of sampling is multiplied by the probability of being selected in the second stage of sampling and further multiplied by probabilities of selection in any subsequent stages. For example, say that we draw an initial sample of 50 students with a goal of getting 25 females, but the sample yields 30 females, so we select 25 for retention. The resulting sample can be treated as a single entity—a random sample of a random sample is a random sample—and the overall probability of selection for any given female in the school is the probability of being selected in the first stage, or $30/N_{female}$, multiplied by the probability of being selected (retained) in the second stage, or $25/30$, which results in an overall probability of $25/N_{female}$. Not surprisingly, this is the same result as if we had dropped 5 instead of keeping 25.

In all of these examples, the sampling is EPSEM (equal probability of selection for every member of the population), and the probability of selection for any given member is n/N, regardless of how we get to n. It should be emphasized that these calculations assume some form of random sampling throughout the process. If any component of the sampling is not random, then the sample may not be EPSEM. For example, say that we draw 30 female students but only need 25, and we use the first 25 that we are able to contact, instead of randomly dropping 5 or randomly choosing 25 to retain. Here, any given student's probability of being retained in the second stage will depend on her availability. We cannot specify this probability, but it almost certainly is not equal across students: It will be higher for students with higher availability, who therefore will be overrepresented in the final sample (or, if you prefer, lower for students with lower availability, who therefore will be underrepresented). For example, if we plan to contact the selected students at school, and some students are less likely to be available because of chronic illness, truancy, participation in extramural activities, or other reasons, then students with these characteristics will be underrepresented in the final sample.

When a sample is drawn in two or more stages, even if sampling is random throughout, the sample may not be EPSEM if probabilities of selection for different members of the population are not equal (or balanced) across stages. For example, assume that we want a sample of 25 female students from a school, and we obtain this sample by randomly drawing 5 classrooms (homerooms), then 5 females within each selected classroom. In this example, the probability of selection for any given female student is the chance that her room is selected in the first stage of selection, $5/N_{classrooms}$, multiplied by the chance that she is selected if her room is drawn, $5/N_{female(j)}$, where $N_{classrooms}$ is the number of classrooms and $N_{female(j)}$ is the number of female students in the jth classroom. For example, if there are 24 classrooms in the school and 11 females in a particular classroom, each female in that room has a $(5/24) * (5/11)$ chance of selection. If there are 14 females in another classroom, each female in that room has a $(5/24) * (5/14)$ chance. This is not an EPSEM sample if the number of females varies across classrooms. (However, the sample might be viewed as "good enough" for practical use, as long as the number of females is pretty similar across classes and there is unlikely to be any biasing pattern in the classes with more vs. fewer females.)

On the other hand, a multistage sample can be EPSEM even if different members of the population have different probabilities of selection at various stages of sampling, as long as the differences balance out across stages. Consider the following case study.

CASE STUDY 1.1

A newspaper held a contest using the theme of "travel" to promote readership. During the contest, each day's newspaper contained an entry form that listed places mentioned in the paper that day. Contestants were to fill out the form by indicating the page on which each place was mentioned

(Continued)

(Continued)

and then mail the completed form (or a copy) to the newspaper. There was no limit on the number of entries: Contestants could send as many mailings as they wanted and include any number of copies with each mailing. The top prizes were expensive trips to popular destinations, and the contest drew thousands of entries.

Winners were selected as follows. All of the envelopes addressed to the contest were dumped into a large bin and stirred around, and a staff member from the newspaper reached into the bin and drew 100 envelopes. The selected envelopes were opened, the entry forms within them were dumped into a basket and stirred around, and the staff member drew individual forms for the various prizes.

A newspaper employee who was familiar with the contest felt that this procedure was unfair. She complained to a friend who worked for a lawyer, and the lawyer filed a lawsuit on behalf of all people who had entered the contest. The complaint centered on the fact that the newspaper had not opened each and every envelope containing entries. It was argued that this was unfair to the people who included multiple entries in their envelopes.

Was it? To illustrate the issue, consider two contestants, one who sends 10 envelopes with one entry each and one who sends 10 entries in a single envelope. For the first contestant, the probability of having an envelope selected in the first stage of sampling is $(100 * 10)/N_{envelopes}$, where 100 is the number of envelopes drawn, 10 is the number of envelopes submitted by the contestant, and $N_{envelopes}$ is the total number of envelopes received in the contest. That is, the first contestant has a chance of $10/N_{envelopes}$ on each draw, and there are 100 such draws. Within any one of the envelopes submitted by this contestant, the probability of having an entry chosen in the second stage, if the envelope is selected in the first stage, is $1/N_{entries}$, where 1 is the number of entries within the contestant's envelope and $N_{entries}$ is the total number of entries in selected envelopes. The overall probability, multiplied across stages, is $(100 * 10)/(N_{envelopes} * N_{entries})$. In comparison, for the second contestant, the probability of having an envelope selected in the first stage of sampling is $100 * 1/N_{envelopes}$, and the probability of having an entry chosen in the second stage, if the envelope is selected in the first stage, is $10/N_{entries}$. The overall probability, multiplied across stages, is $(100 * 10)/(N_{envelopes} * N_{entries})$. Thus, both contestants have the same chance of winning (if we ignore the fact that $N_{entries}$ is somewhat influenced by the number of entries in the contestant's envelope).

From a sampling perspective, these calculations illustrate that a multistage sample may be EPSEM even if there are different probabilities of selection at various stages of sampling, as long as the differences balance out across stages. This principle will be exploited later in the book, in our discussion of multistage cluster sampling. From the newspaper's perspective, these calculations show that the contest was fair. The lawsuit was dropped once this point was realized.

Types of Nonprobability Samples

If you cannot specify probabilities of selection, then you are in the realm of nonprobability sampling. Nonprobability sampling can assume many forms. One form is *judgment sampling,* in which researchers control sampling down to the element level and actively use judgment regarding the representativeness of elements. An example of judgment sampling is test market selection for new products, in which individual cities are judgmentally chosen to be representative of the broader market. The logic of judgment sampling is that expert judgment and past experience can ensure a representative sample.

Another form of nonprobability sampling is *convenience sampling,* in which the researcher studies whichever population members are easily available. If you ever participated in a research project for class credit, you were part of a convenience sample. This type of sampling includes *volunteer samples,* such as people who respond to television news polls that ask viewers to text answers to questions, and catch-as-catch-can samples obtained at places like a shopping mall. The usual logic for convenience samples is that they will produce a sample that is good enough for the research purposes. For example, a researcher might argue that scent preferences are pretty similar across people, and a convenience sample of mall shoppers is therefore just as good as any other sample for testing different scents of furniture polish.

Quota sampling is another form of nonprobability sampling. In quota sampling, data gatherers are given quotas for the number of observations to be gathered in various population groups (e.g., men aged 18–34, men 35–64, men 65+, women 18–34, women 35–64, women 65+) and are told to fill these quotas. The general selection mechanism may be specified—for example, an interviewer might be told to call selected telephone numbers without callbacks or to approach the first available person who passes an interviewing station—but the ultimate composition of the sample is governed by quotas rather than by probabilities.

A sample can contain a mixture of probability and nonprobability elements. Say, for example, that we judgmentally select four schools at which to test the educational performance effects of providing students with tablet computers, and then we randomly select students within those schools to receive the tablets. Ultimately, this is a nonprobability sample, because its judgment components make it impossible to fully specify probabilities of selection.

Comparing Probability and Nonprobability Samples

Probability samples have several advantages over nonprobability samples. Probability samples allow you to use probability-based statistical procedures, such as confidence intervals and hypothesis tests, in drawing inferences about the population from which the sample was drawn. Nonprobability samples do not: While it is common for researchers to apply statistical procedures without regard to the difference, nonprobability samples are technically "nonmeasurable" in that the precision of sample estimates cannot be determined from the selected sample itself, and of even greater concern, there is no objective basis for inference from the sample to the population. Also, nonprobability samples are subject to various possible biases that don't affect probability samples. These possible biases include the following:

- The respondents who are easy to get, or who volunteer for research, may not be typical of the broader population. This is one of the biggest problems in sampling. Even with probability samples, the most common way to go wrong is to settle for easy observations, such as people who tend to be home when you call.

- People might use a judgment sample to promote their own agendas. For example, we encountered a situation in which a software company was planning research to determine why sales were down in certain markets. The marketing executive in charge of the research wanted to blame the problem on poor performance by the technical service department, rather than poor marketing, so he wanted to select certain customers to "prove" that service was a problem. It is much more difficult to bias a probability sample in this way, since chance governs the selection of elements.

- Judgment sampling also relies on the knowledge about the population of the "expert" selecting the sample. That knowledge may not be accurate or may not be relevant to the purposes at hand. And, of course, different experts may disagree as to what constitutes a representative sample.

- Nonprobability samples tend to be biased toward well-known members of the population. For example, if you were asked to choose 10 representative colleges as locations for research on students' social lives, which 10 colleges would you choose? If you are like most people, your selections will overrepresent familiar names, such as major state schools.

- Nonprobability samples also tend to be biased against "oddball" population members. For example, in choosing representative colleges, most people will exclude religious seminaries, because these colleges are perceived as unrepresentative. The effect of these exclusions is to underestimate the true variability in a population.

For all of these reasons, probability samples are less prone to *selection bias* than nonprobability samples. When population members are selected by chance, there is no reason for selection to be biased unless the probabilities of selection are not equal, and it is usually possible to spot and fix such inequalities.

Apart from selection bias, the other sources of sample bias are *coverage bias* and *nonresponse bias*. Probability samples have no intrinsic advantage over nonprobability samples in these regards, because the distinction between probability and nonprobability sampling is only in the way that elements are selected. However, as a practical matter, probability samples often fare better in these regards, as well.

Essentially, it is a matter of process. To draw a formal probability sample, you must define the population and apply some sampling procedure to it; for example, if you wish to draw a sample of 50 students from a school, you might determine that the school has 500 students and take every 10th student after a random start between 1 and 10. You can't establish this type of procedure unless you have (a) defined the student population, (b) estimated its size, and (c) established some means of identifying which student corresponds to which selection. Once these matters are made explicit, you are likely to devise a procedure that covers the entire population, and you are likely to be aware of coverage problems in your sampling materials or procedures. Also, your sample will give fair representation to the people who are difficult to obtain, and you will not be able to report a good response rate unless you make a good effort to gather data from these people. In contrast, these issues may not be transparent in nonprobability sampling. It is common for nonprobability samples to produce higher response rates than probability samples, not because the nonprobability samples are truly less exposed to sample bias but rather because issues of coverage and nonresponse have been buried within the selection procedure, and the sample has been limited to convenient participants.

Given all of these points, our general preference is for probability samples. However, nonprobability samples can provide useful information and are widely used in academic and commercial research, as well as for exploratory or pilot studies. For example, "qualitative" researchers in the social sciences often use nonprobability samples because their samples are small and they wish to control the characteristics of the sample through judgment rather than leave them to chance. We return to the use of nonprobability samples later in the book, particularly in our discussion of model-assisted and model-based sampling in Chapter 7 and our discussion of "how good must the sample be" in Chapter 9.

1.4 GUIDELINES FOR GOOD SAMPLING

Having introduced basic sampling concepts, we now turn to implications of these concepts for sampling practice.

As already noted, a *sample* is a subset of a larger population, and the *population* (or *universe*) is the set of elements about which we would like to draw conclusions. In a sense, we are only interested in the sample as a vehicle for understanding the population. This means that we typically want the sample to provide an accurate representation of the target population, or to put it another way, we want results from the sample to *generalize* to the target population. There are three broad reasons why results from a sample might not generalize: nonsampling error, (random) sampling error, and sampling bias. Sampling bias, in turn, may arise from coverage bias, selection bias, and/or nonresponse bias. Overall, these points have the following implications for sampling practice.

First, efforts should be made to minimize *coverage bias.* The population of interest should be explicitly defined, so it is possible to evaluate the potential for coverage bias in sampling materials and/or procedures, and preference should be given to procedures that maximize coverage. For example, assume that we are interested in a group that constitutes only 5% of the general population. One approach to sampling such a group is to screen for group members within the general population: This approach gives every group member a chance of selection but is expensive because the group is rare. Alternatively, we may be able to sample from a specialized list of group members, such as the members of a certain organization. If the specialized list has limited coverage of the total group— which is almost always the case—then preference should be given to screening the general population, even though this approach is costlier. Higher cost means fewer observations for any given research budget, but a smaller sample with less potential for coverage bias is usually better than a larger sample with more potential for coverage bias.

Second, efforts should be made to minimize or adjust for *selection bias.* Probability sampling is usually preferable to nonprobability procedures, and it should be explicitly considered whether the procedure provides equal probabilities of selection for every member of the population. If the sampling procedure is not EPSEM, weighting should be used to adjust for differences in selection probabilities. For example, if the sampling procedure gives married people half the chance of selection compared with single people, then married people will be underrepresented in the sample accordingly, and their data should be weighted twice as heavily to adjust for this underrepresentation. (We discuss weighting in various places throughout the book, especially in Chapter 7.)

Third, efforts should be made to minimize *nonresponse bias.* Once the sample is drawn, efforts should be made to maximize participation, and preference should be given to procedures that facilitate this goal. Say, for example, that we are planning to survey potential voters in a school board race, and it will be possible to conduct a telephone survey with a 20% response rate or an online survey with a 2% response rate. In this case, preference normally would be given to the telephone survey, even if it is costlier. Higher cost means fewer observations for any given research budget, but a smaller sample with less potential for nonresponse bias is usually better than a larger sample with more potential for nonresponse bias. Again, the guiding principle is to avoid or minimize bias.

Fourth, within the context of unbiased sampling procedures, efforts should be made to minimize *sampling error.* Recall that sampling error concerns the possibility that a sample may differ from the broader population because of random variation in sample composition; also, recall that the level of sampling error relates to the sample size. In some cases, it may be possible to reduce sampling error by using procedures that offer more information from the same sample size (this is the goal of stratified sampling) or a larger sample for the same budget (this is the goal of cluster sampling). Such procedures should be used where appropriate.

As a practical matter, it isn't always possible to get as good a sample as one would like, because of limits on time, funding, or access. For example, a graduate student in education may only be able to conduct research in schools that are within driving distance and willing to provide access. A student in political science may be limited to an online survey with a convenience sample because she lacks the funding for a more expensive study. Fortunately, in most situations, samples need not be perfect to be usable, as we will discuss in Chapter 9.

Whatever your resource constraints, remember that the usefulness and credibility of your research depends at least to some extent on the quality of the sample studied. It is important to understand the issues, to be able to make good decisions, and to be able to evaluate sample quality. This book will be useful to you in that regard. We already have introduced the broad factors used to evaluate samples—the level of exposure to coverage bias, selection bias, nonresponse bias, and sampling error—and as we continue, we will add practical details regarding issues and procedures.

1.5 CHAPTER SUMMARY AND OVERVIEW OF BOOK

This chapter introduced the general topic of sampling. We began with a brief history of sampling in social research and described the evolution from uncontrolled to controlled sampling practices. We cited the failure of the *Literary*

Digest poll in the 1936 presidential election between Roosevelt and Landon and the failure of other polls in the 1948 presidential election between Truman and Dewey as events that convinced social researchers that it is more important to consider *what kinds of people* are selected than *how many.* A smaller, better sample is almost always preferable to a larger, worse sample.

Next, we introduced basic concepts of research error. We described three reasons why data from a sample might not accurately represent the population of interest: nonsampling error, sampling error, and sample bias. *Nonsampling error* consists of all error sources unrelated to the sampling of respondents, including interviewer error, response error, and coding error. *Sampling error,* or sampling variance, refers to the possibility that a sample may not reflect the larger population because of chance variation in sample composition. *Sample bias* refers to the possibility that members of a sample differ from the larger population in some systematic fashion. There are three forms of sample bias: *coverage bias,* which occurs if some segment of the population is excluded from consideration in the sample; *selection bias,* which occurs if some population groups are given disproportionately high or low chances of selection; and *nonresponse bias,* which occurs if failure to respond is disproportionate across population groups. Sample bias is a more serious problem than sampling error, because sample bias guarantees a bad result. Again, this reinforces the idea that *who* is more important than *how many.*

Next, we talked about different types of samples. We described three general types of *probability sampling*—simple random sampling, stratified sampling, and cluster sampling—and we discussed how to calculate sampling probabilities. We also described various types of *nonprobability samples,* including judgment samples, convenience samples, volunteer samples, and quota samples. We indicated why probability samples are less prone to selection bias and therefore preferable to nonprobability samples.

Given this background, we discussed guidelines for good sampling as follows. First, you should explicitly define the population of interest before drawing a sample and give preference to materials and procedures that minimize the possibility for bias in covering this population. Second, you should use probability sampling and adjust the resulting data for any differences in probabilities of selection. Third, you should try to minimize nonresponse bias and not just settle for the easy participants. Fourth, subject to having minimized bias, you should consider procedures that might allow you to reduce the level of sampling error, such as stratified sampling or cluster sampling.

Exhibit 1.2 illustrates the sources of research error that relate to sampling and the practices that mitigate them.

Exhibit 1.2   Possible Sources of Research Error Related to Sampling

Source	Caused by	Mitigated by
Sampling error (sampling variance)	Random variation in sample composition	Larger sample size and/or efficient sample design
Sample bias		
• Coverage bias	Some members of the population are excluded from consideration in the sample	Defining the population in advance and using materials and procedures that maximize coverage
• Selection bias	Some members of the population are given disproportionately high or low chances of selection	Using probability sampling and weighting the results for any differences in probabilities of selection
• Nonresponse bias	Some members of the sample fail to respond	Using procedures that minimize nonresponse and possibly weighting results to adjust for differences in response rates across groups

The remainder of this book elaborates on our guidelines for good sampling practice. Chapters 2 and 3 address the procedural aspects of probability sampling from start to finish: (a) defining the population, (b) framing the population,[5] (c) drawing the sample, and (d) executing the research. Collectively, we call this "the sampling process," as shown in Exhibit 1.3. It is through these steps in the sampling process that one controls, in turn, coverage bias, selection bias, and nonresponse bias.

In Chapters 4 to 6, we turn from the issue of *sample bias* to the issue of *sampling error.* In doing so, we turn from questions of sampling procedure to questions of sample design. We start, in Chapter 4, by detailing the relationship

5. A frame is a symbolic representation that identifies members of the population so that a sample may be drawn. For example, a frame may be a list of the population or just a series of numbers that represent the first population member, second population member, and so on.

Exhibit 1.3 The Sampling Process

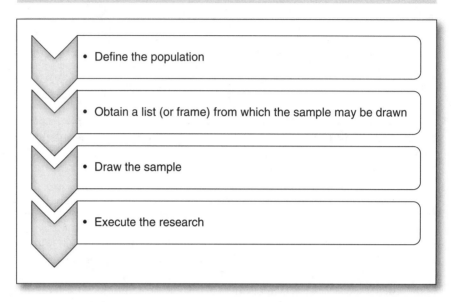

- Define the population

- Obtain a list (or frame) from which the sample may be drawn

- Draw the sample

- Execute the research

between sampling error and sample size, and we show how to set the sample size in line with one's research objectives. In Chapters 5 and 6, we discuss how stratified sampling and cluster sampling might be used to reduce sampling error.

Given this foundation, Chapter 7 addresses issues related to estimating population characteristics from samples, including the theoretical basis for estimation from nonprobability samples. In Chapter 8, we extend our basic ideas about sampling to a variety of special contexts, including sampling rare populations, sampling visitors to a place, sampling organizations or establishments, sampling influence groups or elites, panel sampling, sampling in international contexts, and incorporating new technologies into sampling plans. Finally, in Chapter 9, given all we know at that point, we discuss how to evaluate samples. We describe the information that should be provided in a *sample report* to allow users of the research to evaluate the sample, discuss the question of how good the sample must be, and close with some general advice.

EXERCISES AND DISCUSSION QUESTIONS

Throughout this book, we will provide exercises and discussion questions that allow you to think about the issues that we have covered. You will find answers to the numerical exercises and comments on the discussion questions online at sagepub.com/blair.

Exercise 1.1

A large school district plans to survey parents to measure their opinions on various issues. The survey will be done as follows. A random sample of 20 elementary schools, 10 middle schools, and 5 high schools will be drawn. Within selected schools, classes will be randomly drawn: 5 homerooms per elementary school, 10 homerooms per middle school, and 20 homerooms per high school. A self-administered questionnaire and envelope will be placed in the "home communication" folder of each student in selected classes. Parents will be asked to complete the questionnaire, seal it in the envelope, and send it back to school with their child. Is this an EPSEM sampling procedure? What is the probability of any given student being selected?

Exercise 1.2

A university wants to learn about the problems its freshmen experience in making the transition to college, so it can design and prioritize programs to keep these students in school. The university plans to gather this information from freshmen who sign up for interviews in exchange for extra credit in an Introduction to Psychology class. How do you evaluate this sample in terms of potential coverage bias, selection bias, and nonresponse bias? Overall, is this sample acceptable for the research purpose? Would the university do better if it sent a request to freshmen's e-mail addresses, asking them to participate in the research, and collected the information online?

2

Defining and Framing the Population

hapter 1 introduced the steps of the sampling process: (a) defining the population, (b) obtaining a frame (or list) of the population from which the sample may be drawn, (c) drawing the sample, and (d) executing the research. The extent to which a sample is exposed to coverage bias, selection bias, and nonresponse bias depends on how well these steps are performed.

This chapter addresses the first two steps in the sampling process, defining and framing the population. In this chapter, you will learn the following:

- How to define the population of interest in operational terms
- Possible sources of frames (or lists) of the population
- The various problems that a frame (or list) may have
- How to solve those problems

2.1 DEFINING THE POPULATION

The first step in the sampling process is to define the population. A *sample* is, by definition, a subset of a larger population. The *population*, or *universe*, is the set of elements about which you would like to draw conclusions.

Before selecting the sample, it is necessary to have a clear idea of the population that you wish to study. Failing to think carefully about the population often leads to samples that are convenient but don't match what is needed. For example:

CASE STUDY 2.1

A common error in the field of market research is using information from existing customers to make judgments about the market. Customers are used because they are easy to get, but people who *do* buy a product can't really give you the viewpoint of people who *don't* buy the product.

Consider this example. A chain of nursing homes measured its public image by interviewing every person responsible for registering a patient at one of the chain's nursing homes. These people were asked how they heard of the home and how they rated it on various dimensions. The results were tabulated every month and distributed in an "Image Report." This report showed the chain's image to be stable during a 6-month period in which there was heavy media coverage about poor care in the homes and during which admissions to the homes dropped sharply.

The problem, of course, is that the chain presumably was interested in its image among all *potential* customers, or perhaps the general public, but the population being studied was all *actual* customers. Since people who heard the bad news stayed away from these nursing homes, the research could not capture the company's image problems.

If this example seems extreme, remember that the *Literary Digest* fiasco was, in essence, a case of studying a convenient population (higher income people who appeared on a mailing list) rather than the correct population (all likely voters). Defining the population in advance allows you to avoid such problems.

To define the population for sampling purposes, two questions must be answered:

- What are the population units?
- What are the population boundaries?

2.1.1 Defining Population Units

The first step in defining a population is to define the units. Is it a population of individuals, households, institutions, business establishments, behavioral events, or what?

The definition of population units for any given research project will depend on the nature of the topic and the purposes of the study. For example, if you are doing a study of voting intentions, then you probably will study individuals, because voting is done at the individual level. For a study of home-buying intentions, you probably will study households, because homes are a household-level purchase. However, if you are studying home *buying* as opposed to *buying intentions*, then your population might consist of purchase transactions.

It is important to recognize that the data source need not be the same as the population unit. Individuals may speak on behalf of households, companies, and/or sales dollars. This use of proxy reporters does not change the definition of the population. Consider the following example.

CASE STUDY 2.2

An entrepreneur whose business was organizing corporate parties in a large city was considering a new hospitality service, as follows. When a business was expecting visitors from out of town, such as potential employees or their spouses, it could call the entrepreneur's company and arrange to have the visitor(s) taken on a tour of the city and provided with other entertainment. The entrepreneur was confident that she could provide this service better than businesses could do it for themselves. However, she didn't know whether businesspeople would be willing to buy the service, as opposed to doing it themselves to save money or show personal interest in the visitor.

To test the idea, the entrepreneur did a mail survey of all companies that had used her party services in the previous 2 years. This population contained 75 companies. The entrepreneur sent two questionnaires to each company, one to the manager of human resources (HR) and one to the chief executive officer (CEO). Overall response rate to the survey was 62%. Of the people who responded, 46% said that their companies would be interested in using the planned service.

If the desired population consisted of individual respondents, then the 46% figure would be meaningful. However, the customers for this service will be *companies,* not individuals. The data from this survey must be interpreted in some way to express interest at the company level. For example, a company might be counted as being interested only if the HR manager and CEO both express interest, on the theory that a purchase will require interest from both.

Here's an even bigger issue: Assume that these companies have large differences in size and that 7 of the 75 companies account for about 60% of potential revenues. In this case, if the interested companies include the seven key customers, then this service looks promising, regardless of the other companies' opinions. If the interested companies do not include those seven customers, then the service probably is doomed. To reflect this situation, the data should be weighted to reflect the revenue potential for each company. A company that represents 10 times as much revenue as another company should get 10 times the weight.

When you think about it, the desired unit of analysis in this study is *sales dollars,* not people and not even companies. However, dollars (and companies) can't speak. Only people speak, so the data are gathered from people. It is important to remember, though, that these people speak on behalf of the true units of interest, and the results must be treated accordingly.

In some studies—especially large social surveys used for multiple purposes—there may be more than one population unit of interest. For example, the U.S. National Crime Victimization Survey is interested both in the characteristics of *households* that are touched by crime and in the experiences of *individuals* who may have been victimized. Multiple population units can be accommodated in a single study as long as one unit is nested within another, such as individuals within households, workers within companies, expenditure dollars within shoppers, and so on. Such situations are parallel to the case just given. One population unit is selected as the basis for study design—in Case Study 2.2, that initial unit would have been companies, with two individuals selected to report for each company—and weighting is used to express results on the basis of other population units.

2.1.2 Setting Population Boundaries

Once the population units have been defined, the next step is setting the boundaries of the population. *Population boundaries* are the conditions that separate those who are of interest in the research from those who are not. For example, in a study of candidate preferences for a school board election, you might only be interested in people who are likely to vote in the election. Population boundaries may be defined by demographic characteristics (e.g., persons 18 years or older), geography (who reside in the school district), behaviors (who voted in the last election), intentions (who intend to vote in the next election), or any other characteristics that are relevant to the research.

The Need for Operational Specificity in Population Boundaries

The key point in setting population boundaries is to state them in specific operational terms so that everyone can tell who should and shouldn't be measured. "Adults in the Chicago area" is not an adequate definition, because it doesn't tell interviewers whether they should gather data from an 18-year-old in Hammond, Indiana. "Beer drinkers" is not an adequate definition, because it doesn't tell interviewers whether they should interview someone who drank one beer once in his life. The measurement operations that define the boundaries of the population must be clear and specific. Proper definitions of population boundaries take forms such as "people who are at least 18 years of age and have their principal place of residence in Cook County, Illinois" or "people who have drunk beer at least once during the past 3 months," or "people who are at least

18 years of age, reside within the Oak Creek School District, are registered to vote, and say that they 'definitely' or 'probably' will vote in the upcoming election." These boundaries can be translated into unambiguous screening conditions to separate those who are in the population from those who are not.

CASE STUDY 2.3

Sometimes it is easy to define a population in conceptual terms, but difficult to do so in operational terms. For example, in Case Study 2.1, we said that the population of interest was "all potential customers" of a nursing home chain. This definition is easy to understand in conceptual terms but difficult to operationalize. Should we define the population in terms of age? Geography (e.g., proximity to one of the chain's facilities)? Responsibility? Recent purchase? Intention to purchase?

Here is one possible definition: "people who are at least 18 years of age; have their principal place of residence in the 713, 281, 832, or 409 telephone area codes; and who placed a relative in a nursing home facility within the past 12 months."

Here is another definition: "people who are at least 18 years of age; have their principal place of residence in the 713, 281, 832, or 409 telephone area codes; have a relative who is likely to enter a nursing home facility within the next 12 months; and are the person who would have principal responsibility for choosing that facility."

The logic of the first definition is that (1) people who have already been through the decision process are most likely to have formed the opinions of interest in this research, and (2) previous behavior is more solid than intentions. The logic of the second definition is that the group of ultimate interest is the people who will make this decision in the near future. Neither definition includes the people who will actually enter the homes (essentially presuming that the decision will be made for them). Neither definition includes people from outside the area who might have an elderly relative who was (or will be) placed within the area. Both definitions include people from inside the area who might have a relative who was (or will be) placed in a facility elsewhere.

Is one of these definitions better than the other? Would a third definition be better? Before we can answer these questions, we have to resolve issues such as the following: Who makes the decision regarding selection of facility? Does the answer vary, such that some residents place themselves and others are placed by family members? How long before entry do they make that decision? How long before entry do they begin to gather information? Are "out-of-area" placements a small enough segment to ignore? Once we resolve such issues, the results can be translated into operational criteria, but the task will not be simple.

Other Issues in Setting Population Boundaries

In addition to the need for specificity, population boundaries are often set with an eye toward the cost-effectiveness of the research. This might be relevant for our nursing home example: For example, we might restrict the research to certain telephone area codes that provide a large majority of the chain's admissions, even though it is recognized that some customers from outside the area are missed by this definition. In doing so, we would be making an implicit assumption that the potential coverage bias caused by excluding certain population members is not serious enough to warrant the extra cost of obtaining these observations.

Population boundaries also will implicitly reflect any method limitations. For example, if you do a landline telephone survey, your operational population is limited to people with landlines, whether or not you state that fact in your population definition. If you don't have foreign language interviewers, your operational population in the United States is limited to people who speak English. If you do a mail survey, your operational population is limited to people who can read and write. Also, many studies are operationally limited to adult participants who live in households.[1,2]

In cases where the classification of population members depends on their own reports (as opposed to information from records), the operational boundaries of a population also may be limited by population members' willingness or ability to report qualifying conditions or behaviors. Willingness can be an issue if the qualifying condition is socially sensitive (e.g., being gay or lesbian, having used illegal substances, having been a crime victim, being human immunodeficiency virus [HIV] positive, or even conditions such as having received a traffic ticket, living with an unmarried partner, or having a certain level of income). Ability can be an issue if the condition is unobserved or vague. For example, people who are HIV positive may not know that they are HIV positive. Somebody who has been in a fistfight may not know that it was, technically, a criminal assault.

As a result of these various factors, there is almost always some mismatch between the conceptual population of interest and the actual, operational

---

1. Many studies are limited to adults to avoid legal or procedural complications associated with gathering data from minors. Also, while it has been our experience that children as young as 6 years can be reliable respondents regarding their own behaviors, a restriction to adults may be based in concerns that younger respondents will not be able to provide reliable information. For example, in research designed to measure the psychological response of New York City schoolchildren to the World Trade Center attack of September 11, 2001, researchers limited the study to students in the 4th through 12th grades "mostly to save time and money" but also because the researchers feared that "it would be more difficult to assess the effects on such young children" with the methods employed (Goodnough, 2002, p. A1).

2. The restriction to households excludes people who reside in group quarters. Group quarters are nonhousehold places where people live or stay in a group living arrangement, including places such as college residence halls, fraternities or sororities, military quarters, prisons, nursing homes, rooming houses, convents, and homeless shelters. About 3.5% of U.S. adults live in group quarters, but the rate is around 10% for people ages 18 to 24 (many at college) and 15% for people age 85 and older (many in nursing homes) (U.S. Census Bureau, 2012, Table 73).

population. The usual direction of error is toward undercoverage of the true population. This is one factor to consider in evaluating the quality of a sample.

2.2 FRAMING THE POPULATION

After defining the population, you must obtain a frame of the population before sampling can begin. A *frame* is a list or system that identifies members of the population so the sample can be drawn. A single study may use more than one frame: for example, in the United States, we might use census data to select places where we will do a study and local directories to select people within those places.

Lists generally are the preferred type of frame. With a computerized file or printed directory that lists the population, it is easy to draw selected members. For example, at most universities, a sample of students may easily be obtained by drawing names from the student directory. However, lists are not always available; for example, if you want to sample visitors to a particular website, to learn something about them and get their opinions on the site, you generally will not have a list from which to sample. In these situations, some sort of counting system must be used to keep track of the population members and identify the selections (e.g., every fourth visitor).

We will begin our discussion of sampling frames by discussing the use of lists and then broaden the discussion to include other types of frames.

2.2.1 Obtaining a List

The first and often most difficult step in using a list for sampling purposes is obtaining the list. Existing lists should be used whenever possible because they are cheaper than custom-made lists. For example, if you wish to do a mail survey of the local population to measure opinions for a friend's school board race, one way to get a list of the population is to send someone door-to-door to record the address of every occupied housing unit. A second way is to use the U.S. Postal Service Master Address File if possible. Obviously, it is much easier and cheaper to use the existing list as a sampling frame.

In fact, the availability of a list—or any other frame—can have a strong influence on the method of data collection used for a survey. For example, a survey of visitors to a particular website would typically be conducted online, with a pop-up invitation for selected site visitors to participate in the survey, because it is far more efficient to identify members of the population through their visits to the site than, for example, calling people on the telephone and asking if they visited the website. Even if there is some reason why it is necessary to conduct the survey in person or by telephone, we probably would start with an online request to participate and ask respondents to provide the necessary contact information. On the other hand, a survey regarding general Internet usage might very well be conducted by telephone, because there is no efficient way to identify visitors to every site on the web, and it would be relatively easy to identify members of the population by calling people on the telephone and asking if they use the Internet.

We sometimes use the term *special population* to refer to groups for which a frame is readily available. Visitors to a particular website are an example of a special population, as are visitors to physical locations such as parks or zoos. Other examples include students at a college (who are listed in the college's directory), members of an association (identified through the membership list), inpatients or outpatients of a hospital or clinic (identified through patient records), schools or school districts (identified through state educational agency records), voters in a past election (identified through voter rolls), and many business or institutional entities (identified through directories). Such populations are likely to be sampled and contacted through whatever information is available in the frame; for example, if we have telephone numbers but no postal or e-mail addresses, then we are likely to do a telephone survey or at least start with telephone contacts.

Surveys of the "general population"[3] are most often conducted by telephone or mail because sampling frames with good population coverage are available. Regarding telephone, companies such as Survey Sampling International maintain records of listed landline and cellphone numbers, and it is possible to extend coverage to nonlisted households by incorporating random numbers in the sampling process (as discussed later in the chapter). These companies will draw a random sample of telephone numbers for a reasonable fee, nationally or within a defined area, and this is currently the most common way that telephone sampling is done. Nationally, it is possible to reach more than 95% of

---

3. This includes population subgroups for which no special frame is available, including demographic groups such as men, women, young people, old people, African Americans, whites, high-income people, low-income people, and so on. There are e-mail and postal mailing lists that provide this sort of information, but while mailing lists are useful to direct marketing organizations, they generally do not offer broad coverage. Usually, to get a high-quality sample of a population subgroup, you have to start with a general population frame and screen down to the targeted group.

people via telephone (although, as we will discuss later, there are significant issues regarding landlines vs. cellphones).

For mail surveys, the U.S. Postal Service maintains a Master Address File, and this list can be accessed for sampling purposes. In principle, this list covers all households, as well as all other locations where mail is delivered, such as college dorms, residential hotels, and so on.

Online surveys face two coverage problems with respect to the general population. First, only 75% of the U.S. population currently uses the Internet (U.S. Census Bureau, 2012), and the coverage problem is more severe for some population subgroups. The figure drops to 68% for African Americans, 62% for Hispanics, and only 34% for those with less than high school education. Exhibit 2.1 shows that while Internet usage has grown among all age groups and is virtually universal among younger Americans, older age groups lag behind.

The second and more severe coverage problem for online surveys of the general population is that there is no general directory of e-mail addresses. As a

Exhibit 2.1   Internet Usage Differs Across Age Groups

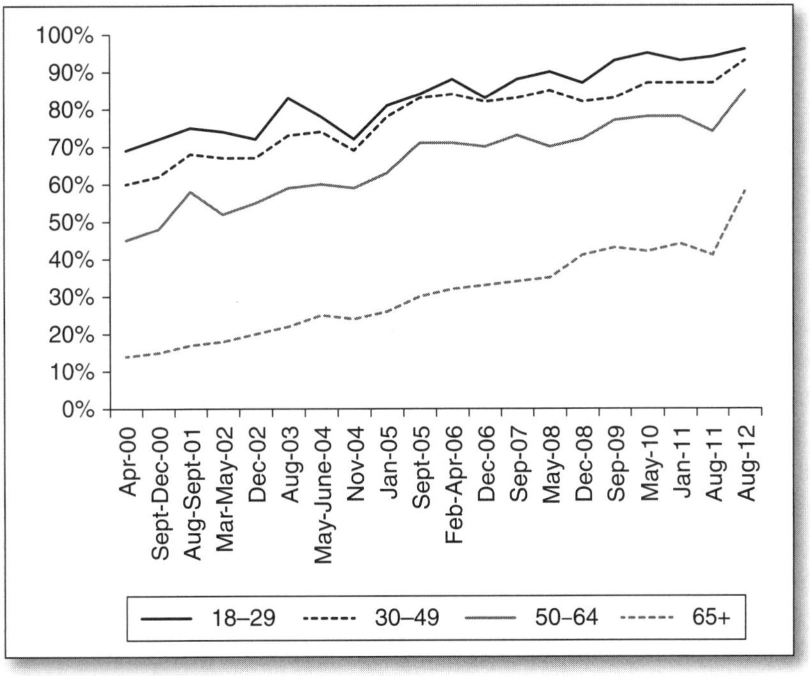

Legend: 18–29, 30–49, 50–64, 65+

Source: Data from Pew Research Center "Internet Use Over Time" Pew Research Center, Washington, D.C. (Published May 2013) http://www.pewinternet.org/data-trend/internet-use/internet-use-over-time/, Accessed on 9/23/14.

result, online surveys of the general population must rely on more limited sampling frames.

One such option is *opt-in panels* offered by a variety of companies such as YouGov. These panels consist of people who have agreed to respond to online questionnaires in return for incentives. Panelists are recruited by means of banner ads on websites, e-mail, direct mail, or word of mouth from other panelists (Baker et al., 2010). Samples drawn from these panels often are subjected to geographic and demographic quotas—that is, their distribution on geographic and demographic variables will be designed to match the U.S. Census—but this is not the same as saying that the samples are randomly drawn from the general population. The panels may have millions of members, but this is only a small fraction of the total population, so while users of these panels find them satisfactory for practical purposes, the theoretical potential for coverage bias is high. One interesting option is the KnowledgePanel (formerly Knowledge Networks) maintained by GfK Research; the premise of this panel is to recruit a random sample of the general U.S. population and provide them with incentives in return for participation in web surveys.

A less expensive option for researchers on a budget is Amazon's Mechanical Turk (*MTurk*), which has a large panel of people who participate in surveys, experiments, or other tasks in exchange for small payments. However, the MTurk panel cannot be viewed as a cross section of the general population, MTurk studies do not allow the outbound sample controls that are typical with the panels described above, and MTurk participants are volunteers who choose studies rather than being chosen, so MTurk samples have arguably more exposure to coverage and selection bias.

A third possibility for online surveys is to recruit respondents through venues such as social media and online forums. Participants in these venues are likely to differ in some ways from the general population, and further bias may be possible to the extent that respondents are attracted by the study topic (in contrast to opt-in panels or MTurk, where respondents are drawn by incentives that are unrelated to the topic of the research). However, social media may have useful sampling purposes, as discussed in Chapter 8.

Overall, online surveys of the general population face substantial frame limitations and, as a result, must be viewed as having some form of nonprobability sampling. This means that estimates drawn from these studies must rely on some form of model-based estimation, which we will discuss in Chapter 7. However, the samples obtained in online research may be as good as or better than the alternatives being considered; for example, a study conducted with a sample of MTurk panelists may be at least as defensible as a study conducted with a sample of college students. Also, online surveys are wholly appropriate for special populations that are found online, such as visitors to a website, and for special populations that have a list of e-mail addresses. Finally, online samples may be good enough for the purposes at hand. We discuss the question "How good must the sample be?" in Chapter 9.

2.2.2 Problems With Lists

Having obtained a list, you must deal with problems in the list. Ideally, a list will contain every member of the population once and only once (i.e., there will be a one-to-one correspondence between the list and the population). Few lists meet this standard, and the sampling procedures must compensate for the list's deficiencies.

It is useful at the outset to point out that almost all lists one is likely to use for sampling have been constructed for some other specific purpose, such as organization membership lists, directories of professionals (such as physicians), or for the purpose of a business service to the population, such as listed telephone numbers. When this fact is noted, it becomes clear why certain characteristics of a list or changes in a list may be of concern for sampling: The processes that produce or change these list memberships do not occur at random but are related to the list's purpose. For example, if we consider the characteristics of categories of physicians who are included on a list, are in the process of being added to a list (newly licensed physicians), or are listed but should not be (deceased), it is clear how a sample chosen from that list may differ from the target physician population of interest and, furthermore, how those differences may be related to the survey variables about which we plan to collect information.

There are four ways that list and population elements can deviate from one-to-one correspondence:

- First, there can be population members that aren't listed. This is called *omission,* because the population element has been omitted from the list.
- Second, there can be listings that aren't in the population. This is called *ineligibility,* because the listed element is not a member of the population and therefore is ineligible for selection into the sample.

- Third, there can be two or more listings corresponding to a given population member. This is called *duplication,* because the population member is duplicated in the list.
- Fourth, there can be two or more population members corresponding to a given listing. This is called *clustering,* because the list member corresponds to a cluster of population elements.

The four list problems and their effects can be illustrated by thinking about a telephone directory (i.e., a list of landline telephones) as a list of adults, as follows.

- The directory *omits* people who have moved to town recently or have unlisted telephone numbers, no telephone, or only a cellphone not covered by the directory. As a result, these people will be omitted from any sample drawn from the directory. This will produce a sample that underrepresents groups such as new residents, schoolteachers with unlisted phones, poor people with no phones, and young people without landlines. More generally, it will create potential coverage bias due to undercoverage of the population.

- Many telephone directory listings are for businesses. These listings are *ineligible* for a sample of households or individuals. Furthermore, if we are interested in a population such as people who are likely to vote in an upcoming election, the telephone directory will contain many listings for people who are not registered or not likely to vote and hence *ineligible* for the purpose at hand. If these ineligibles are included in the survey, they may skew the results, resulting in coverage bias due to overcoverage.

- Some self-employed people such as doctors and lawyers may have two or more listings, without any clear indication that either is an office listing and therefore ineligible. If something is not done about these *duplications,* then the sample will contain a disproportionately large number of professionals. To see why this is true, consider the fact that selections are drawn from the list, not directly from the population. If professionals make up 5% of the population but 10% of the list, then a random sample from the list will be 10% professionals. This is a form of selection bias.

- Most households only have one landline listing, regardless of how many adults live in the household. Adults who live in two-adult households will have only half the chance of being selected that single adults will have. This is because the *clustered* population members (such as married couples) must share one listing and therefore one chance of selection, while the single adult does not share a chance. To put it another way, if single adults make up 5% of the population but 10% of the telephone listings, then 10% of the sample will be single adults. If something is not done about clustering, a sample from the telephone directory will overrepresent single adults, many of whom are relatively young or relatively old. Again, this is a form of selection bias.

Fortunately, even though frame problems are unavoidable in most studies, we have methods for dealing with them, as shown in Exhibit 2.2 and discussed below.

Exhibit 2.2 Snapshot of Problems With Sampling Frames

Problem	Picture[a]	Result	Possible solutions
Omissions (population elements omitted from the list)	P –	Possible coverage bias from undercoverage of omitted elements	• Ignore omissions • Augment the list • Replace the list
Ineligibles (list elements that aren't in the population)	– L	Possible coverage bias from overcoverage of ineligible elements	• Drop ineligibles and adjust sample size
Duplications (multiple listings for population elements)	$P{<}{}^{L}_{L}$	Possible selection bias from overrepresentation of duplicated elements	• Cross-check the list • Subsample duplicates • Weight the data
Clustering (multiple population elements per listing)	${}^{P}_{P}{>}L$	Possible selection bias from underrepresentation of clustered elements	• Take the whole cluster • Subsample within clusters • Weight the data
Ideal (one-to-one correspondence between population and list elements)	P – L		

a. P represents a population element and L represents a corresponding listing.

2.2.3 Coping With Omissions

The most common way of coping with omissions is to ignore them—or attempt to repair them[4]—and hope that the resulting bias is not serious. This approach usually makes sense if the list contains over 90% of the population and does not omit important subgroups. As list coverage declines, however, it becomes more and more necessary to compensate for list deficiencies, on the assumption that omissions do not occur at random; omitted elements are likely to have some characteristics in common. Thus, as the list's omissions increase, so may the potential for introducing bias into a sample selected from it, even though at the time of sampling, one may not know exactly why.

We will discuss various ways of compensating for omissions:

- Random-digit dialing
- Incorporating cellphones
- Address-based sampling
- Registration-based sampling
- Half-open intervals
- Dual-frame sampling

Of course, an evaluation of list coverage requires a reliable outside estimate of the size of the population. Estimates of this type often are made on the basis of U.S. Census reports, but sometimes it is necessary to do a test study to find members of the target population and determine what percentage of them are listed.

Random-Digit Dialing

Many residential landline numbers are unlisted, especially in large cities and among certain types of people. To avoid the coverage bias that might result in telephone surveys, researchers use random-digit dialing (RDD) to reach unlisted as well as listed numbers. *Random-digit dialing* is the dialing of random

---

4. In addition to pure omissions, lists may suffer from incomplete or incorrect information that makes some listings inaccessible, which effectively turns them into omissions. For example, a list might have outdated addresses, or street addresses without telephone numbers or names without e-mail addresses. If the problems are not so severe as to make the list useless, we proceed to draw the sample, and for selected elements that lack the needed contact information, we turn to Google, social media, telephone calls, or whatever means possible to get that information.

numbers in working telephone exchanges so that unlisted numbers can be included.[5]

Researchers who use RDD for the first time often ask, "Won't people with unlisted numbers be upset about the call and refuse to participate?" Actually, cooperation rates for people with unlisted numbers are roughly as high as for people with listed numbers. This also is true for people who have registered for the U.S. Do Not Call list. Most people don't get unlisted or Do Not Call numbers to avoid research interviews, and most don't mind if they are called for this purpose. Some respondents will ask the interviewer how he or she got the number, so interviewers should be given a description of the sampling procedure to read to those who ask, but this is good practice in any survey.

The problem with random dialing is that, while it reaches unlisted numbers, it can be costly because it also reaches a large number of business and nonworking numbers. Several procedures are used to reduce the fraction of unusable numbers obtained in random dialing. A method developed by Mitofsky and Waksberg (Waksberg, 1978) starts with a screening call to a number selected at random from a working telephone exchange. If this first number is a working number, additional calls are made within the bank of 100 numbers until a prespecified number of households, usually three to five, are obtained. For example, suppose the number dialed is 217-555-1234 and it is a working household number. Additional calls will be made at random to the bank of numbers between 217-555-1200 and 1299 until the desired number of households is obtained. If the initial number is not a working number, no additional numbers will be used from that series. The major saving from this procedure is that banks with no working numbers are quickly eliminated. Mitofsky-Waksberg sampling usually yields about 50% working household numbers.

A drawback of the Mitofsky-Waksberg procedure is that it is cumbersome to implement. Having hit a working household number in a telephone bank, you will seek some number of additional households from the same bank: say, for purposes of example, three additional households. So you draw three random numbers within the bank and call them. Not all of the three will be working household numbers, so you replace the nonworking numbers. You continue to repeat this process until you have the desired number of working numbers. The process can be time-consuming, with a lot of back-and-forth between data collection and sampling.

---

5. This section focuses on procedures for sampling residential landlines. Cellphones are discussed in the next section.

A simpler and more common form of RDD is *list-assisted sampling*. Companies such as Survey Sampling International maintain a list of all listed telephone numbers in the United States, sorted into numeric sequence. These companies also have compiled a list of business telephone numbers and can eliminate known business numbers by matching the two lists. The resulting list is used to identify telephone banks that are known to have at least one working household number and to eliminate banks that have no listed household numbers. A sample of random telephone numbers is then drawn from the retained banks. The sample can be completely random from the retained banks or can be allocated in proportion to the number of listed numbers in each bank.

Exhibit 2.3 shows how list-assisted sampling works. Imagine that there are four telephone banks, each with 100 possible numbers. Of the 100 possible numbers in Bank A, 80 are working household numbers with 60 listed and 20 nonlisted; in Bank B, 60 are working household numbers with 40 listed and 20 nonlisted; in Bank C, 4 are working household numbers with none listed and 4 nonlisted; and in Bank D, none are working household numbers. Across the four banks, 144 of the 400 possible numbers (36%) are working household numbers, with 100 listed (69.4% of the 144 working household numbers) and 44 nonlisted (30.6% of the working household numbers). Now, assume that we will draw a sample of 100 numbers from these telephone banks. Here's what we will get under various systems:

- If we use simple RDD without list assistance and simply draw 100 random numbers in the four banks, we expect to draw 25 numbers per bank. Since 80% of the numbers in Bank A correspond to working household numbers (60% listed and 20% nonlisted), we expect 20 of the 25 selections to be working household numbers (15 listed and 5 nonlisted). Likewise, the 25 selections in Bank B should produce 15 working household numbers (10 listed and 5 nonlisted), the 25 selections in Bank C should produce 1 working household number (nonlisted), and the 25 selections in Bank D will produce no working household numbers. In total, we will get 36 working household numbers (36% of the 100 numbers drawn), with 25 listed (69.4% of the working household numbers) and 11 nonlisted (30.6% of the working household numbers). In other words, our sample will perfectly mirror the population (subject to sampling error in the exact composition of the sample).

- If we use simple list-assisted RDD, we will eliminate Bank C and Bank D because they have no listed household numbers, and our 100 selections will be made entirely in Bank A and Bank B. If we draw 100 random numbers in these

Exhibit 2.3 How List-Assisted RDD Works

		Bank A	Bank B	Bank C	Bank D	Total
Total population	Numbers in bank	100	100	100	100	400
	Working HH numbers	80	60	4	0	144
	Listed/nonlisted	60/20	40/20	0/4	0/0	100/44
Simple RDD sample	Numbers selected	25	25	25	25	100
	Working HH selected	20	15	1	0	36
	Listed/nonlisted	15/5	10/5	0/1	0/0	25/11
Simple list-assisted RDD	Numbers selected	50	50	0	0	100
	Working HH selected	40	30			70
	Listed/nonlisted	30/10	20/10			50/20
Proportional list-assisted RDD	Numbers selected	60	40	0	0	100
	Working HH selected	48	24			72
	Listed/nonlisted	36/12	16/8			52/20

two banks, we expect to draw 50 numbers per bank. The 50 numbers in Bank A should produce 40 working household numbers (30 listed and 10 nonlisted), and the 50 numbers in Bank B should produce 30 working household numbers (20 listed and 10 nonlisted). In total, we will get 70 working household numbers (70% of the 100 numbers drawn), with 50 listed (71.4% of the working household numbers) and 20 nonlisted (28.6% of the working household numbers). The sample is much more efficient than a simple RDD sample—it yields many more working household numbers—but nonlisted numbers are slightly underrepresented as a result of omitting working banks that don't have any listed numbers (Bank C in this example).

- If we use proportional list-assisted RDD, we will eliminate Bank C and Bank D because they have no listed household numbers, and our 100 selections will be made entirely in Bank A and Bank B. Since Bank A has 60 listed numbers and Bank B has 40, 60% of the sample will be allocated to Bank A (i.e., 60 random numbers will be chosen in this bank), and 40% of the sample will be allocated to Bank B (40 random numbers). The 60 selections in Bank A should produce 48 working household numbers (36 listed and 12 nonlisted), and the 40 selections in Bank B should produce 24 working household numbers (16 listed and 8 nonlisted). In total, we will get 72 working household numbers (72% of the 100 numbers drawn), with 52 listed (72.2% of the working household numbers) and 20 nonlisted (27.8% of the working household numbers). This sample is even more efficient than simple list-assisted sampling, as a result of shifting selections toward the more heavily populated bank, but it has another source of bias. To the extent that a bank has fewer listed household numbers because it has a higher rate of nonlisted households (rather than simply having fewer households), it will be unfairly penalized in the allocation scheme. In our example, Bank B should have received 3/4 as many selections as Bank A, because it has 3/4 as many working household numbers, but it only received 2/3 as many selections because it had a higher rate of nonlisted households. As with the exclusion of working banks that don't have listed numbers (such as Bank C), the effect is to slightly underrepresent nonlisted numbers.

Like the Mitofsky-Waksberg procedure, list-assisted RDD sampling gains efficiency by eliminating banks of nonworking numbers: Currently, in a national sample, simple list-assisted RDD yields about 55% working household numbers, and proportional list-assisted RDD yields about 65% households. Like Mitofsky-Waksberg, list-assisted sampling has the ability to reach nonlisted households, although it slightly underrepresents these households, with the bias being larger for proportional list assistance. In preference to Mitofsky-Waksberg, list-assisted sampling yields a simple random sample and does not require you to dispose of one number before you can proceed to another.

Somewhat looser RDD methods combine the use of directories with random dialing. Two such methods are to (a) select a sample of numbers from a telephone directory and "add 1" to the last digit of each selected number, so that 555-1234 becomes 555-1235, and (b) select a sample of numbers from the directory and replace the last two digits of each selected number with a two-digit random number. These methods, like Mitofsky-Waksberg, yield about 50% working household numbers.

"Add 1" or "replace two" sampling may be useful for student projects done with local populations, because these methods are easy to implement and allow you to draw an RDD sample without having money to buy one (assuming you have access to a list of local telephone numbers). In general, though, we strongly recommend buying a list-assisted sample if resources are available. The quality of these samples is ensured, and cost efficiencies in doing the research will more than make up for the cost of the sample.

Incorporating Cellphones

Effective telephone sampling strategies must deal with the evolving population of households that are landline only, cell only, or both landline and cell. As of 2012, roughly 35% of American households were cell only, and another 15% received all or almost all of their calls on a wireless phone despite also having a landline (Blumberg & Luke, 2012). The use of "cell only" varies substantially across population subgroups, as shown in Exhibit 2.4. U.S. adults with only wireless service (no landline) are disproportionately younger, poorer, and renters. Clearly, failure to incorporate cellphones into telephone survey designs may lead to coverage bias.

This is not simply an American phenomenon. In explaining why Israeli pollsters badly miscalled the 2012 elections in that country, an editorial in the *Jewish Daily Forward* noted that "(Israeli) pollsters tend to only call landlines, effectively excluding huge swaths of the population ... not coincidentally, mobile phone users are the type of younger voter more likely to support (the party that did better than expected)" (*Jewish Daily Forward*, February 8, 2013).

One conceptually straightforward approach to dealing with cellphones is to select and combine samples from both a landline frame and a cellphone frame. Brick et al. (2007) describe a study specifically designed to evaluate such dual-frame designs. Using samples drawn by Survey Sampling International, a list-assisted RDD sample was combined with a cell sample from 1,000-number blocks identified as cellular in the commercial Telcordia database. In such designs, postsurvey weighting (as discussed in Chapter 7) is needed to adjust for overlap between the frames and any differences in selection probabilities.

Guterbock, Diop, Ellis, Le, and Holmes (2008) have proposed an alternative that dispenses with conventional RDD landline sampling. They argue that households with unlisted landlines and no cellphone are only a few percent of the total U.S. population and that researchers can obtain adequate population coverage by combining a sample of *listed* landline numbers with an RDD sample of cellphone numbers.

The most recent summary of cellphone survey methods is the report by the American Association for Public Opinion Research (AAPOR) Cell Phone Task Force (2010). That report concludes that "it remains premature to try to establish standards on the various issues as it is too soon in the history of surveying respondents in the U.S. reached via cell phone numbers to know with great confidence what should and should not be regarded as a best practice" (p. 16).

A sampling issue addressed in that report is whether to use (a) an overlapping dual-frame design in which respondents in the cellphone sample may also

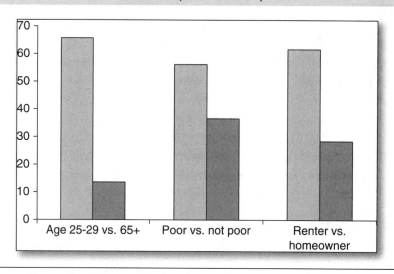

Exhibit 2.4 Percentage of Adults With Cellphone Only (No Landline) Within Selected Population Groups

Source: Centers for Disease Control and Prevention. Retrieved from http://www.cdc.gov/nchs/nhis.htm

have landlines or (b) a dual-frame design with screening of the cellphone sample for cell-only status (and possibly for cell-mostly status). The two types of designs have different implications for how data from the landline and cell samples are combined into overall population estimates. The report does not recommend one over the other and concludes that either design might be the better choice based on the particulars of a given survey.

The AAPOR report notes that nonresponse in RDD cellphone surveys is somewhat greater than in comparable RDD landline surveys in the United States (although the difference has been shrinking over time), which makes cellphone samples somewhat more vulnerable to nonresponse bias. The report discusses various operational issues that affect response rates, including the best times of day for calling (which differ from landline phones), the maximum number and frequency of callbacks, transmitting accurate Caller ID information when dialing a cellphone, and keeping a Do Not Call list for cellphone owners who request that they not be called back.

Finally, the AAPOR report recommends that (1) researchers should explain the method by which the cellphone numbers used in a survey were selected; (2) if RDD telephone surveys do *not* sample cellphone numbers, then researchers should provide an explanation of how excluding cellphone owners might or might not affect the survey's results; and (3) researchers should explain any weighting of cellphone samples, including why the sample was not weighted if that is the case.

Address-Based Sampling

The main alternative to RDD designs for maximizing household coverage in surveys of the general population is address-based sampling (ABS), which uses a frame derived from the U.S. Postal Service (USPS) Computerized Delivery Sequence file (see Roth, Han, & Montaquila, 2013, for an examination of frame quality). It is possible to extend the coverage of this frame with a supplemental file available from the USPS, the No-Stat file, which includes additional rural addresses that do not get direct delivery of mail (Shook-Sa, 2013).

Address-based sampling is a natural fit for mail or in-home surveys. Also, many addresses in the Delivery Sequence file can be linked to phone numbers, which creates the possibility of mixed-mode designs (Iannacchione, 2011). Boyle, Fleeman, Kennedy, Lewis, and Weiss (2012) used such a design in which the ABS addresses were matched to listed telephone numbers. Approximately half of a sample of 10,000 addresses was matched. The remaining addresses (assumed to include cell-only and landline-plus-cell households) were sent a mail survey that included a cash incentive to provide a phone number by return mail. The returned questionnaires included cell-only and dual-use households in about equal numbers. This approach permitted weighted estimates for all population groups. Brick et al. (2012) used a similar approach in a two-state survey.

ABS survey methods are relatively new and continue to be refined. In an article summarizing current ABS methodologies, Iannacchione (2011) suggests that one "read [the] article quickly. By the time you're finished, parts of it will likely be out of date." However, ABS surveys are rapidly becoming more prevalent at research organizations with sufficient resources and expertise.

More generally, sample design for telephone or mixed-mode surveys is currently in flux, and the rapidly changing technical and behavioral context of modern surveys suggests that best practices are likely to remain a moving target.

Registration-Based Sampling

Registration-based sampling (RBS) is a variation on address-based sampling that is used in political surveys. In RBS, lists of registered voters are used as the sampling frame. A typical registration record contains the name and mailing address of each voter along with date of birth and date of registration (Green & Gerber, 2006). This information can be augmented with records of turnout in past elections, including turnout in party primaries.

Registration-based sampling can be implemented in two broad ways. First, the lists may be used "as is" to draw a random sample of registered voters. Second, if the research is being conducted to measure voter preferences in an upcoming election, the lists may be modified to reflect likely turnout in the election. For example, based on turnout records from previous elections, the listed elements may be divided into groups with different probabilities of voting in the upcoming election, and these groups may be sampled in proportion to their probability of voting. This will produce survey results that are implicitly weighted for likely turnout.

As with address-based sampling, registration-based sampling is a natural fit for mail or in-home surveys. However, political pollsters normally prefer data collection modes such as telephone or web that allow more timely results (including overnight polls to gauge public reaction to advertisements, debates, or news events). Using RBS for telephone or web surveys requires a transition from mailing addresses, which are given in voter registration records, to telephone numbers or e-mail addresses, which are not. For example, Green and

Gerber (2006) attempted to link telephone numbers to voter registration records and were able to do so for 65% to 70% of selected voters in Maryland, New York, Pennsylvania, and South Dakota (although some of the phone numbers were outdated). Barber, Mann, Monson, and Patterson (2014) sent a letter to selected voters in Colorado, Florida, and Utah asking them to access a survey website and got response rates of 5% to 7%.

An obvious problem in using RBS for telephone or web surveys is the number of potential respondents lost in translation from addresses to phone numbers or web: more than 30% for Green and Gerber (2006) and more than 90% for Barber et al. (2014). Green and Gerber also report evidence that the loss varied across population subgroups; for example, the Maryland sample underrepresented African Americans, and the New York and Pennsylvania samples underrepresented urban dwellers.

Another problem with RBS is that it may fail to capture newly registered voters. The number of voters missed for this reason will vary from place to place, depending on population characteristics such as age and mobility, how quickly local voting authorities update their lists, and whether the place allows same-day registration. Also, if turnout in prior elections is used to modify probabilities of selection, the result may improperly represent irregular voters who are energized by a particular candidate or issue.

The coverage problems that result from inability to match telephone numbers to registration records, or failure to capture new registrants, can be addressed by supplementing a registration-based sample with a random-digit dialing sample (cf. Mitofsky, Bloom, Lenski, Dingman, & Agiesta, 2005). This is an example of dual-frame sampling, which is discussed later in this chapter.

Half-Open Intervals

Next on our list of possible ways to compensate for omission is the use of *half-open intervals*. In this method, the set of potential population elements is divided into subgroups, and one element in each subgroup is designated as "open." If the open element is drawn for the sample, then the full subgroup is searched for unlisted population members, and any unlisted elements discovered in this process are included in the sample.

For example, in household surveys with personal interviews, you might divide the population into street blocks, and you might designate street numbers ending in "01" as the open elements on each block. So, if you draw the address 3701 Southmore Avenue, then you would search the 3700 block for unlisted housing units and add them to the sample.

The half-open interval gives unlisted elements the same chance of being drawn in the sample as the open element to which they are linked. Of course, if an open element is itself unlisted, then there is no chance of selecting it or other unlisted elements in its subgroup, which may cause some bias in the sample. This potential bias is not a practical problem if the list coverage rate is high but becomes more of a concern as coverage drops.

When using this method, keep the subgroups small, to limit the possibility of swamping the sample with a large number of unlisted elements from a single subgroup. In a household survey, we once had a situation in which an open element led to a new, unlisted high-rise building with hundreds of residents, in a study that was designed to study only 200 households in total. In such situations, the usual response is to take some but not all of the unlisted elements—for example, to take a maximum of three unlisted elements from any open unit and weight those elements as needed to adjust for the full number of unlisted elements in the unit.

While the half-open interval method works well in theory, it may not work so well in practice. Eckman and O'Muircheartaigh (2011) conducted an assessment of the procedure in a sample of housing units in neighborhoods of Seattle, Washington; Providence, Rhode Island; and Oakland, California. They found that interviewers had a low rate of success in reporting housing units that had been deliberately dropped from the area listing given to them. Their overall conclusion is that the half-open interval method does not produce satisfactory results and should not be used unless working from a frame with a "good deal of undercoverage which is believed to lead to undercoverage bias" (p. 130).

Dual-Frame Designs

We have mentioned dual-frame designs in which telephone numbers are drawn from two separate lists, one for landlines and one for cellphones. We also mentioned dual-frame designs in which prospective voters are drawn through a combination of registration-based sampling and random-digit dialing. More broadly, one might compensate for omissions by separating the population elements into two groups, listed and unlisted. Listed elements are drawn from the list, and unlisted elements are pursued by other means.

For example, if you are doing a study on politically active people in a community, and you have a list of members from a local political organization, then members of that organization might be sampled from the list, and politically active people who are not members of the organization might be sampled by screening the general population.[6] Using the list allows you to sample the listed part of the population with high efficiency (hence lower costs), while screening the general population for unlisted members gets you beyond the potential coverage bias of the list. Since the unlisted elements will be more expensive to locate, they probably will be sampled at a lower rate, and overall estimates for the community will be calculated through a weighted combination of the two groups. This is an application of stratified sampling, which is discussed in detail in Chapter 5.

Here is another example of dual-frame sampling:

CASE STUDY 2.4

When Pope Benedict XVI resigned in early 2013—the first time in almost 600 years a Roman Catholic pope had resigned—the *New York Times* and CBS News conducted a survey to learn how U.S. Catholics felt about Benedict's papacy, the extent to which the Church was in touch with their needs, and what the next pope should be like. The survey was conducted with 1,585 adults throughout the United States.

The sample had three broad elements. First, a list-assisted RDD sample of landline telephone exchanges was drawn. Second, this landline sample was supplemented through random dialing of cellphone numbers. Third, self-identified Catholics from previous national polls by the *New York Times* and CBS News were called again for the new poll, and their responses were added to those of Catholics in the new sample. The three samples were combined and weighted as needed to make estimates.

This led to a front-page story, "U.S. Catholics in Poll See a Church Out of Touch." Among the findings, "three-fourths of those polled said they thought it was a good idea for Benedict to resign. Most wanted the next pope to be someone younger, with new ideas" (*New York Times,* March 5, 2013, p. 1).

This survey illustrates two uses of dual-frame sampling (as well as list-assisted random-digit dialing). First, a cellphone frame was used to address omissions in the landline frame. Second, a frame of known Catholics—identified through previous random samples of the general population, and hence presumably a random sample of U.S. Catholics—was used to obtain additional Catholic respondents without the cost of screening the general population.

---

6. In doing so, it will be important to identify whether respondents selected from the general population frame are members of the organization, for two reasons. First, these respondents will be counted with the organization sample. Second, since we probably don't have a good measure of how many people in the community are politically active, the rate of occurrence for organization members in the general population may be used to estimate the size of the nonlisted population. This will tell us how to weight the two groups in generating overall estimates. Similarly, in a dual-frame telephone survey, we will ask members of the landline sample if they have cellphones, and members of the cellphone sample if they have landlines, so we can assign respondents to landline-only, cell-only, and landline-plus-cell groups and weight each group appropriately.

Dual-frame sampling also may be used to address the fact that there is no general frame of online users. For example, Blair and Blair (2006) discuss the possibility of using an online panel to efficiently locate members of a rare population, in conjunction with RDD telephone screening to obtain broader population coverage.

General Comments on Coping With Omissions

All of the procedures that we have described for coping with omissions fall into two broad categories. In some cases, we augment the list (i.e., we use the list and supplement it in some way). Half-open intervals fall into this category, as do dual-frame designs. In other cases, we create or find a better list. Pure random-digit dialing and address-based sampling for telephone surveys fall into this category; we abandon listed telephone numbers for purely random numbers or mailing addresses. The extent to which we augment or replace the list—or simply ignore the problem—depends on practical judgments regarding the extent to which omissions might cause coverage bias, the extent to which the proposed method will mitigate those problems, and the cost-effectiveness of the method.

A review of these procedures also shows the special challenge that omissions pose for online surveys of the general population. In planning an in-home or mail survey of the general population, one can obtain a relatively complete list of addresses or, worst case, send people to list the housing units or establishments in some area. In planning a telephone survey, one can use random dialing to cover the population. In surveys of visitors to a place, one can use a counting frame and count people as they pass a sampling location. But in online surveys, there is no way to cover the general population completely. If the population of interest is a group for which a list of e-mail addresses is available, this is not an issue, but for general populations, the inability to assemble a complete frame means that online surveys ultimately must rely on some form of model-based estimates as opposed to probability-based estimates. We discuss model-based estimates further in Chapter 7.

2.2.4 Coping With Ineligibles

The next framing problem is ineligibles. These are elements that are contained in the frame that do not represent eligible population members. For example, if you are doing a study of political preferences among people who are likely to vote in an upcoming election, and you are using RDD telephone numbers as a sampling frame, those numbers will include many people who are not likely to vote.

Coping with ineligibles is straightforward—don't select them. Since they aren't in the population, they shouldn't be in the sample.

There are two ways to keep ineligibles out of a sample. First, the entire list can be screened for eligibility before sampling, with all ineligible listings being deleted. This often is not practical because the eligibility factor is not visible in the list; for example, a list of RDD numbers will not show whether people intend to vote in an upcoming election. The other approach is to screen selected elements for eligibility *after* sampling, with ineligibles dropped at this time. This is the usual method employed. In some cases, both methods may be used if the population is defined on multiple criteria, and some are visible and some are not. For example, if a population is defined as undergraduate students at a particular university who exercise at least three times per week, it may be possible to drop graduate students when drawing names from the campus directory, then screen selected undergraduates for exercise frequency.

Dropping ineligibles means just that—dropping them, not replacing them. Inexperienced researchers sometimes think that ineligibles should be replaced by taking the next name on the list, but this procedure gives extra chances of selection to the population members who are listed after ineligibles and may cause sample bias. The proper method is simply to adjust the sample size for shrinkage due to ineligibility and drop ineligible listings when encountered.

Adjusting the sample size is done as follows: If e is the proportion of the list that is eligible, the adjusted sample size is n/e, where n is the desired sample size. For example, if you desire a sample of 300 freshmen at a given university, and only 20% of the names in the college directory are freshmen, the adjusted sample size to be chosen from the directory is $300 \div [.20] = 1,500$. A sample of 1,500 names from this directory should yield 300 freshmen.

Estimates of eligibility rates may be obtained either from prior experience or by studying a small pilot sample. Since these estimates may not be exactly accurate, it is a good idea to estimate eligibility on the low side so you are sure to get a large enough sample. Say, for example, that you think that freshmen will account for 20% of the listings drawn from a college directory, but you think the eligibility rate for any given sample could be anywhere from 15% to 25%. Use the 15% figure; in other words, if you want 300 eligibles, draw an initial sample of $300 \div [.15] = 2,000$. Then, if this sample yields 400 eligibles (an eligibility rate of 20%), you can randomly choose 300 for retention or 100 for deletion. The result will still be a random sample: A random sample of a random sample is a random sample, and a random sample minus a random sample is a random sample.

When eligibility will be determined through screening interviews, you should use both the low and high eligibility estimates in planning sample size. In our example, the lowest eligibility estimate, 15%, means that a sample size as large as 2,000 may be needed to produce 300 eligibles. The highest estimate, 25%, means that a sample size as small as 1,200 may be needed ($300 \div [.25] = 1,200$). To protect yourself in this situation, draw a sample of 2,000 but do not release the entire sample for screening. Instead, draw a random subsample of 1,200 from the 2,000; release this subsample and hold the other 800 selections for use if all or part of it is needed. If the first 1,200 selections yield 240 interviews (an eligibility rate of 20%), then draw 300 of the holdout selections to get the remaining 60 interviews ($60 \div [.20] = 300$). This procedure gives you as many selections as you need without producing expensive and unnecessary data.

In studies of rare populations, the potential difference in sample size (depending on variations in the eligibility rate) may be so large that you prefer to draw the smaller sample, work it, and then use the resulting information about eligibility rates to resample as needed. For example, an eligibility rate of 1% would require 100,000 selections to provide 1,000 observations, but an eligibility rate of 2% would require only 50,000 selections. In a recent study of gay urban males that one of the authors worked on, initial samples in various geographic areas were drawn with an assumption that self-identified gay males would be no more than 4% of the population; in general, the correct rate was found to be approximately 2%, so many additional observations were needed, but the first-stage results were very useful in designing the second-stage sample.

A common error is to draw the larger sample (2,000 in our example), release the entire sample for data collection, and simply stop the research when the desired number of eligibles is obtained. This procedure is incorrect, because the first observations obtained will be the observations that are easiest to get; for example, in a survey of the general public, these observations will be homemakers and retired people. Any sample released for data collection should be worked completely to avoid bias in favor of the easy observations.

When adjusting the sample size to allow for ineligibles, it is also appropriate to adjust for the expected response rate. The adjusted sample size is $n/(e*r)$, where n is the desired sample size, e is the eligibility rate, and r is the expected response rate. For example, if you want 300 usable observations, and you expect 20% of the selections to be eligible and 20% to cooperate, then you need an initial sample size of $300 \div [.20 \times .20] = 7,500$.

2.2.5 Coping With Duplications

If a sample is selected from a list that contains duplications of some elements, but none of the duplicated elements are selected more than once, has the duplication caused any problems? The answer is yes.

The basic problem with duplication is that it gives *groups* of population members disproportionate chances for selection into the sample. Even if individual duplicated elements aren't chosen more than once, their *group* is chosen at a higher rate. The group of population members who appear twice on the list is overrepresented by a factor of 2 compared with the group of members who appear once, the group of population members who appear three times on the list is overrepresented by a factor of 3, and so on. This overrepresentation will cause sample bias if the duplicated elements are different from the nonduplicated elements on some variable of interest in the research.

For example, imagine that you are drawing a sample of students at a college, and the procedure is to randomly select classes and then students within classes. Students who are in four classes have four chances that their classes will be drawn, while students who are in two classes have only two chances. The result will be to overrepresent full-time versus part-time students. (Notice that you would not encounter this problem if you sampled students directly from the student directory. The directory might have other problems such as omissions or ineligibles, but each student should be listed only once. This illustrates the fact that different frames for the same population may present different problems.)

There are three ways to correct for duplicate listings. The brute-strength method is to cross-check the list, identify duplicates, and remove them. This will be done if the list is computerized.

A second method is to draw the sample and check only the selected elements to determine how many times they are duplicated in the total population list. Then, to restore equal probabilities of selection, sample members that are listed k times would be retained at the rate of $1/k$ (i.e., members that appear twice in the list would be retained at the rate of 1/2, members that appear three times at the rate of 1/3, etc.). This method is appropriate for noncomputerized lists. It will cause some shrinkage in the sample size, which can be handled in the same way as shrinkage for eligibility.[7]

---

7. This method also provides a way to assess the seriousness of duplication in a list. If the problem is minor, you might ignore it.

The third method, which is usable in surveys, is to ask selected population members how many times they appear in the list. Under this method, all of the data gathered are retained, because it would be wasteful to discard completed interviews, but observations are weighted by the inverse of their number of times in the list. That is, sample members who say they are listed k times are weighted by $1/k$.

This last method obviously requires that sample members know how many times they are listed (e.g., how many classes they are taking). This method should be used only when there is good reason to believe that this assumption is true and when checking the list is difficult or impossible.

Similarly, cross-checking a list works best if the population members have unique identifiers, such as a telephone number. Otherwise, the same household might be represented by people with different first names, and the same person might be represented with variations in the name or address. If you look at the junk mail that comes to your home, you'll probably see these types of variations. Because of these variations, computerized cross-checking usually doesn't remove all of the duplications in a list, but it should reduce them to a level where they cause negligible sample bias.

2.2.6 Coping With Clustering

Our final list problem is clustering. Clustering is similar to duplication in that it involves unfair representation of some group of population members, rather than complete exclusion or inclusion. The difference is that clustered elements are underrepresented in the sample while duplicated elements are overrepresented.

Here is an example of clustering. A town has 100,000 adults: 50,000 married and 50,000 single. The 50,000 married adults form 25,000 households, each with one landline telephone number. The 50,000 single adults form 50,000 households, each with one landline number. A sample of 300 of these numbers for a telephone survey will produce 100 "married" numbers and 200 "single" numbers, because the single people account for 2/3 of the telephone numbers. If one adult is interviewed at each number, the sample will contain 100 married adults and 200 single adults. This is a fair sample of households but not of individuals. Married people account for 1/2 of the adults in town but, because they are clustered on the list, they account for only 1/3 of the adults in the sample.

Clustering arises in mail, telephone, or in-home surveys whenever the desired population unit is individuals (e.g., potential voters) but the sampling frame is a list of households (e.g., a list of residential addresses or landline telephone numbers). Clustering typically does not arise in lists of cellphone numbers or, for the most part, lists of e-mail addresses in online surveys because these lists correspond to individuals. On the other hand, if you have a list of individuals but the desired population unit is households, then individuals from the same household will represent duplicates in the list.

Clustering also arises in surveys of organizations whenever the desired population unit is nested within organizations. An example is Case Study 2.2 in which individual businesspeople gave answers to a survey but the desired population was sales dollars.

There are three basic ways to cope with clustering:

- First, you can gather data from all population elements in the selected clusters. For example, in our married/single example, you would gather data from both adults at each "married" number, which would give you data from 200 married people and 200 single people. Some adjustment to the initial sample size would be needed if the data collection budget allows only 300 observations.

This method provides a fair chance of selection for every member of the population. Unfortunately, as the married/single example shows, it also produces a sample that contains related cluster members. Of 400 population members in that sample, 200 are husbands and wives. This can cause problems of contamination from respondents talking to each other. It also means that the sample is less heterogeneous and hence contains less information than an equal-sized sample of unrelated observations (see the discussion of cluster sampling in Chapter 6). Because of these issues, taking entire clusters is only a good idea when (a) clusters are relatively small and relatively few in number, or (b) it is simply impossible to separate the elements, as with sales dollars within companies.

- Second, you can sample population members within clusters at some fixed rate. The usual rate for sampling individuals within households is 1/2. In the married/single example, you would retain only half of the "single" households (and drop the others), and you would gather data from one randomly chosen person in each of the "married" households. This would produce a sample size of 100 people from the 100 "married" households and 100 people from the 200 "single" households. A sample size adjustment would be needed to get 300 interviews.

This method provides a fair chance of selection for every member of the population. However, it is a relatively expensive procedure, because you pay to locate some number of "single" households, and then you discard half of them.

- Third, you can compensate for clustering by randomly selecting one population member from each selected cluster and weighting that observation by the size of the cluster. In the married/single example, one observation would be obtained from each of the 100 "married" and 200 "single" households in the original sample, but the married observations would be weighted by 2, giving them the weight of 200 people in total.

Sampling Within Households

The original method of randomly selecting individuals within households was developed by Kish (1949), who developed a procedure that requires listing all household members and then selecting one individual based on a preset rule called a Kish Table. This procedure became the standard method for sampling within households for door-to-door surveys.

In telephone surveys, the Kish procedure was found to be less effective, because respondents could not see the interviewer and were less willing to provide a listing of all household members. One alternative was to use a method proposed by Troldahl and Carter (1964). This method required only two pieces of information: the number of adults in the household and the number of males (or females). An individual was then selected through a rotating series of four selection tables. The Trodahl-Carter method eliminated the need to list the entire household, but some bias remained because not all household members had equal probabilities of selection within the four tables and also because of disparities in the gender composition of single-adult households. There tend to be more single-female households, due to widows and single mothers who don't take a roommate or a live-in partner (on the other hand, single-female households tend to be undermeasured, because females who live alone may not tell a caller that there is no male in the household).

A subsequent method has been to select the household member who most recently had a birthday (O'Rourke & Blair, 1983) or the person who will have the next birthday (Lind, Link, & Oldendick, 2000). While unbiased in theory, the last (or next) birthday method encounters some bias in practice because initial respondents disproportionately claim themselves as the proper respondent. Studies have found that the proper respondent is identified 75% to 90% of the time (Lavrakas, Bauman, & Merkle, 1993; Lavrakas, Stasny, & Harpruder, 2000; Lind et al., 2000; O'Rourke & Blair, 1983). While not perfect, this method is now the most widely used procedure for sampling within households in telephone surveys because it is easy to administer.

Most recently, Rizzo, Brick, and Park (2004) have proposed a method of within-household sampling that is minimally intrusive, reducing the effect of the selection process on household response. Their approach takes advantage of the fact that single and two-adult households account for about 85% of all U.S. households. Selection is not at issue in the single-adult households. In the two-adult households, half the time, the adult answering the phone is selected, and half the time the other adult is chosen. More complicated or intrusive methods then have to be used only in the 15% of remaining households.

Weighting Data to the Proper Population Unit

Earlier in this chapter, we gave an example in which individual businesspeople gave answers to a survey, but the desired population unit was sales dollars: see Case Study 2.2. This is a common problem in market research: The unit of interest is expenditures, but the reporting units are people or companies.

From a framing point of view, the problem can be viewed as a form of clustering. Just as there are two adults in each "married" household in our married/single example, there are $X of potential sales at each company in Case Study 2.2. In the married/single example, we can randomly select adults within households if our desired population unit is individuals rather than households, but we cannot sample dollars within companies in Case Study 2.2 because the dollars cannot speak. Instead, we let one respondent speak for all of the dollars in a company, and we weight those answers by the cluster size (i.e., the number of dollars).

2.2.7 Framing Populations Without a List

In some research projects, sampling must be done without a list of the population. For example, if you want to survey visitors to a particular website or shopping mall, you won't find a list of visitors. Sampling without lists is done from "counting frames" as follows:

- Estimate the size of the population.
- Select a sample of numbers between 1 and N, where N is the population size.
- Count the population and gather data from the appropriately numbered members.

For example, in a sample of visitors to a shopping mall, if you expect 10,000 shoppers to enter the mall during the interviewing period, and you wish to select 500 of them, you can randomly select 500 numbers between 1 and 10,000. Alternately, you can take every 20th number after some random start (10,000 ÷ 500 = 20). You then will count shoppers as they enter the center and approach the shoppers with appropriate numbers.

Counting frames are subject to the same problems as lists: omission, ineligibility, duplication, and clustering. Omission results from underestimating the population size (or the sizes of population subgroups). For example, if you estimate the number of visitors to a shopping mall at 10,000, and this estimate is too small, then all shoppers beyond the 10,000th have no chance of selection because they don't appear in the sampling frame.

Ineligibility results from some of the counted elements not meeting population criteria. For example, counting the visitors to a mall is easiest if you count every visitor, but some of the visitors might not meet requirements that have been set for the population (regarding age, gender, product usage, or whatever). Ineligibility also results from overestimating the size of the population (or of population subgroups). Your sample may be smaller than expected because only 9,412 shoppers visited the mall during the interviewing period, and you expected 10,000. In effect, the numbers 9,413 through 10,000 were ineligible elements in your sampling frame.

Duplication and clustering usually result from a mismatch between the counting units and population units. For example, you might want a sample of *people* who shop at some mall, but the implicit counting unit is visits to the mall. Some people visit the mall more than others, and the extra visits constitute duplications in the counting frame if the desired unit is people (Blair, 1983).

In general, the available solutions for problems in counting frames are more limited than the solutions for problems in lists. Omission is solved by simply estimating population size on the high side. Ineligibility is solved by screening for ineligibles. Duplication and clustering are usually solved by weighting data after they are gathered, because the absence of list documentation makes it impossible to clean or check the sampling frame prior to data collection.

2.3 CHAPTER SUMMARY

This chapter discussed issues in defining and framing populations. Regarding population definition, we noted that a sampling population is the set of elements about which you would like to draw conclusions. To define a population, you have to specify (a) the population units and (b) the population boundaries. The boundaries must be stated in specific operational terms.

Regarding sample frames, we noted that a frame is a list or system that identifies every member of the population symbolically. Ideally, the frame should have a one-to-one correspondence with the members of the population. This may not occur because of omissions, ineligibles, duplications, or clustering.

The response to omissions is to ignore them if the problem is small and address them if the problem is likely to cause bias in the sample. Random-digit dialing, dual-frame designs to incorporate cellphones, and possibly address-based sampling or registration-based sampling are used to handle unlisted numbers in telephone surveys. Other methods for dealing with omissions are the use of half-open intervals and more general dual-frame designs.

The response to ineligibles is to drop them when encountered. If ineligible elements cannot be recognized in the frame, it may be necessary to screen for them in the field. Either way, the initial sample size should allow for losses due to ineligibility.

Possible responses to duplicate listings are (1) to delete them from the frame prior to sampling, (2) to retain selected elements at a rate that is inverse to the number of times each selected unit is listed, or (3) to ask each selected participant how many times he or she is listed and weight the observations by the inverse of the number of listings.

Possible responses to clustering are (1) including every member of selected clusters, (2) sampling within clusters, or (3) randomly selecting one element in each cluster and weighting for cluster size.

EXERCISES AND DISCUSSION QUESTIONS

Exercise 2.1

A researcher wishes to study key business leaders to learn their opinions about issues facing a metropolitan area. Define this population in specific operational terms.

Exercise 2.2

The municipal government of a "college town" wishes to survey area residents regarding their park and recreation needs. Define this population in specific operational terms. Should children be eligible to respond? People who live outside the city boundaries? Students at the local university who have access to university facilities? Students who live in dormitories? Students in fraternities or sororities? People in the local jail? People in a homeless shelter? People in nursing homes?

Exercise 2.3

A friend of yours is running for a place on the local school board, and you agree to help her by surveying local voters to learn which issues are most important and what they would like the school board to do. Can you get a list of registered voters who live in the school district? If so, does it contain mailing addresses? Telephone numbers? E-mail addresses? Apart from this, is there a directory of telephone numbers that might be usable for your purposes? A directory of mailing addresses? A directory of e-mail addresses?

3

Drawing the Sample and Executing the Research

O nce you have defined and framed the population of interest, you are ready to draw the sample and execute the research. This chapter discusses how to do so. In this chapter, you will learn the following:

- How to draw a sample so that all population elements have a fair chance of selection
- Methods for controlling possible nonresponse bias
- How to calculate response rates

3.1 DRAWING THE SAMPLE

There are two basic methods for drawing probability samples, and you will want to use the method that is easiest and best for your particular situation. The basic methods are (1) simple random sampling and (2) systematic sampling.[1]

---

1. In Chapter 1, we mentioned stratified and cluster sampling designs. In stratified sampling, we separate the population into subgroups called strata and draw separate samples for each subgroup; see Chapter 5 for details. In cluster sampling, we separate the population into subgroups called clusters and draw a sample of clusters; see Chapter 6. In both cases, when it comes to actually drawing the sample—drawing elements within strata, or drawing clusters and elements within clusters—we use a simple random or systematic selection procedure.

3.1.1 Simple Random Sampling

Simple random sampling uses a chance mechanism to draw population members directly from the sampling frame. This can be accomplished with physical selection procedures or more commonly through the use of random numbers.

An example of physical selection procedures would be to list each population member on a slip of paper, mix the slips of paper in a bowl, and draw slips of paper to get the sample. Another physical procedure would be to number the population members and select numbers by spinning a wheel or drawing numbered balls. These physical procedures are appealing because they are concrete, and everyone is familiar with games of chance that use these mechanisms. However, physical procedures can be cumbersome; for example, imagine how long it would take to make a slip of paper for every adult in your town, then draw 500 slips from a drum if you wanted a sample of 500. Physical procedures also present difficulties in achieving randomness. It is not easy to mix slips of paper so completely that any patterns in them are broken up. For example:

CASE STUDY 3.1[2]

On December 1, 1969, the Selective Service System of the United States conducted a lottery to determine the order of call to military service in the Vietnam War for men born from 1944 to 1950. The "draft" occurred during a period of military conscription from just before World War II to 1973.

The days of the year (including February 29) were represented by the numbers 1 through 366 written on slips of paper. The slips were placed in separate plastic capsules that were mixed in a box and then dumped into a deep glass jar. Capsules were drawn from the jar one at a time.

The first number drawn was 258 (September 14), so all registrants with that birthday were assigned lottery number 1. The second number corresponded to April 24, and so forth. Men with the first 195 birthdays drawn were later called for military service in the order those days were drawn.

People soon noticed that the lottery numbers were not distributed uniformly over the year. In particular, November and December births, or dates 306 to 366, were drawn relatively early in the process and received lower draft numbers. Only 5 days in December (December 2, 12, 15, 17, and 19) were higher than the last call number of 195. This led to complaints that the lottery was not random.

Analysis of the procedure suggested that mixing 366 capsules in the box did not mix them sufficiently before dumping them into the jar. The capsules had been put in the box month by month,

2. Drawn from http://en.wikipedia.org/wiki/Draft_lottery_(1969) and David E. Rosenbaum, "Statisticians Charge Draft Lottery Was Not Random," *New York Times*, January 4, 1970.

January through December, and subsequent mixing efforts were insufficient to overcome this sequencing (the box had been shaken "several times," carried up three flights of stairs, and carried back down).

The results of the drawing were allowed to stand, but discontent with the fairness of the procedure was high—at least among men born in December who found themselves drafted into the army!

A better method for drawing simple random samples is to use random numbers. The traditional way of doing this is to assign numbers to members of the population and draw random numbers to determine which members are selected. For example, assume that we wish to draw a sample of 5 people from a population with 15 members. We first state some rule for numbering the population members—typically the order they appear in the sampling frame (the order they appear in the list, the order in which they enter the site, etc.). We don't have to write the numbers down; we just have to know how they will be applied. We then draw 5 random numbers between 01 and 15 (or whatever numbers have been assigned to the population members). The population members corresponding to those numbers are selected.

The random numbers can come from a variety of sources. Your calculator may have a random number function, Excel has random number functions, you can Google *random number generator* to find random number generators on the web, or you can even use a printed table of random numbers. Depending on the source you use, you may get some numbers that are larger than the size of the population; for example, if you are drawing two-digit random numbers to select elements from a population with 15 members, some of the two-digit numbers will be larger than 15. These numbers will simply be discarded, as will any duplicate numbers until you hit the desired sample size.

Exhibit 3.1 provides a specific illustration. We started with the 15-member population shown in the exhibit. We numbered them 1 to 15 in the order they appeared. We then used Excel's RANDBETWEEN function to draw five random numbers between 01 and 15. The numbers drawn were 7, 5, 4, 15, and 14. The selected elements are marked with asterisks.

Notice that the sample may not seem to be perfectly random. Starting from Element 1 (Ann), we get three misses, then three hits in four elements, then six misses, then two hits. This, of course, is sampling variation in action. The sample is random, but most random samples exhibit some peculiarities (and the smaller the sample, the more likely it will look odd, as we will discuss in Chapter 4). It would be a mistake to reject the sample because it "doesn't look right." Obviously, this would destroy the random character of the sample.

Exhibit 3.1   Example of a Simple Random Sample

	1	Ann
	2	Bob
	3	Carl
*	4	Dave
*	5	Edna
	6	Frank
*	7	Griselda
	8	Hamza
	9	Isabel
	10	Jose
	11	Kevin
	12	Luther
	13	Maria
*	14	Noy
*	15	Opal

A potentially faster way to draw simple random samples is to directly assign *permanent random numbers*[3] to the population elements, sort them, and take the desired sample size (Ernst, Valliant, & Casady, 2000). If the population is listed in an Excel file, this can be done as follows:

- Create a new column in the population list, usually as the first column in the spreadsheet.
- Use the RAND function to create random numbers in that column. This assigns a 15-digit random number to each member of the population.

3. *Permanent random numbers* are numbers assigned once to a set of elements. Each element retains its random number through different needs to sample or subsample the elements for different purposes (e.g., creating a main sample and supplemental samples, dividing the sample into independent random groups to be used at different points in time, etc.).

- Copy and paste that column of random numbers back into itself, pasting it as values. This makes the numbers permanent, so they don't change when you manipulate the list.
- Sort the list based on those random numbers (in either ascending or descending order, your choice). The population elements now appear in random order.
- Take the first *n* elements as the selected sample.

Exhibit 3.2 provides a specific illustration. We took the same population with 15 members, assigned random numbers to each member, sorted them in descending order, and took the first 5.

If, for some reason, you want random numbers with more than 15 digits to sort the population, you can create random numbers in two different columns, make them permanent, and then multiply them.

Exhibit 3.2 A Simple Random Sample Based on Permanent Random Numbers

*	0.95621172263443100	Edna
*	0.95529589891009300	Dave
*	0.95031621511811900	Isabel
*	0.90142567105138400	Maria
*	0.87603942643812900	Kevin
	0.82253995726832500	Frank
	0.60169540845067400	Ann
	0.59862117130896600	Carl
	0.47783527407634200	Jose
	0.42387453801472000	Hamza
	0.37273035992107500	Noy
	0.24560028470083000	Bob
	0.22650088973448900	Luther
	0.17737231327867700	Griselda
	0.03267881450417860	Opal

Once permanent random numbers have been assigned to members of the population, they can be used in multiple sampling stages or if the population is divided into strata. For example, if we decide that we want to divide this population into males and females and draw simple random samples of three males and three females, we can simply divide the two groups and take the three males and three females with the highest (or lowest if you prefer) random numbers.

3.1.2 Systematic Sampling

Systematic sampling is a procedure that samples every ith member of a population after a random start between 1 and i. For example, to draw a sample of 5 from a population of 15, you would do the following:

- First, divide the population size by the desired sample size to get the sampling interval, i, which is truncated to the nearest whole number. In our example, $15 \div 5 = 3$, which means we will take every third population member after some random start.
- Next, draw a random start s between 1 and i. The use of a random start ensures that every population member has an equal chance of selection.
- Proceed to take population members numbered s, $(s + i)$, $(s + 2i)$, $(s + 3i)$, and so on.

Exhibit 3.3 provides a specific illustration. We took the same population with 15 members. We numbered them 1 to 15 in the order they appeared. We divided the population size by the desired sample size to get a sampling interval of 3 and used Excel's RANDBETWEEN function to draw a random start between 1 and 3. The number drawn was 2, so we proceeded to select population members 2, 5, 8, 11, and 14. The selected elements are marked with asterisks.

When sampling from computerized lists, systematic sampling doesn't save much time compared with simple random sampling. After all, the computer is doing the work. In physical sampling, though, systematic sampling can save a lot of time, as discussed in the next section of this chapter. Systematic sampling also can be easier when you don't have a list of the population and have to use a counting frame—for example, in sampling visitors to a place—because you just have to keep track of the interval since the last selection and not the cumulative population count.

Exhibit 3.3 Example of a Systematic Sample

	1	Ann
*	2	Bob
	3	Carl
	4	Dave
*	5	Edna
	6	Frank
	7	Griselda
*	8	Hamza
	9	Isabel
	10	Jose
*	11	Kevin
	12	Luther
	13	Maria
*	14	Noy
	15	Opal

As far as sample quality is concerned, systematic samples are generally considered the same as simple random samples,[4] but differences can occur because of the nature of the procedures. Simple random sampling gives equal probabilities of selection not only to all individual elements in the population but also all possible combinations of elements (i.e., all possible samples). Some of these combinations may look odd; for example, in our example of simple random sampling, we noted that the sample had some peculiarities. Systematic sampling, in contrast, gives equal probabilities to all individual elements but not to all possible samples. In fact, systematic sampling allows only i possible samples. For example, if i = 3, systematic sampling will allow only three possible

4. For example, we usually treat simple random and systematic samples of the same size as having the same sampling error, although strictly speaking, computing sampling errors for a systematic sample cannot be done in such a straightforward manner.

samples: the first element of the population followed by every third subsequent element, the second element of the population followed by every third subsequent element, and the third element of the population followed by every third subsequent element.

Thus, systematic sampling has a potential advantage in that it spreads selections through the sampling frame and will not bunch selections as simple random sampling can. This feature can be exploited if you organize the frame on some variable of interest. For example, if you are drawing a sample of elementary schools from a list, and you order the list based on the percentage of students at each school who qualify for government-assisted lunches, then a systematic sample will ensure that you proportionately represent schools with different percentages of low-income students. (This is called implicit stratification; we discuss stratified sampling in Chapter 5.)

Systematic sampling also has a potential disadvantage. If the frame exhibits *periodicity* (a recurring sequence of population members), and the sampling interval coincides with that periodicity, then systematic sampling can produce an unrepresentative sample. For example, we once saw a list of a social organization that was ordered husband-wife-husband-wife, and so on, which wasn't realized until a systematic sample with an even sampling interval was chosen and all of the selections were women. This type of problem rarely occurs, but it is always a good idea to learn everything you can about the frame and "eyeball" it for periodicities before drawing a systematic sample. Also, if the sampling frame can be reorganized without too much effort, it is a good idea to put the frame in some type of order (women before men, large companies before small companies, etc.), not only to ensure that the systematic procedure will spread selections across different types of population members but also to break up periodicities that might exist.

The initial application of systematic sampling often yields a sample size different from what is needed. For example, if you need a sample of 200 members from a population of 500, the calculated sampling interval is $500 \div 200 = 2.5$. If you truncate this interval to 2, you'll get an initial sample of $500 \div 2 = 250$, which is larger than desired. If you round the interval up to 3, you'll get a sample of $500 \div 3 = 167$, which is smaller than desired.

In this particular example, you could alternate between taking every second and every third element into the sample, but the more general solution is to round in the direction of the larger sample and randomly delete the extra selections. Oversampling and deleting is almost always easier than undersampling and adding. The deletions can be done systematically; for example, if you simply skip every fifth selection, an initial sample of 250 will be reduced to a sample of 200.

You should not stop sampling in the middle of a list when you reach the desired sample size, because this would result in a sample biased toward the earlier part of the list. Sample all the way through, then delete any excess.

3.1.3 Physical Sampling

There are times when sampling is done from physical sources such as printed directories or file drawers containing archival records. In these situations, the fastest way to draw a sample is with systematic sampling based on physical measures.

Sampling From Directories

Systematic sampling from printed directories is done as follows:

• First, divide the needed sample size by the number of pages in the directory to calculate the number of selections per page. For example, if a population with 33,207 members is listed in a directory with 176 pages, and you want a sample size of 500, then 500 ÷ 176 = 2.84 selections per page (round up to 3 selections per page, not down to 2, to oversample rather than undersample).

If the number of pages is larger than the needed sample size, divide the number of pages by the sample size to determine a sampling interval for pages. For example, if you have a directory of 176 pages and a needed sample size of 25, then 176 ÷ 25 = 7.04 pages per selection (round down to 7 for oversampling).

• Second, draw a random sample of as many locations as you need per page. Say, for example, that a directory is printed in four columns per page, with each column containing 104 lines, and you want three selections per page. In this situation, select one random number between 1 and 104 to indicate a selected line in each column and one random number between 1 and 4 to indicate a column you will skip on each page. This will give you three selections per page, as desired.

• Third, make a template to facilitate sampling. Take a piece of light cardboard that is at least as long as the directory pages (manila envelopes or file folders make excellent templates). Align the top of the template with the top of the printed column in the directory, and mark the selected line(s) on the template.

- Fourth, draw the sample by placing the template against the appropriate columns of the directory and selecting the population members indicated by the marks on the template. Align the template with the first printed line rather than the top of the page, because print location can vary from page to page. Repeat this procedure from the first through the last pages of the directory. Do not stop when you hit the desired sample size—work the whole directory and randomly delete excess selections.

This procedure is described in terms of lines rather than listings in the directory, because lines are the basic printed unit.

In some directories, different listings may have a different number of lines. When this occurs, the selection procedure should be geared to the most common listing length. For example, if most listings take two lines, some take three, and a few take four, then the third and fourth lines should be treated as ineligibles. If a selected line corresponds to the first two lines of a listed population member, then the member is taken for the sample; if the selected line corresponds to the third or fourth line of a listing, then the listing is ignored. This will prevent the listings with extra lines from having extra chances of selection. Also, any blank lines should be treated as ineligibles. These factors should be considered when calculating the eligibility rate and the needed sample size.

A directory also may contain completely ineligible items. In general, it is a good idea to look through the directory before using it, so as to spot possible problems and accommodate them within the sampling procedure.

Sampling in this fashion goes much faster than simple random sampling or counting every *i*th listing as long as a directory has regular print, the listings occupy similar numbers of lines, and there aren't a lot of ineligible items. If the printing is irregular, or the listings vary greatly in length, or there are lots of ineligible items, then plain systematic sampling may work best.

Sampling From File Drawers

Physical sampling from other types of frames follows procedures similar to physical sampling from directories. For a simple illustration, we consider selecting a sample of records stored in file cabinets, although it is unlikely you will encounter this specific situation. Say, for example, that archival records of interest are kept in 25 file cabinets, each with four drawers. To draw a sample of 100 records, you would do the following.

- Measure the depth of the drawers: say, for example, 30 inches each.
- Calculate the total length of the records: 25 cabinets × 4 drawers per cabinet × 30 inches per drawer = 3,000 inches of records.
- Divide the total length by the needed sample size to get a physical sampling interval: 3,000 inches ÷ 100 selections = 30 inches per selection.
- Draw a random starting point expressed in fractions of an inch or millimeters.
- Pull the records in the first drawer tight. Lay a tape measure (or a ruler or a yardstick) over these records and locate the random starting point. Take the records that correspond to that point, plus the records that come at appropriate intervals after the starting point.

In order to work with convenient sampling intervals, it may be helpful to round the interval down to the nearest inch. This will produce oversampling, just as rounding the interval down produces oversampling in sampling from directories. Also, the records may be of differing widths; for example, archival medical files may be thicker or thinner depending on the patient's medical history. If an EPSEM (equal probability selection method) sample of files is desired, then it will be necessary to use some standard width and regard widths over that amount as ineligible. This is parallel to the fact that listings may occupy different numbers of lines in a directory.

3.2 EXECUTING THE RESEARCH

With the sample drawn, all that remains is to execute the research. We refer to this step, executing the research, as part of the sampling process because good execution is necessary to preserve the quality of the original sample. Consider the following examples:

CASE STUDY 3.2

An electric utility in the Midwest decided to offer an "energy consulting" service to residential customers. For a fee, a company representative would come to a customer's home, analyze how the home could be made more energy efficient, and show the costs and benefits of possible changes.

(Continued)

(Continued)

The company did a survey to estimate how popular this service would be among customers, to help plan staffing and support levels. Questionnaires were mailed to all residential customers—about 200,000—with their March power bills. Around 10,000 customers responded. The returned questionnaires indicated a very high level of interest in the service, so the power company geared up for heavy demand. However, actual demand proved far less than implied by the survey.

There are at least three possible reasons why this survey produced misleading results. First, the survey was done right after customers had paid a series of winter power bills, so interest may have been inflated above its baseline level. Second, it is easier for people to *say* they want a service than it is for them to *pay* for the service. Third, and of most interest here, the obtained sample is biased because of poor research execution.

Note that we say the *obtained* sample is biased. There is nothing wrong with the original sample: in fact, it's a census. The problem is one of execution and follow-through. The 10,000 customers who responded are only 5% of the customers who received questionnaires and should be viewed as a sample of volunteers rather than a random sample of the population.

In fact, the best way to interpret the data might have been to assume that the 95% who did not respond to the questionnaire were not interested in the service. Cooperation in mail surveys tends to be influenced by respondents' interest in the topic, and unlike telephone and face-to-face surveys, where people usually refuse before they know anything about the topic, you should assume that non-respondents to a mail survey looked at the questionnaire and decided they weren't interested. This bias never vanishes entirely from mail surveys but does become smaller as the response rate increases.

This example shows that a good initial sample is of no use if the researcher fails to protect its integrity in execution, or to put it another way, the value of giving all population members an equal chance of selection is undone if they are not also given an equal chance of being interviewed or observed, which is a function of how the research is executed. The example also shows that a big sample—in this case, a sample of 10,000 people—is not necessarily a good sample. The company would have been better off to spend the same amount of money on a smaller study with less exposure to nonresponse bias.

Nonresponse is a huge issue in modern survey research, at least in the United States. Exhibit 3.4 shows trends in telephone survey response rates as reported by the Pew Research Center. Since 1997, Pew reports that its telephone response rates have fallen from 36% to 9%, because potential respondents are more difficult to contact and less likely to cooperate when contacted. Declines in response rates for other methods of administration such as mail and Internet have not been as severe because contact rates are less of an issue, but response rates are an issue in all forms of surveys.

Exhibit 3.4   Decline in U.S. Telephone Survey Response Rates Since 1997

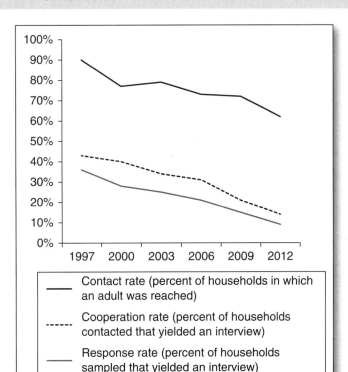

Source: Data from Pew Research Center "Assessing the Representativeness of Public Opinion Surveys." Pew Research Center, Washington, D.C. (May 15, 2012) http://www.people-press.org/2012/05/15/assessing-the-representativeness-of-public-opinion-surveys, Accessed 9/23/14.

3.2.1 Controlling Nonresponse Bias

A variety of methods have been used, alone or in combination, to control nonresponse bias. These methods are listed in Exhibit 3.5 and discussed below.

Maximizing Response Rates

The level of nonresponse bias in a study is a function of two things: (a) the response rate and (b) the extent to which respondents differ from nonrespondents on the characteristics of interest. If the response rate is high, and there are

Exhibit 3.5 Snapshot of Methods for Controlling Nonresponse Bias

- Attempting to maximize the response rate
- Using quotas
- Probability sampling with quotas
- Weighting for differential response
- Comparing early versus late respondents
- Follow-up studies of nonrespondents

relatively few nonrespondents, then it will take large differences between respondents and nonrespondents to bias the results. The lower the response rate, the greater our concern. As a result, the best way to control nonresponse bias is to maximize the response rate.

The first step in maximizing the response rate is to choose a method of administration that tends to get high response. Within any given method, the next step is to use procedures that ensure contact and encourage response. Blair et al. (2013) provide an extensive discussion of these issues, with recommendations for best practices across various types of research. Because the issues concern data collection practices rather than sampling per se, we will not discuss them here, but we note that they are central to controlling nonresponse bias.

Quota Sampling

In some studies, sample composition (and hence nonresponse bias) is controlled through quotas rather than follow-ups. This is common in telephone surveys done by commercial market researchers, intercept surveys done with passers-by in shopping malls or other locations, and surveys done with mail or online panels.

In the context of telephone surveys, quota sampling works as follows. A random sample of numbers is selected and called. If nobody answers the phone, the interviewer discards the number and proceeds to another. This procedure produces high numbers of retired people and homemakers if it is used without controls, because these are the people who are most likely to be available when called. To control this obvious bias, the researcher can set quotas, most often for age and sex. For example, a researcher might set quotas to match population percentages of men younger than 55 years, men 55 years and older, women younger than 55 years, and women 55 years and older. This will prevent getting a sample that is disproportionately 55 and older or disproportionately female.

Quota sampling produces samples that look reasonable, at least for the dimensions on which quotas are set, and data collection is faster and cheaper than with follow-ups. However, if you call different telephone numbers until you find someone available, there is no getting around the fact that your sampling procedure will find the least active and most accessible members of the population, which can be a biasing factor in your research. Consider the following example.

CASE STUDY 3.3

Meet the O'Leary sisters, Bridget and Kathleen. Both are 18 to 34 years old, female, and unmarried.

Bridget is a party girl. She patronizes clubs, movies, and restaurants. When home, she eats frozen food or take-out. She buys clothes, not furniture. Your chance of reaching her when you call is 20%.

Kathleen is a stay-at-home. Her hobby is needlepointing Irish toasts (e.g., "May ye be in Heaven an hour before the Devil knows you're dead"). She buys spices, scratch foods, craft supplies, and things to brighten up her apartment. Your chance of reaching her when you call is 80%.

Imagine that 18- to 34-year-old unmarried women are split 50/50 (half and half) between the Bridgets and Kathleens of the world. Further imagine that you are doing a telephone study with quota sampling and have set a quota of 200 interviews for this group.

Your first 200 calls to group members go to 100 Bridgets and 100 Kathleens. You catch 20 Bridgets at home and 80 Kathleens. If everyone cooperates, this gives you 100 interviews.

Your next 200 calls again go to 100 Bridgets and 100 Kathleens. Again, you catch 20 Bridgets and 80 Kathleens. If all cooperate, you get 100 more interviews, filling your quota for the group. However, the quota has been filled with 40 Bridgets and 160 Kathleens rather than 100/100 as appropriate. What happened?

Sampling can be viewed as a multistage process, in which the probability of a population member appearing in the obtained sample is calculated as their probability of being selected, multiplied by their probability of being contacted if selected, multiplied by their probability of cooperating if contacted. Here, Bridgets and Kathleens had equal probabilities of being chosen and of cooperating if contacted, but the probability of being contacted was four times as high for Kathleens (80% vs. 20%). That is why we got four times as many Kathleens as Bridgets in the sample, despite equal numbers in the population.

Callbacks in a telephone survey are used in an effort to equalize probabilities of contact at 100% for all members of the sample, so that availability is not a source of bias. Essentially, they ensure good outcomes by managing the process. Quotas, in contrast, manage outcomes without addressing process. They can prevent obviously bad outcomes in terms of group distributions, but as the Bridget and Kathleen example shows, they always leave some availability bias within the quota groups. As a result, quotas are not as good as callbacks for controlling nonresponse bias.

The extent to which the availability bias left by quota sampling creates exposure for nonresponse bias depends on the extent to which availability is correlated with the research topic. If we were sampling Bridgets and Kathleens for purposes of a health conditions survey, it might not make a difference, but if we were studying food preparation habits and frequency of eating in restaurants, it probably would.

Also, note that we have described a form of quota sampling that uses probability sampling for the initial and replacement selections. Many forms of quota sampling do not use probability selection: for example, in old-fashioned Gallup polling as described in Chapter 1, and in most shopping mall studies done by market research firms, the selection of individual respondents is not controlled and interviewers can approach whomever they want. Similarly, commercial mail and online panels may be balanced to reflect demographic and geographic quotas but typically consist of volunteers who have been recruited rather than selected. In these situations, quota sampling is a form of nonprobability sampling and is subject to selection bias as well as nonresponse bias. For example, an interviewer in a shopping mall may only approach people who "look nice."

Probability Sampling With Quotas

As seen in our Bridget and Kathleen example, availability bias will arise in a quota sample if there are different probabilities of contact across elements within the quota cells, even if the elements are randomly drawn. Without these differences in contact probabilities, the procedure would not have an availability bias. To illustrate this point, consider the following:

CASE STUDY 3.4

As before, imagine that 18- to 34-year-old unmarried women are split 50/50 (half and half) between the Bridgets and Kathleens of the world. Also, imagine that Bridgets are split 40/60 and Kathleens are split 60/40 between Republicans and Democrats.

Imagine that you are doing a study with quota sampling and have set a quota of 200 interviews for 18- to 34-year-old unmarried women. Because you realize that Bridgets and Kathleens will not be properly represented without a control, you have specifically set a quota of 100 Bridgets and 100 Kathleens (never mind how you will operationalize this requirement!).

Your first 200 calls to 18- to 34-year-old unmarried women go to 100 Bridgets and 100 Kathleens. Within Bridgets, the calls go to 40 Republicans and 60 Democrats, and you reach 8

Republicans and 12 Democrats (20% of each). If everyone cooperates, this gives you 20 Bridget interviews, split 8/12 between Republicans and Democrats. Within Kathleens, the calls go to 60 Republicans and 40 Democrats, and you reach 48 Republicans and 32 Democrats (80% of each). If everyone cooperates, this gives you 80 Kathleen interviews, split 48/32 between Republicans and Democrats.

After 250 calls, you will have called 125 Kathleens and contacted 100 (80%) of them, split 60/40 between Republicans and Democrats. At this point, you have filled your quota for Kathleens.

After 1,000 calls, you will have called 500 Bridgets and contacted 100 (20%) of them, split 40/60 between Republicans and Democrats. At this point, you have filled your quota for Bridgets.

Notice that Republicans and Democrats are properly represented for Bridgets, Kathleens, and in total. Republicans and Democrats are properly represented for Bridgets because contact probabilities were homogeneous within Bridgets: Republican Bridgets and Democrat Bridgets had the same 20% chance of being contacted, so neither group was overrepresented as a result of higher availability. Republicans and Democrats are properly represented for Kathleens for the same reason: Republican Kathleens and Democrat Kathleens had the same 80% chance of being contacted, so neither group was overrepresented as a result of higher availability.

Between Bridgets and Kathleens, the contact probabilities are not homogeneous, and as we have already seen, the difference would have led to availability bias if not controlled. We accommodated the difference between Bridgets and Kathleens by setting quotas for the respective groups and working harder to contact the more difficult group.

As this example suggests, if probability sampling is used to draw the elements of a quota sample, and quota groups can be defined such that probabilities of contact are homogeneous *within* each group, then quota sampling will not be subject to availability bias and will properly represent the population of interest (contact probabilities will not be homogeneous *between* groups and need not be, because quota allocations will ensure proper representation at this level). Sudman (1967) referred to this type of sampling as *probability sampling with quotas*, or *prob-quota sampling*.

Prob-quota sampling offers little in the way of cost savings compared with probability sampling with follow-ups, because there is no reduction in the number of contact attempts. For example, in sampling with follow-ups, if a selection has a contact probability of 20%, it will take an average of five calls to establish contact. In prob-quota sampling, if that selection is replaced by another selection with a 20% contact probability, then another, then another, it will still take an average of five calls to contact a respondent. The only way the number of contacts will be reduced is if the replacement elements have higher probabilities of contact, which means that availability bias is being incurred. To put it another way, the reason that quota sampling usually costs less than probability sampling with follow-ups is because quota sampling has availability bias, and if the availability bias is eliminated, so are the savings. In fact, it may cost *more* to use prob-quota sampling than follow-ups, because first calls in a study with follow-ups may yield information about respondents' schedules that results in higher contact probabilities on later calls.

The big potential advantage for prob-quota sampling is speed. With prob-quota sampling, a telephone interviewing operation could study a careful sample of the population within a single evening, while follow-ups would take at least a week. This would be a big advantage in time-sensitive research such as overnight political polling. For example, one of the earliest applications of prob-quota sampling was to study public reactions in the period immediately after the assassination of President John F. Kennedy (Sudman, 1967). Emergency health surveillance is another area in which this method may be effective. For example, several years ago, an unexpected strain of flu required an alternative vaccine. A quick assessment of people's intention to get the new flu shot was needed to estimate needed production of the vaccine.

The operational problem with prob-quota sampling is being able to define a compact set of quota groups that have homogeneous contact probabilities. If too many groups are defined, it becomes very costly to fill quotas in the hardest to find groups, but if the groups are too large, they lose homogeneity and availability bias becomes a problem. In the mid-1960s, when door-to-door interviewing was the common method for general population surveys, Sudman (1967) advised four quota groups for studies of individuals: employed women, nonemployed women, men ages 18 to 29, and men age 30 and older. Almost certainly, current group definitions would differ because of changing methods and changing social conditions.

Prob-quota sampling is an interesting idea that merits consideration, for example, in situations when a high overall nonresponse rate is anticipated using a strict probability sample, but as far as we know, there is little current usage of the procedure, and it is not clear that groups can be defined that will effectively eliminate the availability bias found in other quota methods.

Weighting for Differential Response

If you maximize the response rate, or if you use quotas, you are controlling nonresponse bias by controlling the composition of the sample. Another approach is to weight observations in an effort at statistical control.

Weighting can be done in various ways. One approach is to weight the sample to an external standard. The obtained sample is compared with known population characteristics on any available variables: for example, a general population sample for which measures of sex, age, and income have been taken might be compared with census data on these variables. If there are no significant differences, this is taken as evidence that nonresponse bias is not a problem, and nothing is done. If significant differences are observed, they are controlled by weighting the data to match the population distribution on the discrepant variable(s). For example, if 40% of the respondents in an observed sample are younger than 55 years and 60% are 55 years and older, and the relevant population is known to have 80% younger than 55 and 20% older, then data from respondents younger than 55 would be weighted by 80 / 40, or 2 (the proportion of the sample they should represent, relative to the proportion that they do represent), and data from respondents age 55 and older would be weighted by 20 / 60, or 1/3. Symbolically, the ith group is weighted by (π_i / p_i), where π_i is the group's proportion in the population and p_i is its proportion in the sample.

Another approach is to weight by response rates. For example, imagine that response rates in a national telephone study are 10% for big city telephone exchanges and 40% for other telephone exchanges, with an overall response rate of 20%. Clearly, the obtained sample underrepresents big cities. In this example, data from the big city exchanges would be weighted by 0.20 / 0.10, or 2 (the response rate they should have had, relative to the response rate they did have), and data from the other exchanges would be weighted by 0.20 / 0.40, or 0.5. Symbolically, the ith group is weighted by (r / r_i), where r is the overall response rate for the whole sample and r_i is the response rate for this group. In the field of online panel research, weighting of this type is called *response propensity weighting*, in reference to individual or group propensities to respond.

A third approach is to weight by probabilities of contact (which works in theory but tends to be unreliable in practice and thus is rarely used). For example, Politz and Simmons (1949) proposed a scheme in which data are gathered without callbacks or quotas, but respondents are asked whether or not they were available on the preceding five evenings, and data are weighted inverse to availability. Respondents who were available on all six evenings (current plus five preceding) receive a weight of 1, and respondents who were not available on any of the preceding evenings receive a weight of 6, on the presumption that only one sixth of respondents of this type would be available on a random evening. Following a similar logic, Nowell and Stanley (1991) proposed that uncontrolled shopping mall surveys be inversely weighted according to self-reported time on site, on the presumption that the probability of being intercepted is proportional to time on site.

At first glance, group weighting appears to be a very attractive way to control for nonresponse bias. No need to pay for careful methods and follow-ups: just do whatever is easy, let the sample be what it is, and fix it through weighting. However, there are some major problems with this approach.

First, group weighting can be viewed as a quota scheme where the quotas are assigned post hoc rather than a priori,[5] and it has the same underlying exposure to availability bias, as well as possible selection bias if the sampling is not random. If your research has a dismal response rate, it is optimistic to presume that there is no response bias just because the demographic characteristics of the sample happen to match the population as a whole, or to claim that you have fixed the problem by weighting for obvious flaws. For example, you may have a fair proportion of 18- to 34-year-old females in the sample, or you may have weighted this group to fair proportion, but do you have Bridgets or Kathleens? It is a mistake to presume that weighting can turn a poor sample into a good sample.

A second problem is that weighting increases sampling error (the level of random variation associated with a sample), in the sense that a disproportionate sample that is weighted to achieve proportionality has higher sampling error than a proportional sample (unless the disproportionate scheme has been designed to take advantage of group differences in variation or cost, as will be discussed in Chapter 5). We discuss the effect of weighting on sampling error in more detail in Chapter 7: For now, we simply note that increased sampling error is a negative consequence of weighting.

A third potential problem is that weights must be reliable to be useful, and problems may exist in this regard. For example, the Politz-Simmons procedure depends on self-reports of availability, and it has been found that respondents are not reliable in providing this information, so the procedure receives little use as a result.

Given these problems, weighting should not be viewed as a primary method for controlling nonresponse bias. Weighting is appropriate to control the possibility of bias resulting from intractable problems, such as irreducible nonresponse, but one's first line of defense against nonresponse bias should always be careful data collection procedures.

---

5. In fact, another name for weighting in this fashion is *poststratification*, or analyzing the data in groups on a post hoc basis. We will mention it again in Chapter 5, on stratified sampling.

Comparing Early Versus Late Respondents

Exposure to nonresponse bias is sometimes evaluated through comparisons of early versus late respondents. The logic is that the earliest respondents are the easiest to get, later respondents are harder to get, and nonrespondents are hardest to get, so there is a trend in difficulty. Under this logic, if key results differ between early and late respondents, the differences indicate a correlation between difficulty and results, and hence exposure to nonresponse bias. Conversely, a lack of differences indicates that there is no correlation and hence that nonresponse bias is not a problem.

Unfortunately, this method is almost always used in the context of mail or online surveys with low response rates, where its plausibility is suspect. For example, if half of the responses to an online study come within 1 day, and most of the rest come within the next 2 days, and the overall response rate is 8%, it is rather heroic to assume that an absence of differences between the 1-day and the 2- and 3-day respondents provides reliable information about the 92% who didn't respond. Overall, we regard this as a weak method.

Follow-up Studies of Nonrespondents

Even if one uses the best possible practices, nonresponse bias may remain a threat. For survey researchers, there has been a steady decline in sample cooperation over the past 20 years. Telephone surveys might have response rates under 15% and mail and Internet-based surveys are often under 10%. In such circumstances, the ultimate way to control nonresponse bias is to measure and adjust for it. This requires that data be obtained from a sample of nonrespondents for purposes of comparison with respondents.

Follow-up studies of nonrespondents usually are not large; for example, in a mail survey with several hundred responses, one might try to obtain a sample of no more than 50 nonrespondents. The goal is not to make precise estimates concerning this group but simply to check whether they are different from respondents. If differences are not observed, one can feel better about the generalizability of the research, regardless of the response rate. If differences *are* observed, then a problem is known to exist. At this point, one can at least document the problem, and if the sample of (initial) nonrespondents is large enough and has a high enough response rate, it may be reasonable to adjust the study results by weighting and combining data from respondents and nonrespondents.

Gathering data from nonrespondents might seem like an oxymoron, but it is not impossible. Some respondents will respond to a different mode of administration; for example, people who don't return a mail questionnaire may respond to a telephone interview, or vice versa. Even within the same mode of administration, the data collectors who are given the task of converting refusals are typically more capable than average, or the second research request may catch the respondent at a better time. Also, an interview of nonrespondents may be limited to a few key questions to make it easier to persuade people to participate. Finally, since it is desirable to get the highest possible response rate in a follow-up of nonrespondents (to try to capture "hard-core" as well as "soft-core" nonrespondents), it is becoming increasingly common to offer cash incentives to induce nonrespondents to participate in the follow-up research.

Online surveys may be particularly amenable to mixed-mode follow-ups of nonrespondents, at least partly because online surveys tend to have lower response rates to begin with. Couper et al. (2007) report a study pertaining to an online weight management intervention in which 85% of the baseline participants did not respond to an online questionnaire at the 12-month measurement period. Three hundred nonrespondents were randomly assigned to a telephone follow-up, and 400 were randomly assigned to a mail follow-up. As Exhibit 3.6 shows, both follow-up methods obtained response rates of more than 50% from people who had previously not responded to the online request.

Follow-up studies of nonrespondents offer significant benefits if they can be done effectively, as in Couper et al. (2007). They obtain direct measures of nonresponse bias, and nonresponse bias on all measured variables can be estimated. On the negative side, follow-ups to nonrespondents extend the data collection period and are costly, with no guarantee of worthwhile return for the delay and costs. Because of their nontrivial cost and time requirements, they must be allowed for in the initial research budget and schedule.

In general, follow-ups of nonrespondents are more likely to be useful in household than in organizational or business surveys. A large proportion of household nonresponse is noncontacts, which are amenable to additional aggressive efforts. In contrast, refusals dominate nonresponse to organizational surveys and often are due to reasons such as company policies that follow-up appeals will not affect.

3.2.2 Calculating Response Rates

Our description of the final, obtained sample will include information about the response rate (see Chapter 9 for a full discussion of what to put in the sample

Exhibit 3.6   Alternative data collection methods may capture nonrespondents.

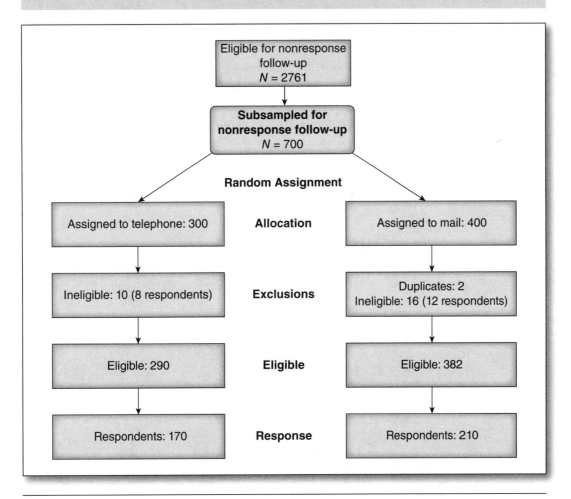

Source: Copyright © Mick P. Couper, Andy Peytchev, Victor J. Strecher, Kendra Rothert, Julia Anderson. Originally published in the *Journal of Medical Internet Research* (http://www.jmir.org, 13.06.2007). Distributed under the terms of the Creative Commons Attribution License.

report). This is not as straightforward as it might seem. The terms *response, refusal, cooperation,* and *completion rates,* among others, are used by different researchers to mean quite different things. Although there have been recommendations for the computation and presentation of these rates (see Council of American Survey Research Organizations; Groves & Couper, 1998; Hidiroglou,

Drew, & Gray, 1993), they have not been universally adopted. The most recent attempt is a publication by the American Association for Public Opinion Research (AAPOR, 2011) that recommends standard definitions and formulas for telephone and face-to-face surveys.[6]

We propose two simple measures of response rates, but more important, we urge that the researcher show exactly how the rates for the particular study were computed and what rules govern the sample dispositions that go into those rates.

Our first measure is a *response rate* that measures how effective you were at obtaining data from all eligible sample members. This figure is calculated as

$$\text{Response rate} = I \,/\, [(I + R + NC + O) + e(U)],$$

where

I = the number of interviews or observations;

R = the number of refusals;

NC = the number of noncontacts believed to be eligible;

O = the number of cases not obtained for other reasons, such as language problems;

U = the number of cases with unknown eligibility;

$e = I \,/\, (I + SO)$, where I is the number of interviews or observations and SO is the number of cases screened out as ineligible.

The second measure of response is a *cooperation rate* that measures how well you did at getting data from selected population members you were able to reach. This figure is calculated as

$$\text{Cooperation rate} = I \,/\, (I + R + O).$$

Notice that noncontacts and refusals must be differentiated to calculate the cooperation rate. This is not possible in mail and online surveys, so the only response rate you will get from those studies is the response rate.

---

6. Both the AAPOR Standard Definitions Report and the AAPOR (Excel) Response Rate Calculator V3.1 are available for download at http://www.aapor.org/Standard_Definitions2.htm.

3.3 CHAPTER SUMMARY

This chapter discussed issues in drawing samples and executing research. We discussed two basic methods of drawing samples: simple random sampling and systematic sampling. With simple random sampling (srs), population members are drawn directly using random numbers to determine which members are selected. With systematic sampling, a random start is followed by every ith population member. In situations where sampling must be done from physical sources such as printed directories, or file drawers containing archival records, the fastest way to draw a sample is with systematic sampling based on physical measures.

The principal sampling issue regarding research execution is nonresponse bias. To maintain sample integrity, try to maximize the response rate: Choose a method that encourages participation from the highest possible percentage of selected population members, use callbacks or follow-up procedures to ensure that virtually all selected population members will be contacted for the research, and follow "best practices" in doing the research. There also are other methods for controlling nonresponse bias, including quota sampling, probability sampling with quotas, weighting for differential response, and comparing early versus late respondents, but these methods are less effective than maximizing response. If the response rate remains low despite your best efforts, try to gather data from a sample of nonrespondents. These data can be compared with data from respondents to test for nonresponse bias and to provide a basis for adjusted estimates.

A description of the final, obtained sample will include information about the response rate. We suggest two measures: the response rate, which measures how effective you were at obtaining data from all eligible sample members, and the cooperation rate, which measures how well you did at getting data from selected population members you were able to reach.

EXERCISES AND DISCUSSION QUESTIONS

Exercise 3.1

Take a class roster—or any list—and draw a simple random sample and a systematic sample from it.

Exercise 3.2

In a survey on parks and recreation, 40% of respondents are younger than 55 years, and 60% are 55 years and older. The relevant population is known to have 80% younger than 55 and 20% older. The unweighted survey results indicate that 26% of area residents want more children's playgrounds in city parks: 50% for respondents younger than 55 years and 10% for respondents 55 years and older. If these results are weighted to correct for age, what percentage of area residents want more children's playgrounds?

SECTION II

Sample Size and Sample Efficiency

In Section I, we gave an overview of the sampling process, from population definition to research execution. We discussed ways that sample bias can arise at each step along the way and described procedures for obtaining samples with minimum sample bias.

In Section II, we turn to questions of sample size and sample efficiency. Where Section I focused on controlling *sample bias*, this section focuses on controlling *sampling error*. Sampling error refers to the idea that chance variation will cause most samples to differ from the population to some extent, even if the sampling procedure is unbiased.

When you finish this section, you should know (a) the relationship between sample size and sampling error, (b) how to calculate a sample size that provides an acceptable level of sampling error, (c) other methods of setting sample size to provide an acceptable level of precision in the results, (d) sampling methods that may allow you to improve the cost-effectiveness of a sample (i.e., sampling methods that may allow you to produce a lower sampling error for the same research budget), and (e) how to implement those methods.

This section assumes that you have taken an introductory course in statistics and are familiar with the concepts of mean, variance, and standard deviation. Even if you have not had such a course, you should be able to follow the discussion if you familiarize yourself with those terms.

4

Setting Sample Size

This chapter begins our discussion of how to control sampling error by discussing how to set sample size. As we will see, the level of sampling error is determined by the sample size, which means that sample sizes can be calculated to produce acceptable levels of sampling error. In this chapter, you will learn the following:

- How sampling error relates to sample size
- How to calculate a sample size that provides an acceptable level of sampling error
- How to calculate a sample size based on hypothesis testing power
- How to calculate a sample size based on the value of information
- Informal methods for setting sample size

The discussion in this chapter presumes the use of simple random sampling. In some situations, it may be possible to make the sample more efficient by using stratified or cluster sampling. These procedures are discussed in subsequent chapters.

4.1 SAMPLING ERROR ILLUSTRATED

The concept of sampling error is best illustrated by showing the samples available from a small population. Exhibit 4.1 shows such a population: five people named Ann, Bob, Carl, Dave, and Edna. Ann is a 24-year-old female, Bob is a 36-year-old male, Carl is a 48-year-old male, Dave is a 60-year-old male, and Edna is a 72-year-old female. The average age of this population is 48, and the population is 60% male.

Exhibit 4.1   A Small Population

Population member	Age	Gender
Ann	24	Female
Bob	36	Male
Carl	48	Male
Dave	60	Male
Edna	72	Female

Exhibit 4.2 shows all of the samples of size 1, 2, 3, 4, and 5 that can be drawn from this population, assuming that no population member is repeated in a sample (i.e., sampling without replacement). A sample of size 5, of course, is a complete census of the population. Exhibit 4.2 also shows (1) the mean age of each sample, (2) the proportion of each sample that is male, and (3) averages across all samples of a given size. Again, these are *all* of the samples that can be drawn from our five-person population.

Exhibit 4.2   All Possible Samples From Our Small Population

	Mean Age	Percent Male
All samples of n = 1		
Ann	24	0
Bob	36	100
Carl	48	100
Dave	60	100
Edna	72	0
Average	**48**	**60**

All samples of $n = 2$		
Ann, Bob	30	50
Ann, Carl	36	50
Ann, Dave	42	50
Bob, Carl	42	100
Ann, Edna	48	0
Bob, Dave	48	100
Bob, Edna	54	50
Carl, Dave	54	100
Carl, Edna	60	50
Dave, Edna	66	50
Average	**48**	**60**
All samples of $n = 3$		
Ann, Bob, Carl	36	67
Ann, Bob, Dave	40	67
Ann, Bob, Edna	44	33
Ann, Carl, Dave	44	67
Ann, Carl, Edna	48	33
Bob, Carl, Dave	48	100
Bob, Carl, Edna	52	67
Ann, Dave, Edna	52	33
Bob, Dave, Edna	56	67
Carl, Dave, Edna	60	67
Average	**48**	**60**
All samples of $n = 4$		
Ann, Bob, Carl, Dave	42	75
Ann, Bob, Carl, Edna	45	50

Continued

(Exhibit 4.2) Continued

Ann, Bob, Dave, Edna	48	50
Ann, Carl, Dave, Edna	51	50
Bob, Carl, Dave, Edna	54	75
Average	**48**	**60**
All samples of $n = 5$		
Ann, Bob, Carl, Dave, Edna	**48**	**60**

Three important facts can be seen in Exhibit 4.2:

- First, when you calculate an average of sample means (or proportions) for all samples of a given size, they have the same average as the population as a whole. This is what statisticians mean when they say that the "expected value" of a sample mean equals the population mean.

- However, the mean (or proportion) for any given sample will not necessarily be the same as the population mean. In fact, *most* sample means differ from the population mean, not because of systematic bias but simply because of variation in sample composition. This type of variation is formalized in the idea of sampling error.

- The distribution of sample means (or proportions) becomes more tightly concentrated around the overall population mean as the sample size increases. That is, the level of sampling error declines as the sample gets larger.

This last point is illustrated in Exhibit 4.3, which shows the range around the population mean that captures 60% of the possible sample means for age. At $n = 1$, 60% of the possible samples fall between 36 and 60, or within ±12 of the population mean of 48. At $n = 2$, 60% of the possible samples fall between 42 and 54, or within ±6 of the population mean. At $n = 3$, 60% of the possible samples fall between 44 and 52, within ±4. At $n = 4$, 60% fall between 45 and 51, ±3. At $n = 5$, where the sample encompasses the full population, there is no sample variation.

The level of *sampling error* is quantified as the standard deviation of the distribution of sample means (or proportions) across samples of a particular size. In statistical notation, this term is written as $\sigma_{\bar{x}}$ (or σ_p for proportions). The formula that relates the sampling error to the sample size is

$$\sigma_{\bar{X}} = \sqrt{\frac{\sigma^2}{n} \times \left(\frac{N-n}{N}\right) \times \left(\frac{N}{N-1}\right)} \qquad (4.1)$$

Exhibit 4.3   Range of Mean Age That Captures 60% of the Possible Samples

$n = 5$	48
$n = 4$	45____51
$n = 3$	44_____52
$n = 2$	42_____54
$n = 1$	36_____60

where $\sigma_{\bar{x}}$ is the sampling error, σ^2 is the variance among population members for the variable being measured, n is the sample size, and N is the population size.

The term $(N - n)/N$ is the *finite population correction (fpc)*, which adjusts for the fact that variation across samples becomes more and more limited as the samples become a larger percentage of the population. Ultimately, if the entire population is taken in the sample, $n = N$, the fpc goes to zero, and by extension the sampling error likewise goes to zero; that is, there is no sampling error if the sample includes the entire population. This is an important concept, but we usually drop the term for computational simplicity unless the sample constitutes at least 10% of the population, which occurs fairly often in surveys of organizational populations but rarely in surveys of household populations.

The term $N/(N - 1)$ is the *correction for sampling without replacement,* which adjusts for the fact that variation across samples is slightly increased by not allowing elements to be repeated. This term is rarely consequential and is almost always dropped for computational simplicity.

If we drop the finite population correction and the correction for sampling without replacement, this leaves us with

$$\sigma_{\bar{X}} = \sqrt{\frac{\sigma^2}{n}} \tag{4.2}$$

So we can see that the level of sampling error is positively related to the level of variance in the population and negatively related to the sample size. Note that neither the size of the population nor the percentage of the population that is sampled influences the sampling error unless the finite population correction becomes relevant.

4.2 SAMPLE SIZE BASED ON CONFIDENCE INTERVALS

The logic of the confidence interval approach to sample size is as follows. We know that a sample mean (or proportion) is likely to vary from the population value because of variation in sample composition. We would like to control our exposure to error from this source, and we can do so through the sample size, based on a desired *confidence interval* (also sometimes called the *margin of error*).

Sample means follow a "normal" distribution across repeated samples, and 95% of the values in a normal distribution fall within ±1.96 standard deviations from the mean of that distribution. We have defined the sampling error, $\sigma_{\bar{x}}$, as being the standard deviation of the distribution of sample means; therefore, 95% of sample means will fall within ±1.96 ($\sigma_{\bar{x}}$) of the average sample mean—that is, within ±1.96 ($\sigma_{\bar{x}}$) of the population mean. To put it another way, there is a 95% chance that any given sample mean will fall within this interval (assuming an unbiased sampling procedure).

In the previous section of this chapter, we gave formulas that relate $\sigma_{\bar{x}}$ to (1) the variance of the variable in question, (2) the sample size, and (3) if we use the finite population correction, the population size. Therefore, if we specify a desired value for ±1.96 ($\sigma_{\bar{x}}$)—that is, if we specify the desired "95% confidence interval," which we will write as $I_{95\%}$—and if we estimate the variance and the population size, then we can use our previous formulas to solve for the sample size needed to produce this result.

Specifically,

$$I_{95\%} = 1.96\,(\,\sigma_{\bar{x}}\,)$$

If we use Equation 4.1 to substitute for $\sigma_{\bar{x}}$:

$$I_{95\%} = 1.96 \times \sqrt{\frac{\sigma^2}{n} \times \left(\frac{N-n}{N}\right) \times \left(\frac{N}{N-1}\right)}$$

Solving for *n:*

$$n = \frac{\sigma^2 \times \left(\dfrac{N}{N-1}\right)}{\left\{\left(\dfrac{I_{95\%}}{1.96}\right)^2 + \left(\dfrac{\sigma^2}{N-1}\right)\right\}} \tag{4.3}$$

If we drop the fpc and the correction for sampling without replacement and use the simpler Equation 4.2, then

$$I_{95\%} = 1.96 \sqrt{\frac{\sigma^2}{n}}$$

Solving for n:

$$n = \left(\frac{1.96 \times \sigma}{I_{95\%}}\right)^2 \tag{4.4}$$

The following points may be noted:

- We normally use Equation 4.4 unless the sample will be at least 10% of the population.
- Equations 4.3 and 4.4 are for 95% confidence intervals. If you prefer to work with 90% confidence intervals, use 1.645 instead of 1.96 in the equations (90% of the values in a normal distribution fall within ±1.645 standard deviations from the mean).
- Equations 4.3 and 4.4 are relevant when the goal of our research is to estimate the *mean* of some variable with an acceptable level of sampling error. Means are averages; when you answer the question, "What is the average value of some variable?" you are estimating a mean. In some cases, we wish to estimate *proportions*. Proportions are percentages; when you answer the question, "What percentage of the population has some characteristic?" you are estimating a proportion. If the purpose of the research is to estimate a proportion, rather than a mean, then the term $\sqrt{\pi \times (1-\pi)}$ is substituted for σ in these formulas, where π is the proportion of the population that has the characteristic of interest. Likewise, if we seek to estimate any other type of statistic—correlations, regression coefficients, and so on—then we would substitute the appropriate formula for the standard deviation of that statistic.
- Means and proportions also form the basis for estimates of group sizes and total amounts. Group sizes, such as the number of Americans who own guns, are obtained via estimates of proportions; take a sample of Americans, estimate the proportion that own guns, and multiply this proportion by the population size of America, N, to get an estimate of the total group size. Likewise, total amounts, such as total dollars spent by Americans on birthday gifts, are obtained via estimates of means; take a sample of Americans, estimate their mean expenditure on birthday gifts,

and multiply the mean by N to get an estimate of the total amount. So if the purpose of a research project is to estimate a group size or total amount, it may be reexpressed in terms of a mean or proportion for application of the formulas given here.

- Solving Equation 4.3 or 4.4 requires us to estimate σ (or π for a proportion); in other words, it requires us to estimate characteristics of the population before we have studied the population! We will discuss how to do this a little later in this chapter.
- Solving Equation 4.3 or 4.4 also requires us to specify a desired confidence interval. If you aren't sure what confidence interval you want, it may be more appropriate to (1) set the sample size in some informal way, as discussed later in this chapter; (2) calculate the associated confidence intervals for variables of interest; and (3) think about whether those confidence intervals are satisfactory given the purposes of your research. If not, try other sample sizes until you are satisfied.

4.2.1 Computational Examples

Here is an example of sample size calculations for the confidence interval approach. Assume that we wish to estimate the mean annual expenditure on birthday gifts within some population, and we would like to have a 95% chance that the sample mean falls within ±$20 of the population mean. Further assume that the population size is approximately 4,000,000, and our a priori estimate of the standard deviation of annual birthday gift expenditures within this population is $400. Using Equation 4.3, the sample size needed to reach our confidence interval goal is

$$n = \frac{400^2 \times \left(\dfrac{4,000,000}{4000000 - 1} \right)}{\left\{ \left(\dfrac{20}{1.96} \right)^2 + \left(\dfrac{400^2}{4,000,000 - 1} \right) \right\}}$$

$$= 1{,}536.05, \text{ or } 1{,}537$$

Using Formula 4.4, which disregards the finite population correction, we get

$$n = \left(\frac{1.96 \times 400}{20} \right)^2$$

$$= 1{,}536.64, \text{ or } 1{,}537$$

The two formulas yield essentially the same result, because the population is large. However, now assume that the population size is 400 instead of 4,000,000. Using Formula 4.3, the sample size needed to reach our confidence interval goal is

$$n = \frac{400^2 \times \left(\dfrac{400}{400-1}\right)}{\left\{\left(\dfrac{20}{1.96}\right)^2 + \left(\dfrac{400^2}{400-1}\right)\right\}}$$

= 317.54, or 318

Using Formula 4.4, we get

$$n = \left(\frac{1.96 \times 400}{20}\right)^2$$

= 1,536.64, or 1,537

The results are substantially different, and the formula that disregards the finite population correction yields a sample size larger than the population size, which obviously is not possible. In this case, it is important to consider the fpc because the population is small.

Here is another example. Assume that we wish to estimate the proportion of some population who favors a social policy initiative, and we would like to have a 95% chance that the sample proportion falls within ±.02 (2%) of the population value. Further assume that the population size is approximately 4,000,000, and our a priori estimate of the proportion in favor of the initiative is .50 (50%). Using Formula 4.4 since the population is large, and substituting $\sqrt{\pi \times (1-\pi)}$ for σ, the sample size needed to reach our confidence interval goal is

$$n = \left(\frac{1.96 \times \sqrt{.5 \times (1-.5)}}{.02}\right)^2$$

= 2,401

Two points about these calculations are in order:

• First, the result may be a sample size that is larger than you can undertake with your resources. If this occurs, then you must accept a wider, less precise confidence interval. In general, you might wish to enter the sample size formula in a computer spreadsheet and then experiment with different values of the confidence interval to find a good balance of precision (from the confidence interval) and cost (from the sample size), given the planned data uses.

- Also, these calculations apply to estimates for an entire population. If you wish to obtain separate estimates for population subgroups, then each subgroup will have its own sampling requirements. For example, if you want separate estimates of the proportion of men and women who favor some policy initiative, and you want to have a 95% confidence interval of ±.02 (2%) for your estimate in each group, then you will need 2,400 men *and* 2,400 women. If you want separate estimates for Anglo men, Anglo women, Hispanic men, Hispanic women, African American men, and African American women, and you want a 95% confidence interval of ±.02 (2%) for each estimate, then you will need a sample size of 2,400 for each of the six groups. Such goals may outstrip the available resources, necessitating a compromise between precision and cost.

Most research projects have many objectives, and some can be achieved with small samples while others require enormous samples. Resource constraints usually require some compromise on the most difficult objectives.

4.2.2 How to Estimate σ or π

To calculate a needed sample size with the confidence interval approach, you need an estimate of σ, the standard deviation for the variable of interest, or π, the proportion of interest. Where will you get these estimates if you haven't done the research?

Let's start with π, because it is the easier problem. There are three ways to get this estimate. One is to use 50% for your estimate, because 50% produces the largest possible value of the term $\sqrt{\pi \times (1-\pi)}$ and hence the largest (most conservative) sample size requirements. Another is to estimate π based on results obtained from other similar studies or for other similar variables. The third is to do a pretest of your study and gather data to estimate π (this pretest also can be used to test the questionnaire, test the field procedures, and evaluate the sample frame). Usually, the safe approach is to assume 50%.

For estimates of σ, the standard deviation of the variable to be measured, you cannot take advantage of the fact that 50% produces a conservative estimate. Your best options, therefore, are (1) to estimate σ based on results from other similar studies or for other similar variables, or (2) to do a pretest to estimate σ.

4.3 SAMPLE SIZE BASED ON HYPOTHESIS TESTING POWER[1]

The "confidence interval" approach to sample size presumes that you wish to estimate some key statistic in a population and that you wish to achieve a certain level of precision in that estimate. However, you may be less interested in estimating a statistic than in testing a hypothesis, particularly if you are engaged in academic research.

For example, assume that you are measuring public opinion on some policy issue, and you wish to test the hypothesis that the percentage of people in favor of this policy differs between women and men. In this situation, it does you no good to say that you want a 95% confidence interval of ±.02 (±2%) around the overall population value. Nor is it helpful to say that you want a 95% confidence interval of ±.02 (±2%) for men and women separately. What you want is to have enough *power* in your hypothesis test to be able to achieve statistical significance if the hypothesis is correct.[2]

This goal is achieved as follows. First, identify the procedure that you will use to test your hypothesis (i.e., *t* test, *F* test, or whatever). Second, estimate the numbers that you expect to have in this test, except for the sample size. Third, solve for the needed sample size.

Assume, for example, that you expect a difference of about .10 (10%) in the proportion of women and men who favor a policy (this estimate might be drawn from general experience or advice, from previous research on similar topics, or from a pilot study). The statistical significance of this difference will be tested by means of a *t* test with the following form:

$$t = \frac{p_1 - p_2}{\sqrt{\left(\frac{p_1 \times (1 - p_1)}{n_1}\right) + \left(\frac{p_2 \times (1 - p_2)}{n_2}\right)}}$$

where *t* is the *t* statistic, p_1 is the sample proportion of women who favor the policy, n_1 is the sample size for women, p_2 is the sample proportion of men who favor the policy, and n_2 is the sample size for men.

---

1. This section of the chapter assumes that you have taken an introductory statistics course that covered hypothesis testing.

2. The power of a statistical test is the probability that it correctly rejects the null hypothesis when the null hypothesis is false—in this case, the probability that we correctly reject the null hypothesis that men and women have the same percentage who favor the policy.

As you will recall from your statistics class, using a two-tailed significance test, you will be able to support your hypothesis at a 95% level of confidence if t is at least 1.96. Enter this value into the equation, along with the estimated value of .10 for $(p_1 - p_2)$, the difference between the groups. Let's also enter values of .50 for p_1 and p_2 in the denominator; we expect a .10 difference between the two proportions, but setting both values at .50 will maximize the $p * (1 - p)$ terms and give us the largest, or most conservative, sample size. The resulting equation is

$$1.96 = \frac{.10}{\sqrt{\left(\frac{.5 \times (1 - .5)}{n_1}\right) + \left(\frac{.5 \times (1 - .5)}{n_2}\right)}}$$

Assuming equal sample sizes for the two groups (i.e., $n_1 = n_2$) and solving for n_1 (or n_2), we get

$$n_1 \text{ (or } n_2) = 192.08 \text{ or } 193$$

So, if the difference between women and men is .10, as expected, and the percentage that favors the policy is in the neighborhood of .50 for each group, then you will need a sample size of 193 men and 193 women to reach statistical significance for the difference.

If you find it difficult to establish a direct computation of this type, you can accomplish the same result through simulation. Make up a small sample data set, or do a pilot study. Duplicate these data—for example, if you have 20 observations, copy them four times to make 100 observations—and test your hypotheses at various sample sizes until you find the point at which statistical significance is achieved.

4.4 SAMPLE SIZE BASED ON THE VALUE OF INFORMATION

The confidence interval approach is the traditional statistical approach to sample size calculation: the approach you might find in an introductory statistics text. However, as we have just seen, it does not directly serve your needs if the purpose of your research is to test hypotheses. It also does not address the costs and benefits of research, as is appropriate in market research, government expenditure decisions, and other commercial and policy contexts. The confidence interval approach does not separate research with a $1,000 cost per observation from research with a $10 cost per observation, or research where huge amounts of money are at stake from research where small amounts of money are at stake. The only factors that drive this approach are the confidence interval goal and the innate variability of the population; factors such as the cost of research and the value of the decision do not enter the calculations unless the confidence interval is made larger or smaller in response to these factors. The "value of information" approach to sample size calculation, in contrast, explicitly considers these factors (Schlaifer, 1959; Sudman, 1976).

4.4.1 Why Information Has Value

To understand the value of information approach to sample size, we first must understand why research has value. We will develop this argument in the context of market research. The idea is that managers make decisions, and because of uncertainty in the marketplace, even the most experienced and judicious of managers are sometimes wrong. The value of information is that it enables managers to be right more often and thus to increase their companies' profits. In a government statistics context, it allows better decisions about the implementation or elimination of regulatory and social programs.

Suppose, for example, that a manager makes 100 new product introduction decisions. Given the manager's experience and judgment, let's say that she can make the right decision 65% of the time without conducting market research. Let's also say that market research will allow her to make the right decision 75% of the time (research information is never perfect, and competitors may react in unexpected ways).

What, then, is the value of information? Assume for simplicity that the profit from a correct decision is $1,000,000 for a specified time period, and the loss of a wrong decision is a negative $1,000,000. Over 100 decisions, being right 65 times makes the firm $65,000,000, while being wrong 35 times loses $35,000,000. The net profit is $30,000,000. With market research, and a 75% rate of correct decisions, the net profit is $75,000,000 – $25,000,000 = $50,000,000. The difference between the firm's profits with and without research is $20,000,000, or $200,000 per decision. This is the value of the research.

Note that we haven't said that the company makes $200,000 from each of the 100 research projects. On average, this is true, but the value of any given research project can vary. Also, the value of any given project is not known for certain in advance. Information has value in a specific project only if it causes a change from an incorrect to a correct decision, and you don't know in advance when this will happen. You can, however, note that information only pays off when decision makers change their minds. If research is designed to "play it safe" and reinforce rather than challenge management assumptions, it will not pay off.

4.4.2 Factors Related to the Value of Information

The following factors relate to the value of information:

- *Prior uncertainty* about the proper course of action. How much would you pay for information on the direction the sun will rise tomorrow morning? Presumably nothing, because you already know the answer. Information becomes more valuable as you become less certain about the best course of action or, to put it in the context of our example, as the a priori chances of a correct decision get smaller.

- *Gains or losses* available from the decision. Who will pay more for a research project: a large company considering a $10,000,000 investment or a small company considering a $10,000 investment? The answer is the large company, because the large company has far more money at stake.
  Note, by the way, that the value of information does not depend on ability to pay. It is not that the large company has more money to spend; it is that the large company has more to gain from a good decision or lose from a bad one.

- *Nearness to breakeven,* which indicates the likelihood that research affects the decision. Suppose, for example, that a company is considering the introduction of a new product, and the breakeven sales volume for this product is 150,000 units. Research is more valuable if the company's best a priori estimate of the likely sales volume is 200,000 units than if the company's estimate is 1,000,000 units. When the estimate is near the breakeven point, whether below or above, new information has a high likelihood of affecting the decision. On the other hand, when the estimate is far above or below the breakeven point, it is unlikely the decision will be affected. This point can be seen in the following example.

CASE STUDY 4.1

We recently consulted on three projects for a major oil company. All three projects concerned new services that the company might introduce.

The first service involved oil well drilling on a contract basis for smaller oil companies. We interviewed 10 potential customers in connection with this project. After talking with these 10 people, it was obvious that the service did not appeal to the market. We discontinued interviewing, and the company dropped the idea.

The second service involved energy management services for certain kinds of factories. We interviewed 15 potential customers in connection with this project. We found some interest in the service, but it appeared that potential revenues were unlikely to exceed $2 million per year. This revenue potential was nowhere near enough to fit the company's requirements for a new business, so we discontinued interviewing and the company dropped the idea.

The third service involved an environmental cleanup service to detoxify former industrial sites. Early interviews indicated that this service might have high revenue potential; however, it was not clear whether revenues would be large enough to justify the substantial costs and risks of entering the market. As a result, we planned a study that allowed us to make a fairly close estimate of revenue potential. This study involved more than 100 personal interviews (which is a large number in an industrial study) and cost well over $100,000.

Together, the three studies illustrate a point about the value of information. If early information shows that a potential product or service is far above or below the revenues needed for introduction, then further research is not needed. If the situation is not so clear, and there is a large amount of money to be gained or lost from good or bad decisions, then expensive research may be justified.

4.4.3 Sample Size and the Value of Information

Information has value, but information also costs money to obtain. As with all economic goods, we seek to maximize the net gain in information after accounting for costs. This gain is maximized as follows. Each new unit of information—for example, each survey interview—provides some marginal improvement in our knowledge about the topic of interest and hence some marginal value. This marginal value decreases from unit to unit, because the more we know, the less value we get from an additional unit of information. Each unit of information also carries some marginal cost. This marginal cost tends to remain constant from unit to unit. The optimal sample size occurs when the marginal gain from one unit of new information is just equal to the cost of that unit of information.

If we quantify the factors that underlie the value of information (i.e., prior uncertainty, gain or loss potential, and nearness to breakeven), and we specify the variable costs of gathering information (e.g., the cost of conducting each survey interview), then it is possible to calculate an optimal sample size where marginal gain equals marginal cost. An example of these calculations may be seen in Sudman (1976) or Sudman and Blair (1998, Appendix 14.2). The calculations are complex, and in our experience, formal calculations of this type are rarely used (if only because decision makers are unaware of the method).

However, decision makers often draw on implicit notions of the value of information in setting project budgets.

4.5 INFORMAL METHODS FOR SETTING SAMPLE SIZE

We have discussed some formal, quantitative approaches for setting sample size in a research project. Several informal approaches also are used by researchers. These methods, which tend to implicitly reflect the same considerations as our formal methods, include the following:

- Setting sample size according to previous or typical practice
- Using the "magic number" to set sample size
- Setting sample size for minimum cell sizes in subgroup analyses
- Setting sample size according to resource limitations

4.5.1 Using Previous or Typical Sample Sizes

It is common for researchers who do repetitive projects to set sample sizes according to what has worked previously. For example, we know of one pharmaceutical company that usually uses a sample size of 50 to measure doctors' opinions about its new drugs. If a new drug is deemed especially important, the company uses 100 doctors. The company's decision makers are accustomed to these numbers and feel comfortable with them.

The simple approach of repeating sample sizes works well if situations are similar and the previous sample size was satisfactory. It is important to recognize, however, that different situations may require different sample sizes. Simply doing the same thing each time can lead to spending too much or too little on information relative to what it is worth.

A related approach is to "follow the crowd" and use sample sizes similar to those that other researchers have used. Copying sample sizes has the same logic as repeating your own sample sizes—"if it worked before, it should work again"—and the same pitfalls. Different situations, including different analyses of the same types of data, may require different sample sizes.

In many situations, sample size norms relate to the confidence interval calculations we discussed earlier in this chapter, along with some sense of the value of information. Exhibit 4.4 shows how the "margin of sampling error" (i.e., confidence interval) around an estimate of a proportion declines as the sample size increases. There is a steep decline up to a sample size of 200 and a less dramatic decline up to a sample size of 1,000, at which point the curve flattens out and reductions in the confidence interval are hard to come by. It is therefore not surprising that, in our experience, 200 is a typical sample size in many types of research, and national political polls often use a sample size of 1,000 to 1,500. The pollster would gain relatively little overall precision from increasing the sample to 2,500 or 5,000, although the precision of estimates for population subgroups might benefit.

Exhibit 4.4 also gives some indication of why "qualitative" researchers with very small sample sizes often use nonprobability sampling so as to control the characteristics of the sample through judgment rather than leave them to chance. As the sample becomes small, sampling error becomes very large.

Exhibit 4.4   Margin of Sampling Error Versus Sample Size

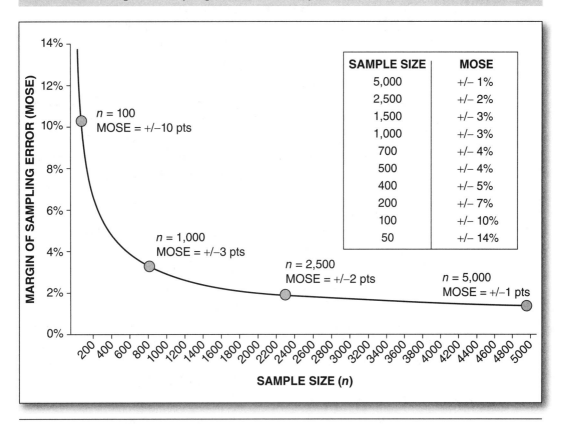

Source: © AAPOR/News U.

4.5.2 Using the Magic Number

Another informal method for sample size determination is to use what we call the "magic number." By this we mean a number that seems appropriate to people who will be asked to support decisions based on the research.

Research is most useful when it challenges conventional thinking and suggests new ways of doing things. After all, you don't need research to tell you to keep doing things the same way. However, research that suggests new ways of doing things almost always faces some resistance. The doubters and opponents of a research conclusion will seek ways to deny or invalidate that conclusion, and one of the most common is to say that the research is based on "only" n number of observations. In the authors' experience, this situation is not infrequent in educational assessments, where an unexpected change in student performance that is inconsistent with past trends can have major repercussions.

To maximize the acceptance of research conclusions and hence make them more valuable, researchers should assess users' beliefs about appropriate sample sizes at the start of a research project. Be blunt—tell them, "You know, sometimes research studies produce unexpected findings," and ask, "If this study produces unexpected findings, what kind of sample size would make you feel comfortable that these findings are legitimate and not a fluke?" Probe until you get answers from the key users who will receive and implement project findings. Then make sure that the sample size exceeds these expectations. This precaution won't forestall all criticisms of the sample size, but it will minimize them, and it is an important part of producing research that satisfies users' intuitive concerns.

In an organization that does a lot of research, the "magic number" is likely to be the same as previous sample sizes. In the pharmaceutical company that measures physician response to new drugs with standard sample sizes of 50 and 100, these sample sizes have become invisible—nobody thinks to question them, and research findings based on them are well accepted. If the research department did a study with some other sample size, such as 40 or 72, then all attention would be on the unusual sample size rather than the results of the study. The research would face resistance because it violates organizational standards that people have accepted.

In academic work, the "magic number" is likely to be whatever is typical for published research in the field. When planning your research, check the journals in which you hope to publish the results to get a sense of sample size norms.

4.5.3 Anticipating Subgroup Analyses

Our third informal method for setting sample size is to anticipate subgroup analyses and set minimum sample sizes in the smallest subgroups. Suppose, for example, that a hospital plans to measure satisfaction among inpatients (people who stayed in the hospital for at least one night) with the treatment and services they received at the hospital. The hospital plans to report separate analyses for various wards (orthopedic, maternity, etc.), and it wants all reports to be based on a minimum of 50 patients. Also suppose that the neurological ward is the smallest distinct ward, accounting for only 4% of inpatients. Under these circumstances, the hospital's inpatient satisfaction study must do one of the following: (1) use a total sample size of at least 1,250 ($50 \div .04 = 1,250$), so the sample should produce at least 50 neurological patients; (2) oversample neurological patients so the subgroup minimum can be met despite a total sample of less than 1,250; or (3) plan not to issue a report for the neurological ward.

This approach to setting sample size is very common in social research, especially for large, multiuse studies that are likely to be subjected to secondary analysis. If you are planning a research project, we strongly encourage you to think about how subgroup data might be used, now and in the future, and to design the sample accordingly. Similarly, try to anticipate cross-tabular analyses, or comparisons of group means, and make sure that your research objectives won't be constrained by a need to collapse cells to get adequate cell sizes (e.g., having to collapse African Americans and Hispanics into an ill-defined "minorities" category).

4.5.4 Using Resource Limitations

Another common way of setting sample size is according to resource limitations. These resources might be time or money. So, for example, your sample size might be defined by the number of interviews you can do in the time available or by the number that you can afford.

A budget-based approach is as follows. Ask a decision maker how much he or she expects to pay for a particular research project (or ask yourself how much you can afford). Subtract the fixed costs of the project from this number. Divide the remaining budget by the expected cost per observation to obtain a resource-based sample size.

Say, for example, that a hospital administrator is willing to spend no more than $25,000 for a patient satisfaction survey to be conducted by telephone. A research company might budget some number of hours to write the question-naire and have it approved by the client, some number of hours for data analysis, some number of hours for report preparation, and some number for report presentation. These hours can be budgeted at appropriate pay rates, including overhead charges and profit. The research company also will budget interview-ers' time for a pretest, supervisory time to plan and supervise the pretest, profes-sional time to conduct training for the pretest and the main study, professional time to prepare training materials, and so on. These are the fixed costs of the project.

Let's say, just for example, that these fixed costs sum to $10,000. This leaves $15,000 for variable costs. Now the research company must estimate the variable cost per interview, which will depend on the screening rate, the length of the screening and main questionnaires, any phone charges, the costs of editing and coding (which depend on the number of open-ended questions), and other vari-able costs. Just for example, say these come to $50 per completed interview for the hospital satisfaction study. Therefore, a $15,000 budget for variable costs will allow a sample size of 300 interviews ($15,000 ÷ $50).

A budget-based approach is, in our experience, the most common method used to set sample sizes where budgets are limited. The approach has intuitive appeal because it allows project funders to talk about research in dollars and cents, a language they understand. The approach also is grounded in financial realities. In contrast to other approaches that essentially budget a study and then ask whether project funders are willing to pay that much, the budget-based approach fits the research effort to the funds available.

The weakness in the budget-based approach is that it doesn't explicitly consider information objectives. For example, 300 interviews may be more than a hospital needs to profile overall patient satisfaction or may be nowhere near enough to develop separate satisfaction profiles for various service areas. Just as statistical calculations must be checked against a budget to see whether the sample is affordable, it is desirable to check a budget-based sample size against information needs to see whether the sample will be satisfactory and efficient.

4.6 CHAPTER SUMMARY

This chapter discussed methods for setting sample size, presuming simple ran-dom sampling. We began by illustrating the idea of sampling error, which is related to sample size. We then discussed how to set sample size based on

(1) confidence intervals, (2) hypothesis testing power, (3) the value of information, and (4) informal methods.

Sampling error refers to the idea that variation in sample composition will cause most samples to differ from the population to some extent, even if the sampling procedure is unbiased. For any given sample characteristic, such as the mean value of some variable, the level of sampling error is quantified as the standard deviation of that characteristic across all possible samples of the same size. This value can be controlled through the sample size.

The concept of controlling sampling error through sample size is implemented through the confidence interval approach to sample size. A 95% confidence interval is a range within which 95% of the values in some distribution will fall. We specify the width of the confidence interval that we are willing to accept for estimates of a mean or a proportion and then solve for the sample size needed to produce that confidence interval.

You may be less interested in estimating a statistic than in testing a hypothesis, particularly in academic research. In this case, what you want is to have enough power in your hypothesis test to be able to achieve statistical significance if the data follow the expected pattern. To achieve this goal, (1) identify the procedure that you will use to test your hypothesis; (2) estimate the numbers that you expect to have in this test, except for the sample size; and (3) solve for the needed sample size. This is a second approach to setting sample size.

A third approach is to set sample size based on the value of information. This approach takes into account the financial importance of the issue being studied and the current level of uncertainty about what to do.

In addition to these formal, computational approaches to sample size, a variety of informal methods are used. Possibilities include the following: (a) use a sample size similar to what has been used in previous research and/or by others, (b) use the "magic number" that will be credible to decision makers or reviewers, (c) anticipate subgroup analyses and plan minimum sample sizes in the small cells, and (d) set the sample size according to available resources.

EXERCISES AND DISCUSSION QUESTIONS

Exercise 4.1

A hospital administrator is planning a patient satisfaction survey. She wants to know the proportion of patients, among a population of approximately 5,000 treated at the hospital during the past 3 months, who say they were "completely satisfied" with various aspects of the hospital's performance. She wants to be 95% confident that her estimates fall within ±.04 (±4%) of the population figure for each measure. How big a sample does she need? If she wanted a confidence interval of ±1% (instead of 4%) for the same estimates, how big a sample would she need?

Exercise 4.2

Given the information in Section 4.4.1, what would be the value of research if the manager never changed her mind and had the same 65% hit rate with or without information? What if the research improved the hit rate to 85%? What if the potential gain from each decision was $10,000 and the potential loss was $10,000?

Exercise 4.3

A college instructor is planning a class project that involves a telephone survey. The instructor has 40 students in the class and wants each student to do a reasonable number of interviews for the project within a 2-week period. What would be a reasonable number of interviews for each student to do? What is the resulting sample size?

5

Stratified Sampling

O ur discussion of sample size in the previous chapter presumes that a simple random sample will be drawn. There also are situations in which the cost-effectiveness of a research project can be improved by using *stratified sampling* to reduce sampling errors or *cluster sampling* to reduce costs. This chapter discusses stratified sampling.

Stratified sampling separates the population into subgroups that are called "strata" and then selects random samples from each subgroup (see Exhibit 5.1 for a graphic depiction). Dividing the sampling effort in this fashion creates some extra work and extra cost. However, under some conditions, the estimates drawn from stratified samples have much lower sampling errors than estimates from simple random samples of the same size. This allows sampling error goals to be met with smaller sample sizes than are needed in simple random sampling and consequently lowers the total cost of research.

In this chapter, we discuss stratified sampling. You will learn the following:

- How stratified sampling may allow you to improve the cost-effectiveness of a sample
- When stratified sampling should be used
- How to draw a stratified sample

5.1 WHEN SHOULD STRATIFIED SAMPLES BE USED?

There are four conditions under which stratified sampling is cost-effective:

Exhibit 5.1 Stratified Sampling Illustrated

Assume companies in a particular industry are of small, medium, or large size. If different-sized companies are to be compared on some dimension, or if there is more variation among larger companies, stratified sampling might be used.

First, the companies are stratified into small, medium, or large strata.

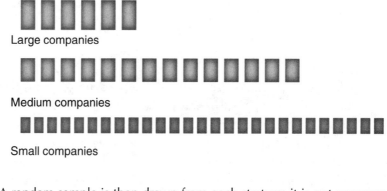

Large companies

Medium companies

Small companies

A random sample is then drawn from each stratum; it is not necessary to sample the same number of companies from each stratum.

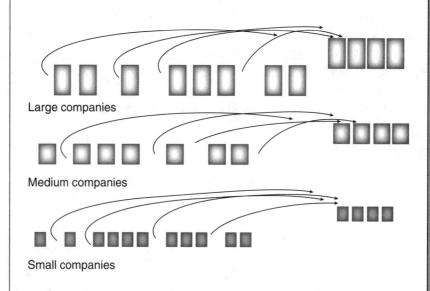

Large companies

Medium companies

Small companies

- The strata are of direct interest.
- The strata have different variances for some variable being studied.
- Costs of data collection differ across strata.
- Prior information about some variable of interest differs across strata.

These conditions are discussed below.

5.1.1 The Strata Are of Direct Interest

The first condition under which stratified sampling is cost-effective is when the strata are of direct interest. This will be the case if your primary research objective is to compare population subgroups or if you plan to make separate estimates for population subgroups and want each estimate to meet targeted confidence intervals.

For example, suppose that you wish to compare the proportions of Hispanics and non-Hispanics who favor some government policy. Assuming equal variances in the two groups, the optimal sample design for such comparisons is one where the sample sizes are equal for each subgroup ($n_1 = n_2$), because this minimizes the sampling error of the comparisons. If the groups differ in size in the population, then they must be sampled at different rates to get equal sample sizes. This, of course, implies stratified sampling.

More generally, stratified sampling is appropriate whenever you have separate confidence interval goals for subgroups, even if your purpose is not to compare the groups. For example, if you wish to report unemployment rates separately for African Americans, Hispanics, and others, and you want the estimate for each group to have the same confidence interval, then the sample sizes needed to reach your goals are the same in each group. The existence of group-specific confidence interval goals creates a need for group-specific sample sizes.

Of course, when the sample is optimized for group comparisons or estimates, it is no longer optimum for estimating the total population. This may not be of concern if one is uninterested in profiling the overall population, but it is common to be interested in the population as well as its subgroups; for example, to be interested in estimating total unemployment *and* unemployment among key subgroups. Sample design options in this situation include (1) to determine a minimum acceptable total sample size for proportional sampling and use remaining resources to augment the smaller subgroups or, more commonly, (2) to determine minimum subgroup sample sizes and use remaining resources to improve estimates of the total.

Here is an example:

CASE STUDY 5.1

The manager of service quality for a hospital chain used stratified sampling to solve a problem in outpatient satisfaction surveys. She says,

> At each hospital in our system, we conduct 2,400 telephone interviews per year with people who received outpatient services. We ask these people to rate our performance on various dimensions, and the results are used to evaluate the performance of each hospital as well as specific care units.
>
> Until recently, we used a random sample of outpatients for these surveys. However, in the course of a year, we might treat thousands of patients in the radiology (X-ray) unit of a hospital and a much smaller number in the occupational therapy unit. Therefore, in drawing a random sample of 2,400 patients, we might get hundreds from radiology and just a few from occupational therapy. This gave us narrow confidence intervals for radiology and very, very wide confidence intervals for occupational therapy. If the occupational therapy unit got poor results, the manager of that unit would complain that the sample was too small to be meaningful.
>
> We've now switched to a system that sets the sample size for each unit separately. This new system goes through the patient records for each hospital and counts the number of patients treated in each unit. It then calculates an initial sample size for each unit that will provide a confidence interval of ±.05 (5%) around estimates of the proportion of patients who were "very satisfied" with our performance. These sample size calculations use the finite population correction, so smaller units get smaller sample sizes. The total initial sample size across all units adds to something less than 2,400, and the remaining available sample size is allocated to units in proportion to their initial sample size.
>
> This system eliminates situations where we only have a few observations for a unit, and it allows me to tell each unit manager that the results have a confidence interval of less than 5%. This has created much better acceptance of the results among the managers.

5.1.2 Variances Differ Across Strata

The second condition under which stratified sampling is cost-effective is when population subgroups have different variances for some variable being studied. Stratified sampling works here because the squared sampling error, or *sampling variance*, for a total sample can be expressed as a weighted combination of sampling variance in various strata, as shown in Equation 5.1 where $\sigma_{\bar{x}}$ is the overall weighted sampling error for the variable of interest, π_h is the proportion of the population contained in the hth stratum (N_h/N), and $\sigma_{\bar{x}_h}$ is the sampling error for this variable within the hth stratum.

$$\sigma_{\bar{x}}^2 = \Sigma \pi_h^2 \sigma_{\bar{x}_h}^2 \qquad (5.1)$$

Since the overall sampling variance is a weighted composite of the strata sampling variances, it is possible to get a smaller overall sampling variance by giving a relatively larger sample allocation to strata in which the variance is higher and a relatively smaller allocation to strata where the variance is lower.

More specifically, Neyman (1934) showed that the minimum overall sampling error is obtained if sample allocations for each stratum are proportionate to the size of the stratum *and* to the standard deviation in that stratum for the variable being studied. Thus, the optimum sample size for a stratum is given by Equation 5.2, where n_h^* is the optimal sample allocation to the hth stratum, π_h is the proportion of the population contained in that stratum, σ_h is the standard deviation for the variable of interest within that stratum, and n is the total sample size planned for the study.

$$n_h^* = \left[\frac{\pi_h \sigma_h}{\Sigma \pi_h \sigma_h} \right] n \qquad (5.2)$$

If variances—and therefore standard deviations—are equal across the various strata, Equation 5.2 can be simplified to show that the allocation for each stratum should be proportional to its size in the population. However, when variances differ across strata, then disproportionate sampling is optimal, with more sampling being done in the higher variance strata.

Whether the benefit is sufficient to cover the inconvenience of stratification depends on the extent to which stratum variances differ. For example, if the key estimates in your research are percentages, such as the percentage of potential voters who favor some policy or the percentage of adults who have received flu shots, then stratification will rarely pay off. Variances of proportions are highly constrained—the variance term $\pi(1 - \pi)$ must always fall between 0 and 0.25— and the differences among strata are typically not large. On the other hand, if the key estimates are means for economic variables such as incomes or expenditures, then stratification may well be productive. The variation among high earners and/or high spenders will typically be much larger than the variation among low earners and/or low spenders.

The biggest differences in strata variances occur in research dealing with organizations (businesses, schools or school districts, hospitals, etc.). As a general rule, large organizations exhibit much more variation than do small organizations. Therefore, samples of organizations almost always should be stratified by size, with higher sampling rates for the bigger organizations.

Very often, stratum variances for organizations are unknown prior to conducting the research. In this case, measures of organizational size can be used to approximate the variances, because size tends to be highly correlated with variance. The equation for optimum sample selection using measures of size is given in Equation 5.3, where MOS is the measure of size to be used and represents a *total amount* for the stratum (i.e., the size of an average stratum element times the number of elements in the stratum).

$$n_h^* = \left[\frac{MOS_h}{\Sigma MOS_h} \right] n \tag{5.3}$$

Size measures may be based on total annual revenues for the organization, number of employees, number of students, number of patients, and so on. If more than one size measure is available, the one most closely related to the critical variables in the study should be used. For example, in a study related to hiring plans or personnel practices, the number of employees would be a better size measure than revenues or assets. However, different measures usually produce similar results.

Here is an illustration of the benefits of stratified sampling when variances differ across strata, drawn from Sudman (1976). Assume that you wish to estimate levels of employment and payroll in a population of hospitals. Also assume that this population has characteristics as shown in Table 5.1. You can see, in this table, the correlation between stratum variances and measures of size (i.e., standard deviations tend to rise as the size of the organizations increases).

Assume that your budget allows a sample of 1,000 from this population. Table 5.2 shows stratum allocations under four different schemes, as well as the sampling variances obtained under each scheme with regard to overall estimates of mean payroll and mean number of employees. The four allocation schemes are (1) proportional allocation, (2) optimum allocation based on standard deviations (or variances) for payroll, (3) optimum allocation based on standard deviations (or variances) for number of employees, and (4) optimum allocation based on number of beds as a proxy for standard deviations. For this last procedure, we used the midpoint of each bed-size category as the measure of size for that stratum, and we assumed that the midpoint of the top category was twice as large as the lower boundary: thus, our size measures were 25, 75, 150, 250, 400, and 1,000, each multiplied by the number of hospitals in that stratum to obtain an MOS_h.

Table 5.1   Information Regarding a Population of Hospitals

Size (in No. of Beds)	No. of Hospitals	π_h	Average Payroll	σ_h for Payroll	Average No. of Employees	σ_h for No. of Employees
Under 50	1,614	.246	266	183	54	25
50–99	1,566	.238	384	316	123	51
100–199	1,419	.216	1,484	641	262	95
200–299	683	.104	3,110	1,347	538	152
300–499	679	.103	5,758	2,463	912	384
500+	609	.093	10,964	7,227	1,548	826
Total	6,570	1.000				

Table 5.2   Stratum Allocations

Size (in No. of Beds)	n Based on Proportional Allocation	n* Based on σ_h for Payroll	n* Based on σ_h for Employees	n* Based on Bed Size
Under 50	246	34	36	28
50–99	238	57	71	83
100–199	216	104	120	150
200–299	104	106	93	120
300–499	103	192	231	191
500+	93	507	449	428
Total	1,000	1,000	1,000	1,000
$\sigma_{\bar{x}}^2$ for payroll	4,908	871	908	941
$\sigma_{\bar{x}}^2$ for number of employees	71.0	17.1	16.5	17.2

In this example, all of the optimum allocation schemes, including the one that is simply based on hospital size, result in similar sample sizes, and all produce overall sampling variances that are less than one fourth as large as those obtained from proportional sampling. Of course, the smallest sampling variance for the estimate of mean payroll is obtained if one optimizes the sample allocation based on stratum variances for payroll, and the smallest sampling variance for the estimate of employment is obtained if one optimizes the sample allocation based on stratum variances for employment—but the results are almost as good if one allocates on other variables, including a simple measure of size. This example shows that optimal stratification can produce very large gains in efficiency for samples of organizations and that it is not necessary to search for a perfect allocation measure to achieve major improvements in sample efficiency. Even if you use a rough or outdated measure of size, you are likely to get major improvements in efficiency.

In some situations, optimum allocation calculations may yield a sample size for a high variance stratum that is larger than the number of elements in that stratum. The solution is simply to take all the elements in this stratum, which is then called a "certainty" stratum because all of its members are included in the sample.

More generally, when the population of interest has a small number of very large organizations that account for a significant percentage of the population's total activity, substantial reductions in sampling error can be obtained without a precise optimization of strata allocations, simply by taking all of the very large organizations so as to eliminate sampling variance from that stratum. Consider our hospital example. If we simply took all 609 of the largest hospitals and allocated the remaining 391 observations randomly (proportionally) to the remaining strata, $\sigma_{\bar{x}}^2$ for payroll and employees would be 2,030 and 44, respectively—not optimal, but only about half of what we would get without stratification.

5.1.3 Costs Differ Across Strata

Neyman (1934) also showed that optimum sample allocations across strata depend on the costs of gathering information in the various strata. When this occurs, it makes sense to buy disproportionately more information in the strata where information is relatively cheap and disproportionately less information in the strata where it is relatively expensive.

Specifically, optimum allocations are inversely proportional to the square roots of variable (per unit) data collection costs in the different strata. Combining this result with Equation 5.2, the more general optimum is given in Equation 5.4, where c_h is the per-unit cost of data collection in the hth stratum, and all other terms are as previously defined.

$$n_h^* = \left[\frac{\frac{\pi_h \sigma_h}{\sqrt{c_h}}}{\Sigma \left(\frac{\pi_h \sigma_h}{\sqrt{c_h}} \right)} \right] n \tag{5.4}$$

If costs, but not variances, differ by strata—which sometimes happens in survey research—then Equation 5.4 reduces to Equation 5.5.

$$n_h^* = \left[\frac{\frac{\pi_h}{\sqrt{c_h}}}{\Sigma \left(\frac{\pi_h}{\sqrt{c_h}} \right)} \right] n \tag{5.5}$$

There are two main situations where costs differ by strata in survey research. The first is when combined data collection methods, such as online surveys with telephone follow-ups, are used to improve the cost-effectiveness of research.

The second situation in which costs differ by strata is when a special population of interest, such as Hispanics or African Americans, is geographically clustered so that there will be large differences in screening costs depending on location. For example, suppose you want to sample Hispanics in a region for a telephone survey. To simplify the example, assume that some Hispanics in this region live in areas that are 100% Hispanic, while others live in areas that are only 5% Hispanic. Assume that the cost of each interview is $25 and that screening households to determine if they are Hispanic costs $10 per completed screen. Therefore, the total cost per completed case is $35 in the areas that are 100% Hispanic, since each $10 screening call will lead to a $25 interview, and $225 in the areas that are only 5% Hispanic, since there will be 20 completed screens at $10 per screen for each completed interview. Since $\sqrt{(\$35/\$225)}$ is .394, the sampling rate in those areas where Hispanics are rare should be 40% of that in the areas that are entirely Hispanic.

5.1.4 Prior Information Differs Across Strata

The final situation in which stratified sampling is cost-effective is when prior information differs by strata. If you start off with more information for some strata than for others, then it makes sense to gather disproportionately more data in the strata where less is known. Ericson (1965) has shown how to determine optimum stratified samples when some information is known already.

We will not go into the details of these calculations; for details and examples, see Sudman (1976). Essentially, they convert your prior information about each stratum into a sample size equivalent. Say, for example, that you wish to estimate the average rise in income that people experience after going through some training program. Assume that the rise in income has a standard deviation (σ) of \$2,500 across people within some stratum, such as people who did not complete high school. Further assume that you believe, based on prior information, that there is a 95% chance that the average rise within that stratum will fall between \$7,000 and \$8,000. Since 95% of the possible sample means will fall within ± 1.96 ($\sigma_{\bar{x}}$) of the population mean, this means that the \$1,000 range between \$7,000 and \$8,000 represents a range of ± 1.96 ($\sigma_{\bar{x}}$). This implies that ($\sigma_{\bar{x}}$) is roughly equal to \$250. Since ($\sigma_{\bar{x}}$) equals ($\sigma/\sqrt{n}$), and σ equals \$2,500, this implies that $\sqrt{n}$ equals 10, or n equals 100. In other words, given the standard deviation of this variable in this stratum, the fact that you can say there is a 95% chance that the average rise within this stratum will fall within a \$1,000 range implies that your prior knowledge is equivalent to 100 observations. Therefore, you will essentially make an optimal sample allocation to this stratum using procedures discussed earlier in this chapter, then subtract 100 from that allocation because you already have that much information.

In some cases, these calculations make it possible that certain strata will not be sampled at all if (a) prior information is available and (b) the cost of gathering additional information is high.

5.2 OTHER USES OF STRATIFICATION

People who don't trust probability sometimes ask that a sample be stratified so that variables such as age, race, gender, or income agree exactly with census data. In other words, they ask for *proportionate stratification* to control the sample, rather than *disproportionate stratification* to make the sample more efficient. This can impose additional sampling and screening costs, and the benefits are minimal. Stratification generally should not be used to ensure that a sample is exactly representative. Given a large enough sample size, uncontrolled chance does a very good job of generating a representative sample.

However, there are circumstances in which proportionate stratification is reasonable. This occurs when the sampling frame can be easily sorted on some variable that is likely to relate to the issues being studied in the research. Suppose, for example, that we wish to study social service expenditures by county governments, and we plan to draw a sample of counties for this purpose. Assume that we have information on the percentage of households in each county with incomes below the poverty line, and we expect this variable to relate to social service expenditures. It is an easy matter to order the counties based on their poverty rates, rather than leaving them in alphabetical or haphazard order. Then, if desired, it is easy to draw a proportional sample of counties with higher and lower poverty rates; in fact, if the list has been sorted on this basis, a proportional sample will naturally arise from using a systematic selection procedure to ensure that all parts of the list are sampled. Sorting a list in this fashion and drawing a systematic sample to ensure proportionate allocations to all groups is called *implicit stratification.*

Researchers also sometimes use *poststratification* after data are collected in an attempt to reduce nonresponse bias. Even if the sample is not designed with disproportionate stratification, differential nonresponse may result in some groups being overrepresented relative to others. Under these circumstances, researchers may weight the groups to bring them back to proportional representation. The logic is similar to weighting for planned disproportionate stratification, but with an important difference. When differences in group representation are the result of the sample design, those differences are planned into the sample a priori, and we know exactly what to do to remove them and bring the sample back to the equivalent of EPSEM (equal probability selection method) representation. When differences in group representation are the result of differential nonresponse, this fact is not a planned outcome but rather is observed a posteriori, and it is not clear that weighting will truly correct for potential biases. We discuss this issue further in Chapter 7.

Exhibit 5.2 summarizes stratified sampling and the conditions under which it is useful.

Exhibit 5.2   Snapshot of Stratified Sampling

What it is	• Separates the population into subgroups and selects samples from each subgroup
Definitely useful when	• The strata are of direct interest (including comparisons among groups) • The strata have difference variances for a key variable • Costs of data collection differ across strata • Prior information about a key variable differs across strata
May be useful when	• The sampling frame can be easily sorted on some variable that is likely to relate to the issues being studied in the research (implicit stratification) • After data are collected in an attempt to reduce nonresponse bias through weighting (poststratification)

5.3 HOW TO DRAW A STRATIFIED SAMPLE

The mechanics of drawing a stratified sample depend on whether the strata are framed separately or together. In some cases, the frames are separate. For example, if a school district wishes to draw a stratified sample of families with children in elementary, middle, and high school, the frame might consist of school-by-school rosters that can be aggregated into separate lists for elementary, middle and high schools. Or, if research is being done to compare employment outcomes for low-income workers who participated in some training program with workers who did not participate, the participants might be listed on an enrollment roster while the nonparticipants are found in the general population. In other cases, the strata are framed together. For example, people with high and low levels of medical expenditures are mixed together in the general population.

If the frames are separate, then strata samples will be drawn separately, in whatever manner best fits each stratum. For example, a sample of training program participants might be drawn by means of a systematic sample from the enrollment roster, while nonparticipants are selected by means of random digit dialing in the general population. This includes the possibility of mixed-mode surveys; for example, if the roster of program participants has e-mail addresses, they might be surveyed online while nonparticipants are surveyed by telephone.

If the frames are separate but not mutually exclusive, then members of one stratum might be selected from another stratum's frame: for example, a training program participant might be selected in the general population sample. The general rule is to treat "wrong frame" selections as ineligible, to avoid the possibility of giving extra chances of selection to population members who are listed in more than one frame. So, for example, a training program participant selected in the general population sample will be screened out.

If the strata are contained in the same frame, then they may be selected separately or together, whichever is more efficient. Usually, selecting them together will be more efficient, especially if stratum membership is not recognizable in the frame. This is done as follows: (1) an initial sample is selected that is large enough to generate the desired number of selections in the stratum with the highest sampling rate, and (2) other strata are subsampled from this initial sample. For example:

CASE STUDY 5.2

A government agency wishes to conduct a study in a low-income area, comparing the work histories, educational backgrounds, and attitudes toward training programs of persons in the labor force who are currently unemployed with those who are currently employed. The agency wants a sample size of 500 in each group.

The total population consists of 100,000 persons in the area who are in the labor force, of whom it is estimated that 90,000 are employed and 10,000 are unemployed. Both groups are spread evenly throughout the area and can be located only by screening, because employment status is not shown in the frame.

To get a sample of 500 people from the 10,000 who are unemployed, a sampling rate of 500/10,000 or 1 in every 20 is needed (apart from any oversampling because of expected noncooperation or ineligibility). If this sampling rate is applied to the entire population of 100,000, it will yield an initial sample of 5,000 respondents, of whom 4,500 are employed and 500 are unemployed. The two groups will be separated in a screening interview, and all of the unemployed selections will be used in the study, while only 1/9 (500/4,500) of the employed group will be retained.

Of course, all of this assumes that the estimate of population composition is correct (90% employed vs. 10% unemployed or underemployed) and that the sample as drawn will reflect the composition of the population. Differences in composition may cause the obtained stratum samples to be larger or smaller than the intended 500, in which case it will be necessary to choose between using the samples as drawn or making adjustments.

5.4 CHAPTER SUMMARY

In stratified sampling, the population is divided into subgroups and separate samples are taken from the various subgroups. Under some circumstances, stratified sampling with disproportionate allocations of sample size to strata can make research more cost-effective. Specifically, stratified sampling is in order when

- the strata are of direct interest,
- variances differ across strata,
- costs differ across strata, or
- prior information differs across strata.

The purpose of stratified sampling is to provide the smallest sampling error, hence the most information, for the available resources.

When the strata are of direct interest, the existence of stratum-specific information objectives creates a need for stratum-specific sample sizes, and the most efficient sample design may be to use the same sample size in all strata regardless of their size in the population. If one wishes to make estimates for the total population as well as for individual strata, it may be appropriate to make some compromise between the most efficient sample for each purpose.

When variances differ across strata, the overall sampling error will be reduced by taking disproportionately larger samples in the high-variance strata and disproportionately smaller samples in the low-variance strata. This situation is particularly common in surveys of organizational populations. When strata variances for such populations are unknown, the use of size measures yields good approximations of variances for the strata, and an easy procedure for substantially reducing sampling error is simply to take all of the largest organizations.

When costs differ across strata, it makes sense to buy disproportionately more information in the strata where information is cheap and disproportionately less information in the strata where it is expensive. There are two main situations when this occurs. The first is when combined data collection methods are used to improve the cost-effectiveness of research, such as online surveys with telephone follow-ups. One will allocate relatively more sample to the inexpensive method. The second situation in which costs differ by strata is when a special population of interest, such as Hispanics or African Americans, is geographically clustered so that there will be large differences in screening costs depending on location. In this case, relatively more sample will be allocated to the low-cost areas.

When prior information is available for some strata, smaller samples should be taken from strata for which there is more prior information. If research costs are high in certain strata, then the availability of prior information may make it optimum to do no sampling in the costly strata.

All of these situations involve *disproportionate* stratification to make the sample more efficient. *Proportionate* stratification to control the composition of the sample usually is not beneficial, but may be used if the sampling frame can be easily sorted on some variable that is likely to relate to the issues being studied in the research. Sorting a list in this fashion and drawing a systematic sample to ensure proportionate allocations to all groups is called *implicit stratification*. Also, even if a sample was not designed as a disproportionate stratified sample, different population groups may exhibit different levels of nonresponse, and the researcher may weight the data to reestablish proportionality. Such weighting is sometimes called *poststratification*.

In drawing stratified samples, one can distinguish among situations where the strata are contained in (a) separate frames that are mutually exclusive, (b) separate frames that are not mutually exclusive, or (c) the same frame. If the frames are separate and mutually exclusive, then strata samples will be drawn separately, in whatever manner best fits each stratum. If the frames are separate but not mutually exclusive, "wrong frame" selections will be treated as ineligibles. If the strata are contained in the same frame, then they may be selected separately or together, whichever is more efficient. Usually, selecting them together will be more efficient, especially if stratum membership is not recognizable in the frame.

EXERCISES AND DISCUSSION QUESTIONS

Exercise 5.1

Refer to Tables 5.1 and 5.2. In Table 5.2, the first two columns show sample allocations based on proportional allocation and σ_h for payroll, as well as the resulting sampling variances for payroll and number of employees. How would these numbers change if the number of hospitals with less than 50 beds, shown in Table 5.1, was 2,614 instead of 1,614?

Exercise 5.2

Following the example given in Section 5.1.3, assume that some Hispanics in a region live in areas that are 100% Hispanic, while others live in areas that are only 2% Hispanic. Assume that the cost of each interview is $25 and that screening households to determine if they are Hispanic costs $10 per screen. What should be the sampling rate in areas where Hispanics are rare compared with the areas that are entirely Hispanic?

6

Cluster Sampling

Cluster sampling, like stratified sampling, can improve the cost-effectiveness of research under certain conditions. In cluster sampling, the population is found in subgroups called *clusters,* and a sample of clusters is drawn. Further sampling of population members may be done within clusters, and multistage cluster sampling is possible (i.e., sampling clusters within clusters). For example, in a study of schoolchildren, we might draw a sample of schools, then classrooms within schools. Exhibit 6.1 provides a graphic depiction of cluster sampling.

Cluster sampling differs from stratified sampling in that cluster sampling uses a sample *of* clusters, while stratified sampling draws a sample *within every* stratum. Cluster sampling also differs from stratified sampling in that stratified sampling is focused on reducing sampling errors, while cluster sampling is focused on reducing costs. Cluster samples actually have higher sampling errors than simple random samples of equal size, but under the right conditions, cluster samples allow a large enough increase in sample size to more than offset their inefficiency, so that overall sampling error is reduced for any given budget.

The logic of cluster sampling can be seen in the context of a national in-home survey of households. Assume that a nationwide sample of 500 households is desired. A simple random sample of 500 households from the nation's more than 100,000,000 households will produce something like the following: one household selected in Cedar Rapids, Iowa; one household in Fort Myers, Florida; one household in Helena, Montana; and so on. The travel and/or training costs for interviewing this sample will be staggering. Interviewers will travel

Exhibit 6.1 Cluster Sampling Illustrated

Assume companies in a particular industry are to be sampled. The companies are located in several different cities. If it is necessary to travel to each company to conduct the research and it is desirable to minimize the number of cities to which researchers need to travel, cluster sampling will be cost-effective.

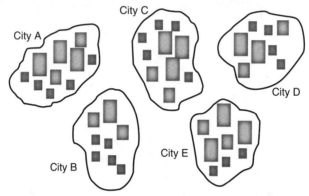

First, the population of companies is divided into clusters (in this case, cities) and a sample of clusters (cities) is drawn. Here, Clusters B and D are selected.

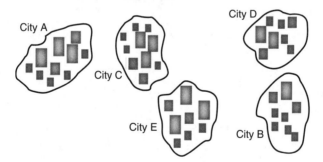

Then a sample would be drawn within each cluster to make up the sample.

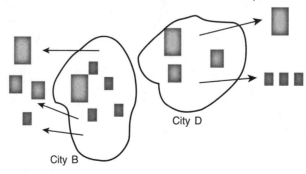

from city to city for each interview, so the cost of each interview will reflect at least one intercity trip (more, if callbacks are needed).

Costs will be greatly reduced if the 500 households are selected in clusters rather than individually. For example, we might draw 25 counties nationwide, four places per selected county, one census tract per selected place, one block per selected tract, and five households per selected block. We still will get 500 households, but interviews will be concentrated in 25 counties with 20 interviews per county, and interviewers will only go to four places in each county. This approach will cost much less than a simple random sample. Or, if the same budget is used, this approach will allow far more than 500 interviews.

In this chapter, we discuss cluster sampling. You will learn the following:

- How cluster sampling may allow you to improve the cost-effectiveness of a sample (in fact, we just described it)
- When cluster sampling should be used
- How to draw a cluster sample

6.1 WHEN ARE CLUSTER SAMPLES APPROPRIATE?

Cluster sampling is cost-effective under four general conditions:

- There are substantial travel costs associated with data collection.
- There are substantial fixed costs associated with each data collection location.
- There is a list of clusters but not of individual population members.
- When clustering can improve the efficiency of locating members of a special population.

We will consider each of these conditions in turn.

6.1.1 Travel Costs

Travel costs are an important consideration in any research project for which data are gathered in person. In such projects, the cost of *getting to and from* the interview (or point of observation) is likely to be higher than the cost of *doing* the interview, and cluster sampling is very likely to be used.

This point is obvious if interviews are in separate cities, as is sometimes the case in industrial marketing research or high-level policy studies. If a researcher is based in Chicago and an interview will be done in Los Angeles, then the cost of airfare, hotel, and travel time will far exceed the cost of conducting the interview. However, travel can be a significant factor even if interviews are done locally. Since professional interviewers are normally paid for all travel time, including to and from their homes, and since they receive a mileage allowance when using their cars, local travel can be an important part of total data collection costs. For example, an interviewer might spend an hour commuting to and from a 30-minute interview appointment.

If the sample is clustered so that several interviews can be done on the same day at the same place, then the costs of going to and from that place are spread out over several observations and the cost per interview is lower. Also, since selected respondents may not be available when the interviewer calls, clustering increases the probability of getting at least one interview from the trip. One of the most expensive and frustrating parts of the interviewing process can be traveling 20 or 30 miles for an interview and finding no one at home, thus wasting the trip.

It should be noted that travel costs are only a consideration when data are gathered in person. Travel costs are not a factor in online, mail, or telephone surveys.

6.1.2 Fixed Costs

Some studies have substantial fixed costs associated with each research location. For example, if you are gathering data from students in schools, and you have to go through a time-consuming approval process to get even one interview at any given school, it makes sense to gather multiple interviews at each location. Similarly, in surveys conducted at shopping malls, there are fixed costs of setup and training regardless of how many interviews are conducted at any given location. Gathering multiple interviews at each mall allows you to spread these fixed costs over the interviews.

6.1.3 Listing Costs

Cluster sampling can affect sampling costs as well as data collection costs. In some research projects, a list of clusters is available, but not a list of individual population members. For example, you might have a list of towns but not a list of people, a list of schools but not a list of students, a list of businesses but not a list of managers or workers, and so on. In these situations, you can select clusters and then obtain (or construct) a list of population elements only within the selected clusters. For example, assume that you wish to draw a sample of school-children in a region, and you have a list of schools but not students. Instead of trying to generate a complete list of students, it will be cheaper and faster to select schools and then list students only within selected schools.

6.1.4 Locating Special Populations

Some studies are concerned with special populations for which no list is available (e.g., low-income Hispanics, gay urban males, etc.). Since there is no list, these populations must be found by screening the general population. This can be very costly if the group is uncommon. For example, if the special population constitutes 2% of the general population, 50 screeners will be needed to find one eligible observation.

Cluster sampling (in conjunction with stratified sampling) may be able to cut screening costs if a rare population tends to be found in geographic concentrations, as often occurs with income and ethnic groups. In such situations, there will be many geographic segments in which no members of the rare population are located and many others with relatively few members of the population. Reductions in screening can be accomplished if empty segments are eliminated and sparse segments are undersampled. We discuss this topic further in Chapter 8, in a section on sampling rare populations.

Exhibit 6.2 summarizes cluster sampling and the conditions under which it is useful.

Exhibit 6.2   Snapshot of Cluster Sampling

What it is	• Separates the population into subgroups and selects a sample of those subgroups
Useful when	• There are substantial travel costs associated with data collection • There are substantial fixed costs associated with each data collection location (such as access or training costs) • There is a list of clusters but not of individual population members (so listing can be limited to selected clusters) • When clustering can improve the efficiency of locating members of a special population

6.2 INCREASED SAMPLE VARIABILITY AS A RESULT OF CLUSTERING

If cost were the only concern in designing cluster samples, the logical approach would be to gather all data in a single cluster. After all, if you can save money by breaking 500 interviews into 25 counties with 20 interviews in each county, why not do all 500 interviews in one county and save even more?

The answer, obviously, is concern about the representativeness of the sample. Households within a single county may have characteristics that are specific to the region. Even if a county appears typical in some characteristics, such as age or income distribution, it cannot be typical for all variables. Consequently, research results from a single county may not provide a good picture of the nation as a whole. As a simple example, think of political surveys where some counties are "red" (Republican) and others are "blue" (Democratic).

The issue here is one of sampling error, not sample bias. If we take all possible county-by-county samples, we will eventually cover the entire country, and the samples will average to the overall population characteristics. However, the county-by-county samples will contain everything from rural Wyoming to downtown Manhattan. The sample-to-sample variation will be larger than in a series of equally sized samples that blend people from around the nation.

In statistical terms, clustering increases sampling error because of correlations among cluster members. Two households in Cedar Rapids, Iowa, are likely to be more highly correlated in their behaviors and attitudes than a household in Cedar Rapids and a household in Fort Myers, Florida. The higher correlation means that a second household from Cedar Rapids adds less new information to the sample than a household from Fort Myers—it is not a second *independent* observation. In fact, if the households in Cedar Rapids were perfectly homogeneous, then a second household from Cedar Rapids would add no new information and thus have no research value. The following example illustrates this concept:

CASE STUDY 6.1[1]

Suppose that you wish to estimate the proportion of African American residents in a city. The cluster sample design calls for a selection of 20 blocks with 10 households per block, or a total sample of

1. Case Study 6.1 and other pieces of this chapter are drawn from Sudman (1976).

200 households. Once in the city, it is learned that all blocks are completely segregated by race. That is, the blocks are either all African American or all non–African American. In this case, how many independent observations does the sample yield?

If the interviewer knocks on the door of the first house of the block and the respondent is African American, then all other households on that block will also be African American; if the respondent is non–African American, then all other households will be non–African American. It is clear that there is really only *one* independent observation per block, so only 20 independent observations from the 20 blocks. Repeated samples drawn with this procedure will exhibit the sampling error associated with $n = 20$, not $n = 200$. In this case, there is no benefit from clustering; or, to put it another way, the optimal cluster size is 1. Taking a second element in the cluster provides no added information to justify the added cost.

Suppose, on the other hand, that the same sample design and blocks are used, but now the purpose of the study is to estimate birth patterns, to discover if births are more likely to occur in some months than in others. As far as we know, there is no relation between race and birth patterns, nor do we expect any relation between birth dates and neighbors. In this case, the sample effectively consists of 200 independent observations, and repeated samples will exhibit the sampling error associated with $n = 200$. Since there is no loss of information from clustering, it would, in theory, make sense to take all of the observations from a single block so as to minimize data collection costs.

This example illustrates that the amount of clustering that should be done depends on the homogeneity of the cluster, and the homogeneity of the cluster depends on the variable being considered. The clusters in our example are completely homogeneous with respect to race but heterogeneous with respect to birth date.

6.2.1 Measuring Homogeneity Within Clusters

The level of homogeneity within clusters, which determines the optimal amount of clustering, is measured by a statistic called the *intracluster coefficient of homogeneity*, expressed as ρ (rho). A ρ value of zero indicates that the elements within clusters are completely uncorrelated, and a ρ value of 1.00 indicates that the elements within clusters are perfectly homogeneous.

It is possible for ρ to be negative if cluster elements are negatively correlated on the variable of interest, but this seldom occurs except in observing the sex of respondents within households. That is, if two interviews are taken from the same household, there is a high likelihood that the sexes of the respondents will be different. The implication is that if one were interested in comparing incidences of medical conditions between men and women, clusters of two respondents per household, one male and one female, might be an efficient design.

More typically, ρ is positive, with values ranging anywhere from near 1.0 to near zero, and mostly below .05. Values near 1.0 are found in organizationally defined clusters, such as workers within companies, if the variable of interest relates to the organization, such as pension plans or job characteristics. For geographically defined clusters, ρ rarely gets above .40 and usually is much lower. In the United States, relatively high values are observed for race (because racial groups tend to live together), housing characteristics (because most neighborhoods have similar housing), and, in rural areas, farm plantings (because farms in any given area tend to plant similar crops). Similarly, economic variables such as household income, asset holdings, and poverty rates tend to have ρ values in the range of .15 to .3, because people who live near each other tend to be economically similar.

Since most social variables are influenced to some extent by economic variables, and since housing choices reflect other similarities among households, some degree of geographic homogeneity is found for most other variables, but ρ is often very small. For example, measures of personal or household expenditures in any given product category typically have ρ values in the range of zero to .05, as do health-related variables such as the incidence of various medical conditions. Political attitude measures may have fairly high ρ values if the attitudes correlate highly with race or economic status; otherwise, most attitude measures will have ρ values of zero to .05.

These guidelines are somewhat dependent on the clustering unit; for example, household income might have a ρ value of .3 at the city block level but less than .1 at the county level, because counties are less homogeneous than blocks. As a general rule, homogeneities are higher for smaller clusters, because people next door to each other tend to be more similar than people across town.

6.2.2 Design Effects From Clustering

We have noted that clustering reduces the number of independent observations and increases the sampling error. The specific increase in sampling error is a function of the size of the cluster and of ρ, the intracluster coefficient of homogeneity. Hansen et al. (1953) provide a useful formula that relates cluster samples with simple random samples of the same size. They show that, if $\bar{n}$

is the average size of the sample from each cluster, then the ratio of the sampling variance for a cluster sample of size n to the sampling variance for a simple random sample of the same size is

$$\sigma^2_{\bar{x}(cluster)} / \sigma^2_{\bar{x}(srs)} = 1 + \rho(\bar{n}-1) \tag{6.1}$$

Although this formula is only approximately true, the approximation is sufficiently accurate for practical use if the clusters are about the same size. The formula does assume that the number of clusters in the sample is small, relative to the total number of clusters in the population. If this is not the case, a finite population correction is applied to the cluster estimate.

According to Equation 6.1, if we use a cluster sample with five selections per cluster, and ρ equals .05, this design will have a sampling variance that is $[1 + .05*(5 – 1)] = 1.20$ times as large as a simple random sample of the same size; in other words, 20% larger. If we increase the cluster size to 25 selections per cluster, and ρ equals .05, this design will have a sampling variance that is $[1 + .05*(25 – 1)] = 2.20$ times as large as a simple random sample. The general term for such ratios of sampling variances (for a particular sample design versus a simple random sample of equal size) is the *design effect*, or *deff*; so, in this example, the clustered design with 5 selections per cluster is said to have a design effect of 1.20, and the clustered design with 25 selections per cluster has a deff of 2.20.

Knowing the design effect allows us to calculate the effective random sample size associated with any given sample design. Recall, from Chapter 4, that the sampling variance for a simple random sample is calculated as σ^2/n (if the finite population correction is ignored); in other words, the sampling variance and sample size are inversely proportional. Therefore, if a cluster sampling design has a sampling variance that is 1.2 times as large as a simple random sample of equal size, it follows that the cluster sample equates to a simple random sample that is smaller in size by the same factor. For example, a cluster sample of 300 with a design effect of 1.20 equates to a simple random sample of $n = 300/1.20 = 250$, and a cluster sample of 300 with a design effect of 2.20 equates to a simple random sample of $n = 300/2.20 = 136$.

6.3 OPTIMUM CLUSTER SIZE

We have seen, from Equation 6.1, that larger cluster sizes lead to higher sampling variances. For example, at $\rho = .05$, a cluster sample with clusters of size 5 will have a sampling variance that is 1.2 times as large as a simple random sample of equal size, while clusters of size 25 will have a design effect of 2.2. This suggests that smaller cluster sizes are better.

However, it is also necessary to consider costs. If there are substantial fixed costs associated with each cluster, such as cluster-specific training costs, then larger clusters will have a lower cost per observation, because they spread the fixed costs of each cluster over a larger number of observations. Therefore, larger clusters will allow a larger total sample for any given research budget. The question is whether this larger sample size will provide more information after taking the design effect into account. Consider the following example.

CASE STUDY 6.2

Assume that you are planning a national, in-home survey to measure various health conditions and health behaviors. The total budget for data collection is $60,000, and you plan to use a cluster sample for cost efficiency. The fixed costs associated with each cluster will be $2,000, mostly for the costs of sending a supervisor to conduct interviewer training at each site. The variable costs of obtaining each interview will be $100 for local travel, interviewer compensation, and respondent incentives. You anticipate that ρ for the primary variables of interest will be approximately .05.

Given this information, if you use clusters of size 5, then each cluster will cost a total of $2,500 ($2,000 in fixed costs plus five interviews at $100 each). The $60,000 data collection budget will accommodate 24 clusters at this cost per cluster. The total sample size will be 120 observations (24 clusters times five observations per cluster). The design effect will be $1 + .05(5 - 1) = 1.20$. Therefore, this design will produce the same sampling variance as a simple random sample of size $120/1.20 = 100$.

If you use clusters of size 10, then each cluster will cost a total of $3,000 ($2,000 in fixed costs plus 10 interviews at $100 each). The $60,000 budget will allow 20 such clusters, for a total sample size of 200 (20 clusters times 10 per cluster). The design effect will be $1 + .05(10 - 1) = 1.45$. The equivalent srs sample size will be $200/1.45 = 137$. This is an improvement over the srs equivalent of 100 that will result from a cluster size of 5.

Table 6.1 shows the same calculations for clusters of size 5, 10, 15, 20, 25, 50, and 100. Among these alternatives, the best choice is clusters of size 20, which allow a total sample size of 300 that equates to an srs of size 153. Cluster sizes of 25, 50, or 100 will allow larger total samples but provide less information because of their higher design effects.

This example illustrates a general characteristic of cluster samples: a trade-off between cost and sampling variance that leads to an optimum cluster size. Up to the optimum cluster size, the decrease in costs resulting from increased cluster size outweighs the increase in sampling variance, while beyond the optimum cluster size, the increase in sampling variance outweighs the decrease in cost.

Table 6.1   An Example of Cluster Sampling Designs and srs Equivalents

Cluster Size	Cost per Cluster	No. of Clusters	Total Sample Size	Design Effect	Equivalent srs Sample Size
5	$2,500	24	120	1.20	100
10	$3,000	20	200	1.45	137
15	$3,500	17	255	1.70	150
20	$4,000	15	300	1.95	153
25	$4,500	13	325	2.20	147
50	$7,000	8	400	3.45	115
100	$12,000	5	500	5.95	84

The optimal trade-off between cost and variance depends on two factors: (1) the ratio of fixed to variable costs in each cluster, which determines the relative value of spreading the fixed costs over a larger cluster size, and (2) the level of intracluster homogeneity, which determines the extent to which larger cluster sizes cause higher sampling variance. Specifically, Hansen et al. (1953) showed that the optimum cluster size may be calculated as

$$n_c^* = \sqrt{\frac{c_1}{c_2}\left[\frac{1-\rho}{\rho}\right]}$$
(6.2)

where n_c^* is the optimum sample size per cluster, c_1 is the fixed cost associated with each cluster, c_2 is the variable cost of each observation within clusters, and ρ is the intracluster coefficient of homogeneity for the variable of interest.

For example, given the information in Case Study 6.2, the optimal cluster size may be calculated as

$$n_c^* = \sqrt{\frac{\$2,000}{\$100}\left[\frac{1-.05}{.05}\right]}$$

$$= 19.49$$

It is no surprise, therefore, that Table 6.1 showed the best results at a cluster size of 20, since this is very near the optimum.

Whatever the optimum cluster size, it is not necessary to set cluster sizes at this exact level to gain most of the benefits of cluster sampling. For example, in Table 6.3, note that cluster sizes of 15 or 25 produce "srs equivalent" sample sizes that are very close to what is obtained at a cluster size of 20. In general, the efficiency of most samples declines very slowly in the neighborhood of the optimum cluster size.

6.3.1 Typical Cluster Sizes

Having established the formula for calculating an optimum cluster size, let us now consider the implications for cluster sizes in various types of research.

In-Home Surveys

Sudman (1976) suggests that optimum cluster sizes in the range of 15 to 30 are common for in-home surveys of the general U.S. population. The ratio of c_1 to c_2 in such studies typically ranges from about 15 to 50, so if $\rho = .05$, optimum cluster sizes will be roughly in the range of 15 to 30. As a result, a national cluster sample of 1,000 U.S. households might feature 50 counties with 20 observations per county.

Repetitive Studies

If interviewers can be hired and trained for a repetitive study, the fixed costs of training can be spread over the expected length of the interviewer's employment (Sudman, 1976). For example, assuming monthly interviews, as in the Census Bureau's Current Population Survey, and assuming that the average interviewer stays about a year, the ratio of c_1 to c_2 for a national survey might drop from 15–50 to approximately 2–4. In this case, assuming $\rho = .05$, the optimum cluster size is in the range of 5 to 10.

Shopping Mall Studies

When marketing researchers in the United States do studies that require face-to-face data collection from consumer populations, they are far more likely to gather the data in shopping malls than from in-home interviews. People might be recruited via telephone and asked to come to the mall to participate in the research (usually, a substantial financial incentive is offered in this type of research). More commonly, people are intercepted as they move through the mall and are asked to participate in the research (with a smaller financial incentive). The logic of using mall interviews is that (1) a broad cross section of the consumer population is available in shopping malls; (2) therefore, sample bias is expected to be within bearable levels; and (3) mall interviews are cheaper than in-home interviews.

The ratio of c_1 to c_2 in mall intercept studies is very high. The fixed cost associated with each mall may be elevated by engagement fees, as well as training and supervision costs, and the variable cost per interview is low because interviewers do not have to travel to reach the participants. As a result, the c_1/c_2 ratio can hit a range of 100 to 200 or even higher. At these levels, if $\rho = .05$, optimum cluster sizes will be in the range of 40 to 60 or higher. Thus, a total sample size of 400 interviews might feature eight malls at 50 interviews per mall.

If people are invited to come to the mall for research purposes and are given an incentive for doing so, then the ratio of c_1 to c_2 typically drops to a range of 15 to 50 because of the higher cost per observation caused by the incentive. At this level, optimum cluster sizes are in the range of 15 to 30.

Graduate Student Projects

For some small studies, it may be possible to justify extremely heavy clustering if one considers only out-of-pocket expenses. Thus, a graduate student or individual researcher might do all the interviewing and other activities related to a project and consider this time as completely or virtually cost free. In this case, only out-of-pocket travel expenses will be of real importance, and heavy clustering will be desirable. Even when heavy clustering is justified in this way for small studies, it should be recognized that at least two clusters must be selected to make any estimate of sampling variance that extends beyond the cluster, and, if the number of clusters selected is small, the reliability of variance estimates will be low.

Clustering Within Households

When households are the desired unit of investigation, there is, of course, no clustering within them. If, however, the population is of individual people, then households represent natural clusters of people, and one must decide how many observations to take from each household cluster.

For some studies, information about all household members is obtained from one household informant. This is highly efficient because the cost of obtaining information about all household members is only slightly higher than the cost of only measuring the respondent. However, the added information is only valuable if (a) the informant knows the information and (b) the household members are not highly correlated with respect to the phenomenon of interest.

If data must be gathered from each household member separately, then costs increase considerably, along with the possibility of contamination of responses as individual members discuss the survey with each other. In this situation, the general procedure is to choose only one respondent per household, unless one of the research goals is to compare responses between husbands, wives, and/or other family members.

Selecting individuals within households can result in bias against people in larger households. A person within a one-person household has a 1/1 chance of being selected within the household, while a person in a two-person household has only a 1/2 chance, a person in a three-person household has a 1/3 chance, and so on. A common practice is to interview one person within each household, then weight that interview by the number of adults in the household to offset the reduced chances of selection for each respondent.

If the topic of sampling within households seems familiar, it is because we first addressed it in Chapter 2, in our discussion of clustering in the sampling frame.

6.4 DEFINING CLUSTERS

In moving through this chapter, we have given various examples of clusters that might be used in sampling. We have talked about students clustered within schools, workers clustered within companies, individuals clustered within households, and households clustered within counties and/or city blocks. These are just some of the possibilities. Table 6.2 lists various populations and ways in which they might be clustered.

In fact, deciding *how* to cluster a population may be more important than deciding how large the clusters should be. The choice of how to define clusters depends on the following factors:

- The clusters should be sufficiently small so that some cost savings are possible; otherwise, the point of clustering is lost. Using counties as

Table 6.2 Possible Clusters for Sampling Purposes

Population	Possible Clusters
General population	Counties Standard Metropolitan Areas Census tracts City blocks Telephone exchanges Political precincts Shopping malls Households
College students	Universities Housing units Classes
Elementary or high school students or teachers	School districts Schools Classes
Businesses	Counties Facilities
Hospital patients	Hospitals Wards
Air travelers	Airports Planes (flights)
Visitors to a place	Time period in which visit occurs (e.g., weekday vs. weekend, or 9:00–10:00 vs. 10:00–11:00)

clusters for personal interviewing usually makes sense; using states as clusters usually does not.

• Clustering schemes that are associated with high levels of intracluster homogeneity should not be used, because the resulting increase in sampling variance will negate the benefits of clustering. For example, there is no point to clustering workers within companies in a study of pension plan arrangements, because all workers within any given company are likely to have the same pension plan.

• The clustering scheme should be one for which a list of clusters is available. In fact, as noted earlier in the chapter, cluster sampling is often motivated by the fact that we have a list of clusters but not a direct list of the population.

- The clusters should be well defined, such that every element of the population belongs to one and only one cluster. If some elements belong to more than one cluster—for example, some special education teachers are on the faculties of more than one school—then these elements will have more than one chance of selection. This may not be a severe problem but should be recognized.

- If we plan to sample within clusters, the number of population elements in each cluster should be known (or a reasonable estimate should be available) to ensure that equal probabilities of selection are maintained for all population elements. We discuss this issue later in this chapter in the section on multistage sampling.

It is not necessary that clusters be defined identically everywhere. For example, in sampling individuals or households in urban areas, clusters will usually be blocks or groups of blocks, while in rural areas, the clusters will be geographic segments bounded by roads and natural boundaries such as rivers and lakes.

Neither is it necessary that all the clusters be the same size. In general, natural clusters will vary enormously in size, particularly as the average size of the clusters increases. For example, some U.S. counties have millions of residents, while other counties have a few thousand. We will address how to accommodate these differences in our discussion of multistage sampling.

6.5 HOW TO DRAW A CLUSTER SAMPLE

There are two general approaches to drawing cluster samples. One approach is used if (1) the entire cluster will be taken when selected *or* (2) the clusters are approximately equal in size. The other approach is used if sampling will be done within clusters *and* the clusters vary widely in size.

6.5.1 Drawing Clusters With Equal Probabilities

If the entire cluster will be taken when selected, it is appropriate to select clusters with equal probabilities, using simple random sampling or a simple systematic sample. For example, assume that we need a sample of students within a school district, and we plan to use a cluster sample of students within the district's 1,247 homerooms. Further assume that we plan to draw 50 rooms and gather data from every student in the selected rooms. In this situation, we will use simple random sampling (or a simple systematic sample) to draw 50 rooms from the list of 1,247. Each room will have an equal chance of selection, 50/1,247, and each student will have the same 50/1,247 chance of selection because the student's chance of selection corresponds exactly to the chance that his or her room is selected.

Now, instead, assume that we plan to draw 100 rooms and 10 students within each room. If the rooms are of approximately equal size, then it still should be acceptable to draw them with equal probabilities. Consider two students, one in a class of 23 and the other in a class of 27. If we draw a simple random sample of 100 rooms from the list of 1,247, then both students' rooms have a chance of selection equal to 100/1,247. Then, if we randomly select 10 students in each selected class, the student in a room of 23 has a within-class chance of selection equal to 10/23, and the student in a room of 27 has a within-class chance of selection equal to 10/27. The student in the smaller room has an overall selection probability of $[(100/1,247) \times (10/23)]$, and the student in the larger room has an overall selection probability of $[(100/1,247) \times (10/27)]$.[2] These probabilities are not equal, but the variation across all of the rooms might be small enough so as not to raise concerns about bias in the resulting sample.

6.5.2 Drawing Clusters With Probabilities Proportionate to Size

If sampling will be done within clusters and the clusters vary widely in size, then it is not appropriate to select clusters with equal probability. The problem with doing so may be seen as follows.

Suppose that you wish to draw a cluster sample of 2,000 students at U.S. degree-granting 4-year colleges. Assume there are about 10,000,000 students in the total population, and you want a sample of 1,000, so your overall sampling rate is 1/10,000 (1,000 ÷ 10,000,000 = 1/10,000).

Further suppose that you plan to do your research at 50 universities (i.e., you will have 50 primary clusters). Assume there are 2,500 colleges and universities in

---

2. This calculation uses the idea that probabilities of selection in multistage sampling equal the product of probabilities at each stage. In our case, the probability that a student's room is chosen, multiplied by the probability that this student is chosen given that the room is selected, equals the overall probability that the student is chosen.

America. Therefore, if all institutions are given an equal probability of selection, the probability of selection for any given college will be $50 \div 2,500 = 1/50$.

To preserve equal probabilities of selection for individual students and obtain a sample size of 1,000, it then is necessary that the sampling rate within institutions be 1/200, since $[1/50] \times [1/200] = 1/10,000$, the desired overall sampling rate. Again, we are using the idea that overall probabilities of selection in multistage sampling equal the product of probabilities at each stage.

Using a sampling rate of 1/200 within colleges, the sample selected from a college with 30,000 students would be $30,000 \times (1/200) = 150$ students, while the sample selected from a small liberal arts college with 1,000 students would be $1,000 \times (1/200) = 5$.

This is undesirable. It can be shown that sampling errors are minimized when the same sample sizes are taken from each cluster. Equal sample sizes also facilitate administrative issues such as the number of interviews to be scheduled and conducted at any given location and the workload for each interviewer. Therefore, if our goal is 1,000 observations from 50 colleges, we would like to have 20 observations per college.

However, if we draw colleges with equal probabilities, large and small colleges will have the same chance of selection despite large disparities in population. If we then draw a fixed number of students within each selected college, students from larger colleges will have a much lower chance of selection. The effect will be to bias the overall sample toward students from small colleges.

The trick in drawing cluster samples, therefore, is to draw equal sample sizes in each selected cluster, yet preserve equal probabilities of selection for population members within big and little clusters. The procedure for doing so is called *sampling with probabilities proportionate to size*, or *sampling PPS*. It works as follows.

If there will be 50 colleges drawn, and a college with 30,000 students is given a probability of selection equal to 30,000/10,000,000 on each draw (the size of that college relative to the total student population), then the college has an overall probability of selection equal to $50 \times (30,000/10,000,000)$. If the college is drawn, and we select 20 students within it, then the probability of being selected within the college is 20/30,000 for each student. The overall selection probability for each student is $[50 \times (30,000/10,000,000)] \times [20/30,000]$, the probability of selection for the college multiplied by the probability of selection for the student within the college. The size of the college will cancel out, leaving $(50 \times 20)/10,000,000$, or 1,000/10,000,000 (which reduces to 1/10,000).

Likewise, if a college with 1,000 students is given a probability of selection equal to 1,000/10,000,000 on each draw (the size of that college relative to the total student population), then the college has an overall probability of selection equal to [50 × (1,000/10,000,000)]. If the college is drawn, and we select 20 students within it, then the probability of being selected within the college is 20/1,000 for each student. The overall selection probability for each student is [50 × (1,000/10,000,000)] × [20/1,000]. The size of the college will cancel out, leaving (50 × 20)/10,000,000, or 1,000/10,000,000.

In this example, students at the larger college have a lower probability of being selected within their school, but the school is given a correspondingly higher probability of selection. Likewise, students at the smaller college have a higher probability of being selected within their school, but the school is given a correspondingly lower probability of selection. The result is an EPSEM sample with the same number of students taken at each selected college.

Probabilities of selection for any given member of the population under two-stage cluster sampling with PPS may be written as

$$\left(\frac{m \times N_{clus_j}}{N} \right) \times \left(\frac{n_c}{N_{clus_j}} \right)$$

where m is the number of clusters to be drawn, N_{clus_j} is the number of population members in the jth cluster, N is the total population size, and n_c is the number of elements drawn within each cluster. As can be seen, the cluster population sizes cancel, leaving all population members with a selection probability of $(m \times n_c)/N$, the total sample size divided by the total population size, regardless of the size of their cluster.

If a PPS cluster sample is drawn in more than two stages, then probabilities proportionate to size are applied throughout the stages. For example, imagine that we draw a statewide sample of 200 households by selecting 10 counties, then two cities or places within each selected county, then two census tracts within each selected city or place, then one block within each selected tract, then five people within each selected block. The following probabilities would be applied:

$$\left(\frac{10 \times N_{cou_j}}{N} \right) \times \left(\frac{2 \times N_{pla_j}}{N_{cou_j}} \right) \times \left(\frac{2 \times N_{tra_j}}{N_{pla_j}} \right) \times \left(\frac{1 \times N_{blo_j}}{N_{tra_j}} \right) \times \left(\frac{5}{N_{blo_j}} \right)$$

Larger counties would be given a proportionately higher chance of selection, then larger places would be given a proportionately higher chance of selection within their counties, and so on, until the final selection of five people per selected block. At every stage, the cluster population sizes cancel, leaving an EPSEM sample.

PPS sampling is implemented as follows.

- The clusters are listed.
- A cumulating measure of population size is recorded next to each cluster until all clusters have been cumulated and the entire population is accounted for.
- A sampling interval is calculated by dividing the population size by the desired number of clusters.
- A random start between 1 and i (the sampling interval) is chosen.
- A systematic sample is drawn using the random start and the calculated interval. A cluster is selected if a selected number falls into its sequence of numbers—that is, if a selected number is greater than the cumulative sum of all previous clusters but less than or equal to the cumulative sum including this cluster.

Several points should be noted. First, we have suggested a systematic sample. A simple random sample may be drawn if preferred at any given stage, but a systematic sample allows implicit stratification as described below.

Second, in a multistage cluster sample, this process would be relevant to every selection stage. For example, when selecting counties within a state, we would cumulate county populations until the full state population was accounted for. When selecting cities or places within a county, we would cumulate city/place populations until the full county was accounted for. When selecting census tracts within a city or place, we would cumulate tract populations until the full city or place was accounted for. And so on.

Third, any clusters that are larger than the sampling interval will fall into the sample with certainty, and some of these clusters may be selected more than once. If a cluster is selected more than once, then the sample size within that cluster is increased correspondingly. For example, assume that we are drawing a statewide sample by selecting 10 counties, then two cities or places within each selected county, then two census tracts within each selected city or place, then one block within each selected tract, and then five people within each selected block. If a large county is selected twice, then we would simply draw four cities or places within that county. If a large city is selected twice, then we would simply draw four census tracts within that city.

If we want to be sure to get a mix of large and small clusters in our sample—for example, if we want to be sure that a statewide sample captures small rural as well as large urban counties—we can organize the clusters in order of size before we draw the sample. This is called *implicit stratification* and will keep us from jumping over the small clusters as we move through the list.

Exhibit 6.3 provides an illustration of PPS sampling. Assume that we want to draw a statewide sample of Maryland residents, and the first stage is to select 10 counties. Exhibit 6.3 lists the 26 Maryland counties, their populations (as estimated by the U.S. Census Bureau in 2013), and their cumulative populations. The total population is 5,928,814. Since we want 10 counties, our sampling interval (i) is calculated as 592,881 (i.e., 5,928,814/10). Using the RANDBETWEEN function in Excel to draw a random start between 1 and 592,881, we got a random start (s) of 403,641. The next selection would be 996,522 ($s + i$), then 1,589,404 ($s + 2i$), and so on. Our 10 selections are as follows:

403,641

996,522

1,589,404

2,182,285

2,775,167

3,368,048

3,960,929

4,553,811

5,146,692

5,739,574

Since the first selection, 403,641, falls within the cumulative range covered by Anne Arundel County, that county is selected (Allegheny County covers the range from 1 to 73,521, and Anne Arundel covers the range from 73,252 to 629,264). The next selection, 996,522, falls within the cumulative range covered by Baltimore County (which covers from 629,265 to 1,452,279). And so on.

Note that Prince George's County receives two selections. Also note that none of the counties with populations under 100,000 are selected.

Exhibit 6.3 Example of Sampling With PPS

County	Population	Cumulative Population	Selection
Allegany	73,521	73,521	
Anne Arundel	555,743	629,264	x
Baltimore County	823,015	1,452,279	x
Calvert	90,484	1,542,763	
Caroline	32,693	1,575,456	
Carroll	167,564	1,743,020	x
Cecil	101,913	1,844,933	
Charles	152,864	1,997,797	
Dorchester	32,660	2,030,457	
Frederick	241,409	2,271,866	x
Garrett	29,889	2,301,755	
Harford	249,215	2,550,970	
Howard	304,580	2,855,550	x
Kent	19,944	2,875,494	
Montgomery	1,016,677	3,892,171	x
Prince George's	890,081	4,782,252	xx
Queen Anne's	48,517	4,830,769	
St. Mary's	109,633	4,940,402	
Somerset	26,273	4,966,675	
Talbot	37,931	5,004,606	
Washington	149,588	5,154,194	x
Wicomico	100,896	5,255,090	
Worcester	51,620	5,306,710	
Baltimore City	622,104	5,928,814	x
Total	5,928,814		

Exhibit 6.4 repeats the exercise, but this time with implicit stratification. The counties are sorted from largest to smallest, with corresponding changes in cumulative totals. All other aspects of the sample remain the same; the sampling interval remains at 592,881, the random start at 403,641, and the 10 selections are 403,641, 996,522, 1,589,404, 2,182,285, 2,775,167, 3,368,048, 3,960,929, 4,553,811, 5,146,692, and 5,739,574.

As before, selections are concentrated in the larger counties, and this time Montgomery and Baltimore Counties are selected twice. Unlike before, one of the smaller counties (Queen Anne's) is selected.

If it seems unfair that most of the selections are going to the larger counties, remember that the people within those counties will have a much lower chance of selection within the county compared to people in smaller counties. As we have seen, the probabilities will balance out exactly across stages of the sample.

6.5.3 Drawing Stratified Cluster Samples

Stratification and clustering are different, as noted at the start of this chapter, but they are not mutually exclusive. It is possible to have a stratified cluster sample. For example, in a study of Maryland residents, we might wish to over-sample the smaller counties to get a larger sample of rural residents for purposes of comparing urban and rural areas. Such samples are drawn as follows.

If it is possible to separate the strata in the sampling frame, then clusters are drawn within strata. For example, in drawing a sample of Maryland residents, we might classify counties as urban or rural, then proceed to draw two separate cluster samples from each group.

If it is not possible to separate the strata in the sampling frame, then strata are sampled within clusters. For example, assume that (1) we are planning an in-home survey on health conditions, (2) we plan to use cluster sampling for cost efficiency, (3) we wish to stratify on age such that half the sample is 65 years or older and half the sample is younger than 65, and (4) we do not have a list that separates older and younger people. In this situation, we will draw a cluster sample that is large enough to provide the desired number of people in the smallest stratum (the 65+ group), and we will then proceed to fill strata allocations within clusters.

There is a potential problem with this procedure. If fixed strata allocations are used, but clusters vary in their strata composition, then probabilities of selection for individual population elements will vary accordingly. For example, if we seek 20 people in the 65+ stratum in each selected county, and this group represents 30% of the population in some counties and only 10% of the population in other counties,

Exhibit 6.4   Example of Sampling With PPS and Implicit Stratification

County	Population	Cumulative Population	Selection
Montgomery	1,016,677	1,016,677	xx
Prince George's	890,081	1,906,758	x
Baltimore County	823,015	2,729,773	xx
Baltimore City	622,104	3,351,877	
Anne Arundel	555,743	3,907,620	x
Howard	304,580	4,212,200	x
Harford	249,215	4,461,415	
Frederick	241,409	4,702,824	x
Carroll	167,564	4,870,388	
Charles	152,864	5,023,252	
Washington	149,588	5,172,840	x
St. Mary's	109,633	5,282,473	
Cecil	101,913	5,384,386	
Wicomico	100,896	5,485,282	
Calvert	90,484	5,575,766	
Allegany	73,521	5,649,287	
Worcester	51,620	5,700,907	
Queen Anne's	48,517	5,749,424	x
Talbot	37,931	5,787,355	
Caroline	32,693	5,820,048	
Dorchester	32,660	5,852,708	
Garrett	29,889	5,882,597	
Somerset	26,273	5,908,870	
Kent	19,944	5,928,814	
Total	5,928,814		

then individual members of the group will have a lower chance of selection in counties where the group is common than in counties where the group is rare.

There are two ways to deal with this problem. First, you can try to define the clusters in a way that minimizes cluster-to-cluster variation in strata composition. This typically implies bigger clusters; for example, the percentage of people who are 65+ years of age will vary less from county to county than from neighborhood to neighborhood. If the variation becomes small enough, you can ignore it for practical purposes. Second, if you feel that the variation is too big to ignore, you can keep track of the screening rates needed to find the various strata within each cluster and use those rates to weight each observation for a probability of selection that is specific to the cluster as well as the stratum.

In some cases, the strata cannot be separated in the sampling frame, but information is available regarding the strata composition of each cluster. For example, we may not have a list that separates older and younger people, but we may know the percentage of people in each county who are 65 years or older. In this case, we can group the clusters (counties) on the basis of this percentage to form groups of clusters that are relatively similar with respect to this variable. The definition of such groups should allow us to weight the resulting data on a group basis rather than a cluster-specific basis.

We will discuss the analysis of data from complex samples in more detail in Chapter 7.

6.6 CHAPTER SUMMARY

Cluster sampling, like stratified sampling, can improve the cost-effectiveness of research under certain conditions. In cluster sampling, the population is divided into subgroups called *clusters,* and a sample of clusters is drawn. Further sampling of population members may be done within clusters, and multistage cluster sampling is possible (i.e., sampling clusters within clusters).

Cluster sampling is cost-effective under four general conditions: (1) there are substantial travel costs associated with data collection, (2) there are substantial fixed costs associated with each data collection location, (3) there is a list of clusters but not of individual population members, or (4) clustering may allow us to find a rare group more efficiently. Under any of these conditions, cluster sampling will allow a substantial reduction in the cost per observation, so more observations can be obtained for any given research budget.

While clustering may reduce the cost of research, it also results in a higher sampling variance, because repeated observations within clusters may not be completely independent. The extent of increase, which is measured by the "design effect," depends on (1) the extent to which population elements are homogeneous within the clusters being considered and (2) the number of elements to be taken within each cluster. Homogeneity is measured by a statistic called ρ, which represents the average correlation among all possible pairs of cluster elements.

The trade-off between cost and sampling variance results in the existence of an optimum cluster size for any given situation. The optimum cluster size for national in-home surveys in the United States is typically in the range of 15 to 30. On the other hand, shopping mall intercept surveys have larger optimum cluster sizes, as large as 50 or more.

The appropriate procedure for drawing a cluster sample depends on whether the entire cluster will be taken and the extent to which clusters vary in size. If the entire cluster will be taken when selected, or if the clusters are approximately equal in size, then it is appropriate to select clusters with equal probabilities. In other words, it is appropriate to take a simple random sample of clusters. However, if sampling will be done within clusters, and the clusters vary widely in size, then it is appropriate to draw clusters with probabilities proportionate to size. Sampling with PPS was described and illustrated.

EXERCISES AND DISCUSSION QUESTIONS

Exercise 6.1

Given the information in Case Study 6.2, what would be the optimum cluster size if ρ is .25 instead of .05? What would be the optimum cluster size if ρ is .05 but the variable cost per observation (c_2) is $20 instead of $100? What would be the optimum cluster size if ρ is .05, c_2 is $20, and the fixed cost per cluster (c_1) is $4,000 instead of $2,000?

Exercise 6.2

Assume that you want to draw a statewide multistage cluster sample of residents in your state, and the first stage is to select 10 counties (or 10 places if your state does not have 10 counties). Draw a PPS sample of 10 counties as we did in Section 6.5.2.

SECTION III

Additional Topics in Sampling

After finishing Sections I and II, you should know (a) how bias arises in samples, (b) how to control sample bias, (c) how to control sampling error through sample size, (d) how the cost-effectiveness of samples might be improved through stratification or clustering, and (e) how to draw various kinds of samples.

Given this foundation, in Section III, we address miscellaneous other topics related to sampling and the use of sample data. When you finish this section, you should know (a) issues related to estimating population characteristics from samples, (b) how to apply sampling principles in a variety of special survey contexts, and (c) how to determine how good a sample is, how good it needs to be, and guidelines for obtaining better even if imperfect samples.

7

Estimating Population Characteristics From Samples

We began this book by asking you to imagine the following situation. A friend of yours is running for a place on the local school board. You agree to help her by surveying local voters to learn which issues are most important to them and what they would like the school board to do.

We introduced the idea that you would rely on a sample of the population, and your sample should provide an accurate representation of the broader population; for example, if your data show that 64% of the respondents want the school district to place more emphasis on reading skills, you want this 64% figure to be an accurate reflection of feelings among the population at large. There are three reasons why it might not be: nonsampling error (which is outside the scope of this book), sampling error stemming from random variation in sample composition, and sample bias stemming from population coverage failures, selection biases, or nonresponse.

Chapters 1 to 3 of this book addressed how sample bias can be controlled through the sampling process, and Chapters 4 to 6 addressed how sampling error can be controlled through sample size and sample design.

In this chapter, we consider some additional issues related to the accuracy of estimates drawn from samples.

- First, we return to the topic of weighting, which has been mentioned at various points in this book. We review how weighting might be used to compensate for differences in probabilities of selection or response, and we discuss associated issues.
- Second, we address the broader topic of using mathematical models to guide sampling and estimation. As we will see, such estimation may allow us to improve the cost efficiency of our research, generate estimates from nonprobability samples, and deal with failures in probability sampling assumptions.
- Third, we discuss how to measure the uncertainty of estimates that are drawn from complex or nonprobability samples.

In this chapter, you will learn the following:

- How to weight sample data
- When to weight sample data
- How models may be used to reduce the variance of estimates drawn from samples
- How models may be used to cope with violations of probability sampling assumptions
- How to measure the uncertainty of estimates from complex or nonprobability samples

7.1 WEIGHTING SAMPLE DATA

There are two broad reasons for weighting survey data: (a) to adjust for unequal probabilities of initial selection across respondents and (b) to adjust for unequal rates of nonresponse after respondents are selected. Unequal probabilities of initial selection may stem from the sample design, such as disproportionate stratified sampling, or from duplications or clustering in the sampling frame. Unequal probabilities of nonresponse may stem from differences in contact or cooperation rates across population subgroups.

As noted in Chapter 3, there are two basic approaches to weighting. One is to weight sample groups toward their known proportions in the population. For example, if 40% of the respondents in an observed sample are younger than 55 years and 60% are 55 years and older, and the relevant population is known to have 80% younger than 55 and 20% who are 55 and older, then data from respondents younger than 55 would be weighted by 80/40, or 2 (the proportion of the sample they should represent, relative to the proportion that they do represent), and data from respondents 55 years and older would be weighted by 20/60, or 1/3. Symbolically, members of the ith group are weighted by (π_i / p_i), where π_i is the group's proportion in the population and p_i is its proportion in the sample. Alternately, aggregate characteristics of the groups (such as means, proportions, or totals) are simply weighted by π_i and summed to provide estimates for the population as a whole. This type of weighting is typically used to correct for disproportionate selection probabilities in stratified designs and may be used in adjusting for differential nonresponse.

A second approach is to weight by probabilities of selection, including contact probabilities or response rates. For example, imagine that response rates in a national telephone study are 10% for big city telephone exchanges and 40% for other telephone exchanges, with an overall response rate of 20%. In this example, data from the big city exchanges would be weighted by 0.20/0.10, or 2 (the response rate they should have had, relative to the response rate they did have), and data from the other exchanges would be weighted by 0.20/0.40, or 0.5. Symbolically, the ith group is weighted by (r/r_i), where r is the response rate or probability of selection for the whole sample and r_i is the response rate or probability of selection for this group. This type of weighting is typically used to correct for differential probabilities of selection in non-EPSEM cluster designs (including situations where respondents have unequal chances of selection within households or unequal chances of selection in half-open intervals) and in designs that feature both stratification and clustering. It also may be used to adjust for differential nonresponse or noncontact rates across groups.

If more than one variable is to be used for weighting, an overall weight might be constructed by simply multiplying the weights for each variable. For example, if a sample is stratified with disproportionate probabilities of selection based on income category, and respondents also have different selection probabilities based on the size of their households, then the relevant weights for income category and household size might be multiplied to construct an overall weight for any given respondent.

Multiplying weights in this fashion implicitly assumes that the weighting variables operate independently. This is usually a good assumption for initial selection probabilities; for example, there may not be any strong reason to believe that any given respondent's reduction in selection probability from being in a large household depends on whether that household is high or low income. The assumption is less tenable for differences in response rates, where respondent characteristics may interact to influence contact or cooperation probabilities; for example, males may be less likely than females to respond to a survey, and this difference may be particularly strong among younger males.

If such interactions are of concern, a variety of approaches might be used. One approach is to multiply the weights but use different weights for one variable conditional on the category of another (e.g., the weight for males varies across age categories). A second approach is to define multivariate cells, or *weighting classes,* each of which receives its own weight (e.g., younger males, older males, younger females, older females). A third approach is to develop an individual-level model that predicts the probability of response based on multivariate respondent characteristics (and any desired interactions of those characteristics) and weight respondents according to their scores on that model. This is called *response propensity weighting.* At a broad conceptual level, all of these approaches do the same thing, but the methods may differ in operational specifics.

Multivariate weighting to match known population distributions may follow a sequential process called *raking.* The researcher begins with the variable (assume it is age) on which the sample and population distributions differ most, computes weights to adjust for that variable, and applies those weights. The researcher then checks the distributions of other potential weighting variables. Those distributions will usually be closer to the population than they were before. If desired, the researcher selects the variable with the next highest difference from the population (assume it is gender), computes weights to adjust for it, and applies those weights. This process continues until the weighted characteristics of the sample are deemed close enough to the population. The process is iterative, because as each weighting variable is included, the distribution of the previous variables is affected, but in most applications, only a few iterations are needed. See Battaglia, Hoaglin, and Frankel (2009) for a good discussion of raking.

As a practical matter, weighting for nonresponse requires either (a) that we can compare the characteristics of nonrespondents and respondents based on information in the sampling frame (e.g., the frame allows us to classify selected telephone numbers as big city vs. other), (b) that we can compare the characteristics of the obtained sample to the broader population of interest (e.g., we can compare the age distribution of the obtained sample with the age distribution of the population), or (c) that we can identify differences in selection probabilities from data provided by respondents (e.g., respondents tell us their household size). This means that weighting is limited to variables for which we have such information. An implication is that survey designers may wish to look ahead when they are designing questionnaires and include measures that may not be of direct interest in the survey but may be useful in weighting if needed.

7.1.1 Should Data Be Weighted?

In general, data always should be weighted if the sample design incorporated unequal selection probabilities (e.g., through stratification). In these cases, differences in probabilities of selection were consciously planned so as to gain efficiencies in the research, we know exactly what to do to remove those differences and bring the sample back to the equivalent of EPSEM representation, and weighting to correct for those differences is part of the plan.

Weighting to correct for differences in nonresponse or noncontact rates is more problematic. It seems only natural to correct for obvious flaws in the sample, but as noted in Chapter 3, there are some major problems with using weights for this purpose.

First, weighting for differential nonresponse can be viewed as a quota scheme where the quotas are assigned post hoc rather than a priori, and it has the same underlying exposure to availability bias as any quota sample. If your research has a dismal response rate, it is optimistic to presume that there is no response bias just because the demographic characteristics of the sample happen to match the population as a whole, or to claim that you have fixed the problem by weighting for obvious flaws. To return to an example given in Chapter 3, you may have a fair proportion of 18-to 34-year-old women in the sample, or you may have weighted this group to fair proportion, but do you have Bridgets or Kathleens? It is a mistake to presume that weighting can turn a poor sample into a good sample.

More generally, weights are effective in addressing nonresponse bias only if the nonrespondents are *missing at random* and do not differ systematically from the respondents. In an example given earlier in this chapter, we might weight on age because respondents younger than 55 years had lower response than did respondents 55 years and older. That weight is wholly successful only if the under 55 respondents are similar to the under 55 nonrespondents. To put it another way, when we weight the under 55 group by 2, we act as if we had obtained twice as many observations from that group, and the additional respondents would have answered in the same manner as the ones we interviewed. This is true if nonresponse was random, but that is typically a questionable assumption. If nothing else, the nonrespondents may be busier than the respondents and hence more difficult to contact or less likely to cooperate.

Since respondents and nonrespondents may differ in a variety of ways, the effects of weighting on bias are likely to have corresponding differences. This is illustrated in Exhibit 7.1. Imagine, as before, that 40% of the respondents in an observed sample are younger than 55 years and 60% are 55 years and older, and the relevant population is known to have 80% younger than 55 and 20% who are 55 years and older. Imagine that the population as a whole and the respective age groups have mean values as shown in the top portion of the exhibit for (a) a scale measuring social conservatism, (b) number of hours per week spent exercising, and (c) a 7-point measure of interest in buying a new car. Finally, imagine

Exhibit 7.1   Differential Effects of Weighting on Nonresponse Bias

	Younger Than 55	55 and Older	Total[a]
Population			
Proportion of population	0.8	0.2	
Mean social conservatism	40	60	44
Mean weekly exercise hours	20	15	19
Mean interest in car buying	3	3	3
Observed sample (respondents)			
Proportion of sample	0.4	0.6	
Mean social conservatism	40	60	52
Mean weekly exercise hours	15	15	15
Mean interest in car buying	4	3	3.4
Weighted sample			
Weighted proportion of sample	0.8	0.2	
Mean social conservatism	40	60	44
Mean weekly exercise hours	15	15	15
Mean interest in car buying	4	3	3.8

a. The mean for each group multiplied by the proportion in that group and summed over groups.

that the observed sample has mean values as shown in the middle portion of the exhibit.

If we compare the top and middle portions of Exhibit 7.1, we can see that all three observed sample estimates are biased for the total population. For the social conservatism scale, this bias stems entirely from disproportionate representation of the two age groups; respondents within each group match their respective population means. For the number of hours spent exercising and car-buying interest, there is an additional source of bias in that the under 55 respondents differ from the under 55 population at large; they are less active and more interested in buying a car. In the case of exercising, this bias brings the under 55 respondents closer to the 55 and above group, and in the case of car-buying interest, it moves them farther away.

The bottom portion of Exhibit 7.1 shows the results of weighting the sample data to match each age group's actual proportion in the population. For social conservatism, the bias is removed, because weighting corrects for the disproportionate representation that caused that bias. For number of hours spent exercising, the bias remains unchanged, because correcting for disproportionate representation of the age groups does not address the difference between respondents and nonrespondents within the under 55 group. For car-buying interest, the bias *increases,* because letting the under 55 respondents speak for the nonrespondents has the effect of overweighting people with higher interest.

To complicate matters, if we weight these same data by gender instead of age, we might get a different pattern of results; for example, we might get more bias reduction in estimates of exercising and less in estimates of social attitudes. The effects of weighting on bias vary not only across different substantive variables of interest but also across different weighting variables. In truth, therefore, we do not know how effective any given weighting scheme is in addressing nonresponse bias for any given variable.

A second problem is that weighting increases sampling error, because a disproportionate sample that is weighted to achieve proportionality has higher sampling error than a proportional sample (unless the disproportionate scheme has been designed to take advantage of group differences in variation or cost, as in disproportionate stratified sampling). The design effect due to weighting is calculated as $\Sigma(\pi_i k_i) * \Sigma(\pi_i / k_i)$, where π_i denotes the proportion of the population sampled at a given rate and k_i is the ratio of the weight for that group to a baseline weight (Kish, 1965). A simple rule is to take the group with the lowest weight as the baseline ($k = 1$) and express the sampling rates in all other groups relative to that one. For example, if 40% of the respondents in an observed sample are younger than 55 years and 60% are 55 years and older, and the relevant population is known to have 80% younger than 55 and 20% who are 55 and older, then k would be set at 6 for the under 55 group and 1 for the 55 and over group,[1] π would be 0.8 for under 55 and 0.2 for 55 and over, and the design effect associated with weighting the sample to proportionality would be 1.67 (i.e., weighting would increase the variance of estimates drawn from the sample by 67%).

A third potential problem is that weights must be reliable to be useful. For example, if estimates of sampling rates are based on respondents' estimates of how long they spent on site (Nowell & Stanley, 1991) or how many times they are likely to appear in a list, systematic errors in these responses may introduce bias into the weights, and random errors will exacerbate the increase in sampling error produced by weighting.

Overall, then, weighting for nonresponse is a two-edged sword. It *may* reduce nonresponse bias, but it *will* increase sampling error, and the net effect may be to increase total survey error. Because of its problems, weighting for nonresponse should be undertaken only when (a) differences in nonresponse are fairly dramatic across groups, (b) the weighting produces substantial and credible changes in important variables, and (c) there are no obvious adverse effects of the weighting. We suggest a process of sensitivity testing to guide these decisions; essentially, try any weighting schemes you are considering, see how they affect the data, and decide whether they seem beneficial. As part of this, consider *trimming* weights. If a large weight needed to correct for severe undersampling of some group has an explosive effect on sampling error, consider reducing the size of the weight so that you only partially correct the undersampling but you also reduce the impact on sampling error, thus balancing between levels of potential bias and sampling error.[2] Similarly, if a small group will be heavily weighted, consider whether that group can be merged with others to manage the size of the adjustment.

Because of its problems, weighting should not be viewed as a primary method for controlling nonresponse bias. Weighting is appropriate to control

---

1. The weight for the under 55 group is 2 and the weight for the 55 and over group is 1/3, so the weight for the under 55 group is six times as large. If it is easier, you can use relative sampling rates instead of relative weights to determine k values.

2. Trimming is often done by looking at the distribution of weights and assigning an ad hoc cut point such that weights outside that boundary are trimmed to the cut point; for example, Chowdhury, Khare, and Wolter (2007) describe a procedure of calculating weights for data from the U.S. National Immunization Survey, taking the interquartile range (IQR) of those weights, and trimming any weight that is more than six times the IQR from the median weight. It also is possible to explicitly introduce trade-offs between bias and sampling error into the calculation of the trimming boundary (e.g., Elliott, 2008).

the possibility of bias resulting from intractable nonresponse, but one's first line of defense against nonresponse bias should always be careful data collection procedures.

We should note that weighting for nonresponse may be more common in political polling than in other research contexts. Political preferences often correlate with demographic variables, so if one weights to correct for a demographic mismatch between a sample and the broader population, there is a good chance that one is also correcting for a mismatch in preferences.

7.2 USING MODELS TO GUIDE SAMPLING AND ESTIMATION

Our focus in this book has been probability sampling, which "uses the sample selection probabilities to provide the basis for its inferences" (Brewer, 1999, p. 36). The great strength of probability-based inference is that it can be applied to any finite population without prior knowledge about that population's distributions. To generate estimates of population characteristics (such as means or proportions) from sample data, all we need to know is the design that produced the sample (e.g., simple random, stratified, cluster, etc.). For this reason, probability sampling is sometimes called *design-based* sampling, which allows design-based inference.

There are conditions under which alternative methods to simple design-based sampling should be considered, such as the following:

- When there is information available about the population that can be used to improve the efficiency of the sample design.
- In situations where it is simply impossible to implement a design-based sampling plan, as in online surveys where a sampling frame does not exist
- When the design-based sample implementation leaves an unacceptable portion of population elements without known, nonzero probabilities of selection, as in surveys with high nonresponse rates where it cannot be assumed that nonrespondents are missing at random
- If the main research objectives do not require a design-based sample

There are two general categories of methods to improve or replace design-based sampling, both of which rely on mathematical models. Methods used in conjunction with design-based sampling are referred to as *model assisted*. Methods used instead of design-based sampling are referred to as *model based*. Both types of methods can apply to sample design, estimation, or both, as we will see.

7.2.1 Examples of Using Models

To illustrate the possible use of models, let's start with an example of design-based sampling and estimation to provide a point of comparison. Say that we wish to estimate quarterly production volume for some industry. We have production reports from a survey of firms in the industry, and we know that the sample was designed as a disproportionate stratified probability sample whereby the industry was stratified into larger versus smaller firms and the larger firms were sampled at a higher rate. Given this knowledge about the sample design, we (a) separate the survey responses by stratum, (b) use the data to estimate production in each stratum, (c) sum the stratum estimates, and (d) voila, we have an unbiased estimate of total production in the industry (assuming that the reports are not biased).

Now, let's consider the use of models to adjust sample design and estimation. Assume that historical data have shown that the larger firms typically account for 80% of total industry production, and the smaller firms account for 20%. Therefore, we can state a model that

$$\text{Total production} = \text{Large firm production}/0.80$$

Given this model, we could sample *only* the larger firms, use the survey data to estimate production in this stratum, and use the model to estimate total production and/or production by smaller firms. For example, if the survey produces an estimate that quarterly production in the large firm stratum was 1,000,000 units, the model will produce an estimate that total industry production was 1,250,000 units and small firm production was 250,000 units. We will subsequently refer to this as Model Example 1.

Let's consider some more examples. For Model Example 2, imagine that (a) a mixture of census and business sources allows us to estimate the total number of people employed in the industry; (b) we can identify the larger firms and sample them, but many are not willing to answer questions about production volume; and (c) the smaller firms are more willing to respond, but we don't have a good list from which to sample them. In this case, we might take whatever responses we can get from the larger firms, sample from whatever smaller firms we can identify, use the combined data to calculate production volume per employee, and multiply that figure by the total number of people employed in the industry to get an estimate of total production volume. Here, we are using the following model:

$$\text{Total production} = b * \text{Total employment}$$

We are using whatever information we can get to estimate b, and we are implicitly assuming that b is constant across sets of firms regardless of the sampling process. To state this assumption more gently, we are assuming that we will obtain a reasonable estimate of b as long as we have a mix of larger and smaller firms, even if those data suffer from population coverage and nonresponse problems.

For Model Example 3, imagine the same situation, except that we do not know the number of people employed in the industry. We only know the total number of firms, and by count the number of larger firms (since we can identify them), and by subtraction the number of smaller firms. In this case, we might (a) take whatever responses we can get from the larger firms, calculate average production volume for these firms, and multiply this average by the total number of larger firms to estimate total production in this stratum; (b) likewise, sample from whatever smaller firms we can identify, calculate average production volume for these firms, and multiple this average by the total number of smaller firms to estimate total production in this stratum; and (c) add the two to estimate total industry production. Here, we are using the following model:

$$\text{Large firm production} = b_L * \text{Number of large firms}$$

$$\text{Small firm production} = b_S * \text{Number of small firms}$$

$$\text{Total production} = \text{Large firm production} + \text{Small firm production}$$

We are using whatever information we can get to estimate b_L and b_S (average production per firm in each stratum), and we are implicitly assuming that b_L and b_S are constant across sets of firms regardless of the sampling process.

Two points may be obvious from these examples. First, model-based estimates are only as good as the model that produced them. In our first modeling example, if large firms accounted for something other than 80% of industry production in the quarter of interest, our estimates of total production and/or small firm production will be biased accordingly. In our second and third examples, if the bs are not constant across sets of firms, our estimates may be biased. Such bias in estimates is referred to as *model bias*.

Second, there are a variety of ways that models might be used to augment or replace probability samples. One can imagine examples beyond those given here, including complex multivariate models. Just as researchers might consider a variety of probability sampling designs for any given project and choose the one they think will yield the best estimates given available resources and constraints, researchers might similarly consider a variety of modeling approaches to augment or replace probability samples and choose the one they think will yield the best estimates.

Survey researchers use models principally to (1) reduce the variance of estimates or (2) cope with severe violations of probability sampling assumptions, including situations where it is simply impossible to implement a design-based sampling plan and situations where the design-based sample implementation is seriously flawed. Examples of the former include (a) sample allocation in stratified probability designs, (b) cutoff sampling, and (c) small area estimation. Examples of the latter include (a) dealing with the lack of an adequate frame, (b) dealing with high nonresponse, and (c) making estimates for nonfinite populations. We will consider each in turn.

7.2.2 Using Models to Reduce the Variance of Estimates

Sample Allocation in Stratified Probability Designs

Say that we wish to estimate quarterly production volume for some industry, and we accomplish this goal by using a disproportionate stratified probability sample with larger firms sampled at a higher rate. The reason for using such a sample is that the variance in production volumes is expected to be higher among large companies than among small companies, and by allocating relatively more of the sample to the high-variance stratum, we can reduce the variance of our total industry estimates. In other words, we can make the sample more efficient and reduce sampling error.

As noted in Chapter 5, the optimal allocation of sample across strata, to make the sample as efficient as it can possibly be, will be proportional to the variances in production volume in each stratum. However, until we do the survey, we won't know these variances. Instead, we will use some available variable that we expect to correlate with production variance and allocate the sample on that basis. For example, if we know the total number of people employed in each stratum, we might use this measure of size as a proxy for variance. In doing so, we are assuming a model that the ratio of total employment to variance in production volumes is constant across strata, and we are using this model to substitute employment for variance in the calculation of optimal sample allocations.

This model is presumably incorrect to some extent, and to the extent it is, the sample allocation will not be truly optimal. However, as long as our measure of size is correlated with stratum variance, the resulting sample will be more efficient than a proportionate sample (as seen in the hospital example in Chapter 5), and if employment is the best proxy available to us, it will be the best we can do. And since we will conduct probability sampling within all strata, we will be able to generate unbiased estimates for the strata and the total population once we do the survey. The variances may be slightly higher than optimal, but the validity of the survey estimates is not affected and the estimated sampling errors will reflect the true sampling errors, because the probability design remains the basis for inference (Kalton, 1983).

This might be labeled as an example of model-aided sampling, where a model has been used to provide information needed to optimize the sample design, but the sample itself is design based. In this case, the model allows us to improve efficiency without suffering bias in our estimates of industry production volume.

Cutoff Sampling

Model Example 1 given earlier, where we surveyed *only* the larger firms and used a model to estimate total industry production based on large firm production, is an example of cutoff sampling. The logic is an extension of the rationale for stratified sampling. Populations of organizations or establishments often have a small number of very large entities that are crucial to the estimation, along with a much larger number of small entities. For many variables of interest—such as production volume—variance among the entities is strongly related to their size, and by allocating relatively more of the sample to the high-variance stratum, we can reduce the variance of total population estimates. In fact, if we have information that allows us to state a reasonably accurate model of how the total population (or the smaller entities) relates to the larger entities, the lowest possible variance of estimates may be obtained by allocating all data collection resources to the larger entities. A cutoff sample does so, selecting the larger entities down to a point at which sampling is truncated.

As already noted, a cutoff sample is vulnerable to model bias, so it presents us with a trade-off between sampling error and possible sample bias. Our willingness to make this trade-off depends on three factors. First, how much we can reduce the variance of estimates, which typically depends on the extent to which population elements differ in size. Second, how good we feel about our model, which typically depends on the strength of its empirical support. For example, is the idea that large firms account for 80% of total industry production based on historical records, or on subjective estimates from trade journals? Third, our willingness to trade off bias for variance depends on the extent to which model bias could affect our estimates, which typically depends on how much of the population we capture. For example, if the captured sample typically accounts for 80% of industry production, leaving 20% uncovered, the uncovered entities would have to increase or decrease their share of production by 5% of their base share to have an impact of 1% on the total estimate. At 95% coverage, the uncovered entities would have to increase or decrease by 20% of base to have an impact of 1%.

Taking these factors into account, cutoff sampling is typically used to estimate business data such as revenues, production, or employment in highly concentrated industries where there are huge differences in firm size, a small number of firms account for a very high percentage of activity, and there is substantial historical and/or ancillary data to guide modeling. In some of these applications, the smaller entities are more costly to survey—for example, larger entities will respond online while smaller entities are more likely to require a telephone call or a visit—and/or the smaller establishments account for a large proportion of the survey nonresponse, so cutoff sampling offers the further benefits of reducing costs and/or reducing exposure to nonresponse bias. For a detailed treatment of cutoff sampling, see Knaub (2008).

Small Area Estimation

Design-based sampling may be perfectly suitable for total population estimates but inefficient for subgroups. For example, providing estimates for small geographic areas is often an important, but secondary, objective of a large-scale survey. We not only wish to estimate the characteristics of interest for the nation as a whole but also for states, counties, or even smaller areas. The design-based approach is perfectly capable *in theory* of providing such estimates, because the small area samples are a subset of the main probability sample. The main estimation problem is that the small area samples are too small; they can produce unbiased estimates but with sampling errors too large for the intended uses. A sample that is large at the national level may become problematic at the state level and hopeless at the county level.

For example, if we wish to estimate quarterly production volume for some industry, and we have a stratified probability sample that covers the full population, we are likely to use design-based estimates at a national level. However, if we seek to estimate production at the state (or lower) level, the variance of design-based estimates may be too high to be useful, and we may use model-based procedures (such as estimating production as a ratio of employment) to reduce the variance of these estimates.

7.2.3 Using Models to Cope With Violations of Probability Sampling Assumptions

Dealing With the Lack of an Adequate Frame

Probability sampling presumes that we have an adequate population frame from which we can draw the sample, with every member of the population given a known, nonzero chance of selection. But what if the available frames have serious omissions, or we have no frame at all? For example, we typically do not have complete frames for populations of Internet users from which to draw samples for web surveys. In such situations, model-based approaches are preferable to hoping, without basis, that design-based sampling will produce reliable results.

Model Examples 2 and 3 are relevant here. In both examples, we lacked an adequate frame for smaller firms. We also had severe nonresponse among larger firms. In the second example, we took whatever data we could get, used those data to fit a model that related production to the number of employees, and estimated production on this basis. In the third example, we took whatever data we could get, used those data to fit a model that related production to membership in the large or small firm stratum, and estimated production on this basis. The resulting estimates are certainly open to model bias, but at least the process is transparent. We know what assumptions were made, and we can give a realistic appraisal of the result.

Model Example 3 is parallel to what happens in quota sampling. Quota sampling rests on assumptions that selection within the defined quota categories can be nonrandom, and the quota weighting model will produce unbiased estimates.

Dealing With High Nonresponse

Low response rates are an increasing threat to the validity and/or reliability of survey estimates. Researchers often use weighting and imputation models to address this issue. Model Examples 2 and 3, especially Model Example 3, again are relevant.

Nonresponse weighting adjustments are based on models of the distribution of nonrespondents (e.g., weighting class adjustments) or models of the mechanism that produces the nonresponse (e.g., response propensities). For example, the weighting class adjustment model assumes that within each class (e.g., a demographic subgroup), nonrespondents are missing at random, meaning that there are essentially no differences within a class between the respondents and nonrespondents. This is the assumption made in Model Example 3, where respondents in the large and small firm strata are treated as representative of nonrespondents in those strata. If this assumption is largely correct, *and* the weighting class variables correlate reasonably well with the survey's dependent variables, then weights applied to the respondents will reduce nonresponse bias. If not, this method of reducing nonresponse bias will be less effective, as discussed earlier in this chapter.

Making Estimates for Nonfinite Populations

Design-based sampling provides a theoretical basis for estimating characteristics of the finite population from which the sample is drawn. But what if we don't want to make inferences about this particular population?

In some cases, it may be more useful to conceive of the population as infinite (often called a *superpopulation*) than finite. For example, Kalton (2002) describes a situation in which a sample of eighth graders, selected in 2001, will be used to make inferences about the population of eighth graders in 2002, an entirely different set of individuals. In this case, "for inferences about the 2002 population, a model is . . . needed. One way to construct this model is to assume a superpopulation model, from which [both] the 2001 and 2002 student populations are drawn as random realizations" (p. 133).

7.2.4 Conclusions About the Use of Models

Survey researchers may use model-based methods to improve sample selection or estimation when design-based sampling is inefficient or flawed. The great strength of design-based inference is that it can be applied to any finite population without prior knowledge about that population's distributions. However, given the costs and constraints of any given project, the realized sample for which data are obtained may differ radically from the conceived probability sample. The great strength of model-based inference is that there is no disadvantage in using that realized sample.

The Achilles heel of model-based estimation is that its accuracy is crucially dependent on the correctness of the model. Several considerations are relevant in this regard:

- A model is rarely entirely correct or entirely wrong.
- A fair amount of effort may be expended in choosing between alternative models.
- Because a model's assumptions are likely *not* to be perfect, a question of immediate concern is how sensitive is it to some amount of deviation from its assumptions. If the assumptions are not quite on the mark, will the estimates for the independent variable remain close to their true values or differ substantially from them? This sensitivity to deviation from the model's assumptions is sometimes described as its *robustness*. Clearly, model robustness is highly desired.
- If the model's assumptions fail, how do we know that has happened, and what can be done about it?
- Models are typically variable specific. Some simple models may serve to estimate different population values. However, the more complex the model, the less likely it will apply to more than one dependent variable.

The fact that design-based inference can be applied to any finite population without prior knowledge about that population's distributions led to probability sampling becoming a dominant paradigm in survey research, widely used in academics, business, and government statistical agencies to estimate population parameters. This paradigm has remained dominant in survey research for several reasons, many of which have to do with the primacy of large-scale surveys whose main requirement is the estimation of descriptive measures for a finite population.

However, the nature of most large-scale surveys may differ greatly from the needs of an independent researcher. For example, the research cultures of academic disciplines differ in ways that are directly relevant to the need for design-based sampling. In a very insightful discussion on reconciling the needs of researchers from multiple disciplines in arriving at a sample design for a particular survey, Michael and O'Muircheartaigh (2008) contrast how disciplines differ on issues such as (a) the amount of reliance on predetermined hypotheses, (b) the key types of expected analyses, (c) the emphasis on internal versus external validity of the research, and (d) how the populations of interest are conceptualized, all of which influence the need for design-based estimates.

Model-based sampling and estimation are complex methodologies, with a large literature. Only a general sense of the issues can be provided here. Readers seeking a more comprehensive treatment might start with the series of papers by Kalton (1983, 2002) and the classic text, Model-Assisted Survey Sampling (Sarndal, Swensson, & Wretman, 1992).

7.3 MEASURING THE UNCERTAINTY OF ESTIMATES FROM COMPLEX OR NONPROBABILITY SAMPLES

Confidence intervals (also called margins of error) are the most commonly reported measure of the uncertainty associated with survey estimates. As seen in Chapter 4, confidence intervals are calculated from the sampling error; for example, a 95% confidence interval for any given estimate is calculated as ±1.96 times the sampling error associated with that estimate, which in turn is calculated from the variance of the variable of interest, the sample size, and (perhaps) the finite population correction. The sampling error is an incomplete measure of uncertainty, because measurement error or other nonsampling errors may also be present in an estimate, but the sampling error at least provides information about the level of uncertainty associated with random variation in sample composition.

If the sample in our study is a simple random sample, the task of calculating sampling errors and hence confidence intervals is simple. Statistical packages provide sampling errors (often labeled standard errors) routinely in their output, and these sampling errors presume that the data were obtained through simple random sampling (srs). However, our sample design may differ from srs. The design may involve stratification or clustering, along with possible weights for nonresponse, or may be a nonprobability sample. In these cases, simple random sampling errors will misstate (sometimes greatly) the precision of the measures.

One option for dealing with data from complex probability samples is to use software that is designed for such data and will compute sampling errors that take into account the specific sample design and weighting procedures. The best-known packages for this purpose are SUDAAN (SUrveyDAtaANalysis) from Research Triangle Institute and WesVar (http://www.westat.com/wesvar/) from the Westat Corporation. Details of their implementation are beyond the scope of this book, but written manuals and short course instruction are available.

Another option is to use pseudo-replication procedures such as *bootstrapping* or *jackknifing* that empirically estimate standard errors by drawing subsamples of the data at hand. Common statistical packages such as SAS or SPSS offer these procedures. To learn more, simply Google *bootstrapping in SAS*, *jack-knifing in SAS*, and so on.

When estimates are produced through model-based rather than design-based procedures, it is increasingly common for researchers to convey levels of uncertainty around their estimates by referring to *credibility intervals* rather than confidence intervals. In broad terms, the difference between these terms is as follows. A 95% confidence interval starts with a population characteristic (such as a mean or proportion) and expresses a range within which sample estimates of that characteristic will fall 95% of the time for repeated samples of the given size. A credibility interval is a Bayesian concept that starts with the characteristic of interest in the one sample that we actually have, estimates the conditional probability of any particular population value given that sample information, and takes the range that captures 95% of the cumulative conditional probability. To make these conditional probability estimates, the analyst must rely on some model.

The good news is that credibility intervals can theoretically accommodate data from nonprobability as well as probability samples. The not so good news is that one must assume that the sample design is conditionally ignorable, meaning that there is not a relationship between the probability of appearing in the survey and the variables being measured. Also, as with any model-based procedure, the results are only as good as the model. Because of these issues, when you see something labelled as a credibility interval, the safest course of action is simply to take it as a sign that the findings are based on a nonprobability sample and not necessarily as the equivalent of a standard error from a probability sample.

The American Association for Public Opinion Research (AAPOR) has made the following statement about credibility intervals: "While the adoption of the credibility interval is an appropriate use of statistical model-based methods, the underlying biases associated with non-probability online polls remain a concern. As a result, the public should not rely on the credibility interval in the same way that it can with the margin of sampling error." For the full AAPOR statement on credibility intervals, see https://aapor.org/AM/Template.cfm?Section=Understanding_a_credibility_interval_and_how_it_differs_from_the_margin_of_sampling_error_in_a_publi&Template=/CM/ContentDisplay.cfm&ContentID=5475.

7.4 CHAPTER SUMMARY

This chapter considered three general topics related to the accuracy of estimates drawn from samples: (1) weighting to adjust for differences in probabilities of selection or nonresponse, (2) the use of mathematical models to guide sampling and/or estimation, and (3) the measurement of uncertainty for estimates that are drawn from complex or nonprobability samples.

Differences in probabilities of selection or nonresponse can lead to selection bias or nonresponse bias in the results of a survey. These differences can be corrected by weighting.

In general, data always should be weighted if the sample design incorporated unequal selection probabilities (e.g., through stratification). However, weighting to correct for differences in nonresponse or noncontact rates is more problematic. Weighting for differential nonresponse assumes that respondents are missing at random, which may not be true. Weighting also increases sampling error, offsetting possible reductions in bias. Any unreliability in the weighting measures will exacerbate this increase in sampling error. Because of these issues, weighting for nonresponse should be undertaken only when (a) differences in nonresponse are fairly dramatic across groups, (b) the weighting produces substantial and credible changes in important variables, and (c) there are no obvious adverse effects of the weighting.

Model-based estimation offers researchers a way to (1) reduce the variance of estimates or (2) cope with severe violations of probability sampling assumptions, including situations where design-based estimation is problematic. Examples of the former include (a) sample allocation in stratified probability designs, (b) cutoff sampling, and (c) small area estimation. Examples of the latter include (a) dealing with the lack of an adequate frame, (b) dealing with high nonresponse, and (c) making estimates for nonfinite populations.

The big plus of model-based estimation is that it can cope with problematic samples. The big minus is the possibility of model bias and the fact that estimates are only as good as the model that generated them.

Regarding the uncertainty of estimates, the task of calculating sampling errors and confidence intervals is simple if we have a simple random sample. Statistical packages provide sampling errors (often labeled standard errors) routinely in their output, and these sampling errors presume that the data were obtained through simple random sampling. However, if we have a complex or nonprobability sample, srs sampling errors will misstate (sometimes greatly) the precision of the measures.

One option for dealing with data from complex probability samples is to use software that is designed for such data, such as SUDAAN (SUrvey DAtaANalysis) from Research Triangle Institute and WesVar (http://www.westat.com/wesvar/) from the Westat Corporation. Another option is to use pseudo-replication procedures such as *bootstrapping* or *jackknifing* that empirically estimate standard errors by drawing subsamples of the data at hand.

When estimates are produced through model-based rather than design-based procedures, it is increasingly common for researchers to convey levels of uncertainty around their estimates by referring to *credibility intervals* rather than confidence intervals. Credibility intervals are theoretically distinct from confidence intervals, but the purpose is similar. The good news is that credibility intervals can theoretically accommodate data from nonprobability as well as probability samples; the not so good news is that one must assume there is not a relationship between the probability of appearing in the survey and the variables being measured. As with any model-based procedure, the results are only as good as the model.

EXERCISES AND DISCUSSION QUESTIONS

Exercise 7.1

In a survey on parks and recreation, 40% of respondents are younger than 55 years, and 60% are 55 years and older. The relevant population is known to have 80% younger than 55 and 20% older than 55. The unweighted survey results indicate that 26% of area residents want more children's playgrounds in city parks: 50% for respondents younger than 55 years and 10% for respondents 55 years and older. If these results are weighted to correct for age, what percentage of area residents want more children's playgrounds? Would you weight these data for age?

If 70% of the survey respondents are younger than 55 years, and 30% are 55 and older, and the percentage of respondents in each group who want more children's playgrounds remains as 50% and 10%, respectively, what would be the unweighted percentage of all survey respondents who want more children's playgrounds? What would be the weighted percentage? Would you weight these data for age?

8

Sampling in Special Contexts

Previous chapters have covered general issues in sampling. In addition to these general points, any given research context is likely to present its own specific sampling issues. Here, we discuss various contexts that are of interest to many social researchers. We consider the following:

- Sampling for online research
- Sampling visitors to a place
- Sampling rare populations
- Sampling organizations
- Sampling groups such as influence groups or elites
- Sampling for panel research
- Sampling in international contexts
- "Big data" and survey sampling
- Incorporating new technologies

Each of these contexts presents its own special sampling problems and its own characteristic procedures. In this chapter, you will learn about those problems and procedures.

8.1 SAMPLING FOR ONLINE RESEARCH

As noted earlier in this book, online data collection is increasingly common and may present significant sampling problems.

The first sampling problem associated with online surveys of the general population is the potential for coverage bias because many people are not online. Only 75% of the U.S. population currently uses the Internet (U.S. Census Bureau, 2012), and the figure is lower in most other countries. Coverage is disproportionately low for elderly people, African Americans, Hispanics, and people with lower levels of education and income, which implies corresponding coverage biases in general population surveys (Couper, 2000).

A second problem in general population surveys is the potential for coverage bias because available sampling frames cover only a fraction of the online population. As noted in Chapter 2, one can buy demographically balanced samples from opt-in online panels: however, these panels are typically assembled through volunteerism rather than random selection, and even if they contain millions of names, this is still a relatively small fraction of the general population, so the theoretical potential for coverage bias is high. Alternatives such as using Amazon MTurk or assembling a frame through social media may present additional coverage and selection problems, as discussed in Chapter 2.

It must be emphasized that these coverage problems relate to surveys of the general population. If the population of interest is found online, such as visitors to a website or members of a social media site, or if it is a special population for which a list of e-mail addresses is available, such as students in a college directory, then coverage is typically not an issue.

The third sampling problem in online data collection is the potential for nonresponse bias stemming from low response rates. In our experience, response rates in online surveys are often less than 5%. Response rates are better for special populations surveyed on topics of interest, such as teachers surveyed about educational issues or college students surveyed about campus issues: here, response rates for well-executed surveys may be 40% or better. Response rates also are better for samples drawn from opt-in panels, typically 25% or better, but one must consider that people are in the panel because they have already agreed to participate in research.

Overall, we can say the following:

• The problems of sampling online populations are lowest when (a) the target population has high levels of online access, which minimizes potential coverage bias from this source; (b) one has (or can assemble) a relatively complete list of e-mail addresses for the population, which minimizes potential coverage bias from this source; and (c) the research topic is of interest to the target population and the study is well executed, which minimizes potential nonresponse bias. These conditions may be met for special populations such as professional groups or college students at a particular campus.

- Online studies of the general population are more problematic; however, in this context, panel samples are generally the best option because of their ability to provide balanced samples for which historical norms may be available. (Online panel samples also may be useful in the context of dual-frame designs when rare groups are of interest, as discussed later in this chapter.)

- Because of frame and nonresponse problems, online surveys of the general population typically must be viewed as having some form of nonprobability sampling, so estimates drawn from these studies must rely on some form of model-based estimation as discussed in Chapter 7.

Despite the problems associated with online samples, researchers increasingly rely on them. In defense of online samples, as noted in Chapter 2, the samples obtained in online research may be as good as or better than the alternatives being considered; for example, a study conducted with a sample of MTurk panelists may be at least as defensible as a study conducted with a sample of college students. Also, online surveys are wholly appropriate for special populations that are found online or for which a list of e-mail addresses is available. Finally, online samples may be good enough for the purposes at hand. We discuss the question "How good must the sample be?" in Chapter 9.

Some online studies are done by posting an invitation to participate on a listserv, discussion board, or Facebook page. Samples obtained in this manner are, of course, nonprobability samples—samples of volunteers with no controls on sample quality. They may be acceptable in contexts where other volunteer samples are accepted: for example, in academic experimental research where participants are randomly assigned to experimental conditions and wide latitude is given regarding sample quality, or perhaps for exploratory purposes. However, these samples are not appropriate for situations in which one wishes to generalize numerical estimates from the observed sample to a specifically defined population.

8.2 SAMPLING VISITORS TO A PLACE

Intercept samples (also called *location samples* or *site samples*) are samples of visitors to a place. Intercept samples might be taken of visitors to a shopping mall, a store, a business district, a museum, a park, a stadium, a street fair, a polling place, and so on.

The most common examples of intercept research are shopping mall studies, also known as mall surveys or mall intercept surveys. These are used as an inexpensive form of market research, especially for studies that require the presentation of physical stimuli such as products, advertisements, or trademarks. In this type of research, the intercept sample is not meant to profile visitors to the specific place: Rather, it is meant as a convenience sample of a broader population, and nonprobability methods are the norm. If multiple sites are used, the selection of locations is based on judgment; for example, in a study concerning the likelihood of confusion between two trademarks, data might be gathered in four shopping malls in different regions of the country, with the selection of specific malls being based on the availability of interviewing services. Within sites, interviewers are usually left to their own devices, subject to any quota requirements.

There may be a desire for intercept samples with higher quality, especially when the research is meant to profile visitors to the particular location. A common example is political exit polling, where the goal is to characterize voting in selected precincts for purposes of analyzing the election and predicting the result. Other examples that we have seen include (1) profiling the trade area from which a store, shopping mall, or business district draws patrons; (2) profiling the characteristics and/or interests of visitors to a street festival, amusement park, athletic event, museum, play, symphony concert, zoo, and so on; (3) profiling how visitors to a place move through it and use the facilities; and (4) in public health surveys, profiling people who visit places with certain health risks, such as gay men who frequent establishments where sex is permitted. In these situations, since the intercept sample is intended to be specifically representative of visitors to the particular place, better sample quality may be desired.

It is possible to use standard sampling procedures to select careful intercept samples, both in the selection of data collection sites and the selection of visitors within sites, as follows.

8.2.1 Selecting Places for Intercept Research

In many applications of intercept research, a single place is of interest. For example, if the purpose of the research is to map the trade area of a particular retail store or to learn the characteristics of visitors to a local arts festival, then the research location is set by definition and there is no need to draw a sample of places (although one may wish to sample places within the place, as described below).

In other applications, the places where data will be collected are intended to represent a broader population of sites. For example, in exit polling, the voting precincts in which data are gathered may be intended to represent the entire state. Here, the sites can be viewed as clusters and either (a) chosen with equal probabilities if one plans to apply a fixed sampling rate within sites, such as every 20th voter, or (b) chosen with probabilities proportionate to size if one plans to gather a fixed number of observations at each site. For example, in an exit polling context where all votes in a state are of interest, the votes can be viewed as being clustered by precinct, and precincts (clusters) can be selected for purposes of polling. Such samples also can be stratified if desired; for example, in election research, "swing" precincts that historically have shown more variation in party preference and/or turnout levels might be assigned to a separate stratum and sampled at a higher rate than "safe" or stable precincts.

A problem that may arise is inability to obtain access to selected places; for example, in drawing a careful sample of shopping malls, one will encounter the problem that malls are private business establishments and many will not permit interviewing on their premises. If this problem becomes too large to ignore, one's general options are to weight the data for place characteristics or substitute places in the same general location with similar characteristics.

8.2.2 Sampling Visitors Within Places

Within sites, the simplest way to obtain a probability sample is to sample people systematically as they enter or leave the site. For example, if 100 interviews are desired at a particular site, and 3,600 people are expected to visit during the interviewing period, one might select every 36th visitor after a random start.[1] Sampling issues that arise in this context include the following:

- *How long should the intercept period last (and when should it be)?* In some cases, there may be a natural period in which data should be collected; for example, in exit polling, data should be collected on election day while the polls are open. In other cases, the intercept period may not be obvious; for example, in studying visitors to a shopping center, there is no natural start and end to the

---

1. This is easiest to do if the task of sampling is separated from data collection—in other words, if the person who counts and selects visitors is not also responsible for soliciting participation or gathering data.

research period. Should data be collected in a single morning? A single day? Three days? A week? More? Obviously, this decision will affect the sampling interval, as the total number of visitors will increase with the length of the intercept period. A rule of thumb is that the intercept period should capture any hourly or daily variations that one might expect in the nature of visitors: for example, one might expect differences in employment status, age, and sex between voters who visit the polls during normal office hours and those who come early or late, and Blair (1983) shows differences between weekday, weeknight, and weekend visitors to shopping malls. It also may be desirable to capture broader time differences, such as differences in museum visitors during the school year versus vacation periods or the tendency of lower income workers to shop around payday.

• *What if you don't have an estimate of population size?* To establish a sampling interval or sampling rate, you have to know how many visitors to expect. This information may or may not be available. In sampling voters, there should be historical data on voter turnout at the precinct level. In sampling visitors to a zoo, or amusement park, or museum, there should be historical ticket and/or turnstile counts. In sampling visitors to an athletic event or symphony performance, there should be data on advance sales and historical walk-up sales. In sampling customers at a store, there should be historical transaction counts. However, in sampling visitors to a shopping mall, business district, or open-air street festival, there may not be any close estimate of population size. In such situations, a preliminary traffic count is needed. If such a count is not possible— for example, if one cannot count the visitors to a 3-day street festival until it is time to do the research—then one must rely on rough estimates or use another sampling method as described later in this section.

• *How should the sample size be adjusted for nonresponse?* Some people will refuse to participate in the research, and the sampling plan must be adjusted accordingly. For example, if you desire a sample size of 100, and you expect a 50% response rate, you need to intercept 200 people to get the desired 100, and the sampling interval should be set accordingly. Response rates for intercept studies can vary widely depending on the nature of the place, the quality of the interviewers, the time of day or year, and the nature of the task, and the best way to estimate response for any given study will be through a pilot test.

• *What if your estimates of population size or response rate are wrong?* Since any estimate of population size will be based on historical data, it is likely to contain some level of error, and you are likely to encounter more or fewer visitors than expected. Likewise, your estimate of response rate may be off. As a result, you may reach the desired sample size before the end of the intercept period or reach the end of the period without enough observations.

If you reach the desired sample size before the end of the intercept period and the discrepancy is not large, carry on with the sampling plan to avoid bias against later time periods. If the discrepancy is large and you cannot afford the larger number of observations, hopefully such a large discrepancy will be apparent early in the data collection process and the sampling plan can be adjusted; otherwise, if you stop data collection early, you risk bias. Similarly, if you reach the end of the intercept period without enough observations and the discrepancy is not large, accept the discrepancy rather than oversampling later time periods, and if the discrepancy is too large to accept, hopefully this will be apparent early in the process and the sampling plan can be adjusted.[2]

- *What if the number of entrances and exits is large?* In trying to draw a probability sample of visitors to a place, our preference is to intercept them as they enter or leave. There may be various advantages in doing so—for example, people may be less rushed and more likely to participate when they first arrive, and people who are leaving can report completely about their activities at the site—but our primary reason from a sampling perspective is that everyone is likely to enter and leave once, so we can account for the entire population of visits with equal probabilities at the points of entrance or exit.

Sampling visitors as they enter or leave is easy if the place has a single entrance or exit, and not too difficult if the place has a small number of entrances or exits, but becomes increasingly difficult as the site becomes more complex. Shopping malls, for example, may have dozens of entrances (including those directly into stores). For these situations, where it may not be practical to sample continuously at every entrance, Sudman (1980) proposed a scheme in which visitors are grouped into clusters based on entrance and time period (e.g., Entrance 1 from 10:00–11:00 a.m. on Saturday), and clusters are sampled with probabilities proportionate to size. A major drawback to this scheme is that it requires separate estimates of population size (number of visitors) for each

---

2. In theory, some protection from large errors may be allowed by sampling over several days or even weeks, which allows time to adjust the sampling plan. However, this doesn't always work. For example, if visitor counts are influenced by the weather, it may be difficult to predict counts from one day to the next.

entrance by each time period. Such estimates are unlikely to be available, and generating them may be costly; as a result, this procedure receives little use. We discuss other methods for sampling at complex sites, including sites that do not have formal entrance and exit points, later in this section.

- *How should children and groups be treated?* Visitors to most places will include a mixture of adults and children, as well as individuals and groups. Their treatment depends on the nature of the research and the corresponding definition of the population. In some cases such as exit polling, the population of interest consists of adult individuals. Here, children are ineligible and should be ignored, both for purposes of counting and selection. Likewise, groups are irrelevant, and people who enter in groups should be counted and selected as individuals. In other situations, children and group composition may be of interest: For example, in profiling visitors to the zoo, there is a good chance that we will be interested in the number of children who attended, their ages, and other information. In these situations, we might define a population of adults, count only individual adults, and essentially treat the number and nature of children as a characteristic of the adult; alternately, we might define a population of groups, count and select groups, and use a single adult respondent to provide information about the group.

- *Are visits the desired population unit?* In sampling visitors to a place, the implicit sampling unit is the visit, not the person or the money they might spend (Blair, 1983). Consider, for example, Person A who visits a store 50 times a year and Person B who visits once a year. Holding aside systematic patterns in the timing of these visits, if we intercept visitors to the store on any given day, the chance of catching A is 50 times larger than the chance of catching B. This is entirely appropriate if we wish to describe the population of *visits:* From this perspective, each of A's visits is a separate population unit that deserves its own chance of selection. However, if we wish to describe the population of *people* who visit the place, then A and B should have equal chance of selection; from this perspective, A's multiple visits can be viewed as duplicate elements in the sampling frame, which produce selection bias in favor of the more frequent visitor. This bias can be corrected by measuring visit frequency—for example, by asking respondents how many times they have come to this place within the past year—and weighting for the inverse of frequency. Similarly, if one is interested in a population of dollars spent on a per annum basis, it will be appropriate to measure visit frequency and level of spending, weight down for visit frequency to get to the level of people, and then weight back up for each person's expenditure (see Blair, 1983).

- *Should data be weighted for length of visit?* Nowell and Stanley (1991) suggest that visitors' probabilities of being intercepted at a place are related to the length of time spent on site, so intercept data should be weighted for (the inverse of) visit length. In general, though, we do not recommend "length weighting." If intercepts are conducted at entrance or exit points, most people will pass these points once as they enter and/or once as they leave, regardless of how long they stay, and the probability of being intercepted will not relate to visit length: Therefore, length weighting will not reduce bias. If intercepts are conducted elsewhere, such as the central court of a shopping mall, then the probabilities of people passing an intercept point may indeed correlate with visit length: However, (a) since the visit is not yet complete, people may not be able to give good estimates of its length, and (b) for length weighting to reduce bias, visit length must also correlate with the variables being adjusted, which may be problematic. Background variables such as age, income, and home ZIP code typically do not correlate well enough with visit length to justify weighting. Variables that clearly relate to time on site, such as the probability of visiting any particular store within a mall or the total number of stores visited, correlate better with visit length, but we have found that the reduction in bias resulting from weighting is not consistent or large enough to justify the associated increase in sampling error.

If there is no reliable estimate of the number of people who will visit a place, a procedure that might be used is to sample systematically by time. For example, if 100 interviews are desired, and the interviewing period is scheduled for 10 hours or 600 minutes, one might select a visitor every 6 minutes after a random start. The advantage of this approach is that it does not require any estimate of the population size (number of visitors). The disadvantage is that it implicitly samples visitors from low-traffic time periods at a higher rate than visitors from high-traffic periods, which might result in selection bias. This bias can be managed by counting the number of visitors while the research is being done and weighting data from different time periods accordingly; for example, if it turns out that weekend visitors were sampled at half the rate of weekday visitors, then weekend observations should be weighted up by a factor of 2.

At complex sites, time sampling can be combined with the entrance-by-time-period clustering suggested by Sudman (1980). Clusters are defined in a similar manner (e.g., Entrance 1 from 10:00–11:00 a.m. on Saturday), selected with equal probabilities, and a fixed time-sampling scheme is applied within each cluster. The advantage of this procedure is that it allows one to draw a probability sample even at a complex site without estimates of population size. The disadvantage is that it implicitly applies a higher sampling rate to visitors from low-traffic time periods and low-traffic entrances compared with high-traffic times and high-traffic entrances. Again, this bias can be managed by counting visitors and weighting.

In some cases, it may not be possible to intercept visitors at points of entrance and exit. This might occur at places that do not have formal points of entry and exit, such as a business district or a street fair or a park, or at places where intercepts are allowed only in constrained areas, such as the central court of a shopping mall. In these situations, one can at least try to establish intercept points that cover different geographic areas and different time periods. For example, in a shopping mall with an east-west orientation, one might establish western and eastern intercept points and collect data at each point during weekday, weeknight, and weekend periods, to capture differences among visitors that are likely to occur across locations and time (Blair, 1983). Traffic counts can be taken at each intercept point for each time period and the data weighted accordingly. This is essentially a quota sampling procedure with quotas defined on location and time, whether or not an effort is made to sample individual visitors at each intercept point through some random procedure.

8.3 SAMPLING RARE POPULATIONS

Rare groups are often of interest to researchers. By rare groups, we mean groups that account for no more than 20% of the general population and usually much less. Examples include men who have sex with men, who are of interest for (HIV) health risk studies; low-income households, who are of interest for welfare policy research and other purposes; and purchasers of specific goods or services.

In sampling a rare population, the first thing to determine is whether a good list is available. If so, sampling and locating respondents is straightforward. However, this is the exception rather than the rule. In most cases, screening of the general population is necessary, and the costs of screening can equal or far exceed the costs of interviewing. For example, if the target group comprises 2% of the general population, 50 screeners are needed to locate each group member unless sampling efficiency is improved in some way.

Exhibit 8.1   Snapshot of Methods for Locating Rare Populations

Method	Conditions in Which It Might Be Useful
Telephone cluster sampling	There are a substantial number of telephone exchanges with no members of the target population
Disproportionate stratified sampling	Prevalence of the target population varies substantially across geographic areas such as telephone exchanges
Network sampling (multiplicity sampling, snowball sampling, respondent-driven sampling)	Members of the target population can be accurately identified and reached through others in a well-defined network such as members of their immediate family
Dual-frame sampling	A special frame is available that has high prevalence of the target population
Location sampling	Members of the target population tend to congregate at identifiable locations
Use of online panels	You are willing to treat the online panel members as representative of a broader population such as all online users

As a result, survey researchers have long been interested in cost-effective methods for sampling rare groups within the general population. Methods that have been used in this regard include telephone cluster sampling, disproportionate stratified sampling, network sampling, dual-frame sampling, location sampling, and, most recently, online data collection (cf. Kalton, 2001). All of these methods are useful under certain conditions, as indicated in Exhibit 8.1 and discussed below.

8.3.1 Telephone Cluster Sampling

Telephone cluster sampling (TCS) for rare groups, a variation of Mitofsky-Waksberg sampling (see Chapter 2), was described by Blair and Czaja (1982) based on a suggestion from Sudman, and further described in Sudman (1985). It works as follows. A random number is dialed within a bank of telephone numbers: This number can be selected via list-assisted random-digit dialing or any other probability sampling procedure.[3] If the number is found to be a working household number, the household (or person) is screened for membership in the target group. If the household is not a member of the target group or if the number is not a working household number, then no further sampling is done within the bank. However, if a group member is found, further sampling is done within the bank until a prespecified number of group members is identified.[4] This procedure has the effect of rapidly dropping telephone banks with no target group members and "fishing where the fish are."

The potential usefulness of TCS for rare groups depends on two factors: (a) the extent to which members of the target population are clustered within telephone exchanges and (b) how rare the group is. The harder it is to find the group in the general population, and the greater the extent to which group members are clustered, the greater the benefits of searching near one group member for another.

If TCS is used, one faces the question of an appropriate cluster size. Sudman (1985) suggests that the optimal number of group members to be taken within each telephone bank is typically in the range of 8 to 10. However, it is difficult to reach cluster sizes of 8 to 10 rare group members in banks of 100 telephone numbers. For example, Blair and Czaja (1982) used TCS to sample African Americans, who comprised about 9% of working household numbers at the time of their study, and found that 18% of the retained telephone banks could not produce a cluster size of 10. If some banks fall short of the desired cluster size, the total sample will likewise be smaller than desired. This is easily addressed through additional sampling or by increasing the initial sample size. More important, TCS requires equal cluster sizes for the sample to be EPSEM and hence unbiased. If some clusters fall short, weights must be used to compensate, and sampling variance increases as a result. In the case of Blair and Czaja (1982), the need to weight respondents from "short" banks produced an increase in sampling variance that threatened to completely offset the increase in screening efficiency (Waksberg, 1983). Sudman (1985) suggested dealing with this problem

---

3. The original purpose for Mitofsky-Waksberg (M-W) sampling was to find working household telephone numbers and eliminate banks of nonworking numbers, as discussed in Chapter 2. For this purpose, list-assisted RDD (which also eliminates nonworking banks) and M-W sampling are competing alternatives. However, when the goal is to find members of a rare group, the two procedures are complementary. List assistance almost completely eliminates banks of nonworking numbers, and telephone cluster sampling can further eliminate working banks in which the target group does not occur.

4. The cluster size is defined as identified, not cooperating, eligible households or individuals. If the cluster size is k, then calling in the bank stops after k group members are identified by screening, whether or not they consent to the main interview.

by increasing the size of the telephone banks; for example, defining banks of several hundred rather than 100 telephone numbers. Alternately—or in addition—one can cut the cluster size, and our experience is that cluster sizes of 2 to 3 are more appropriate than the 8 to 10 suggested by Sudman (1985).

While TCS for rare groups is theoretically appealing, it has not worked well in practice and is rarely used. Furthermore, as people switch from landlines to cellphones, geographic clustering within telephone exchanges declines. However, Blair and Blair (2006) suggest some conditions under which TCS may be useful in dual-frame designs that also use online panels to locate rare groups.

8.3.2 Disproportionate Stratified Sampling

Disproportionate stratified sampling for rare groups may be effective if the prevalence of the target group is higher in some areas than in others. The high-prevalence areas can be assigned to a separate stratum and sampled at a disproportionately high rate to raise the overall efficiency of the design. For example, in sampling men who have sex with men, which is of interest in public health studies, certain areas such as the Castro district in San Francisco have higher than average prevalence of the target group, and the relevant telephone exchanges can be given disproportionate assignments (cf. Blair, 1999). Likewise, groups such as affluent households, households living in poverty, or buyers of specialized products may be disproportionately prevalent in identifiable areas.

The usefulness of disproportionate stratified sampling for rare groups depends on the extent to which the prevalence of the target group varies across geographic areas. One also would like to have prevalence data for the target group (or some reasonable proxy) by telephone exchanges (or some reasonable proxy) to define strata a priori and make efficient strata allocations; however, if such data are unavailable or of poor quality, it is possible to use a two-phase adaptive sampling in which prevalence information acquired in Phase 1 is used to determine near-optimal strata definitions and allocations in Phase 2, where most of the data collection will be done (cf. Blair, 1999). For example, the number of calls needed to find a member of the target group within an area (or the number of calls between group members) provides information about the group's prevalence. The adaptive approach may be generally useful in addressing the common problem in sampling rare special populations—that there are often insufficient or poor-quality secondary data to use in developing the sample design.

Note that the conditions under which disproportionate stratified sampling (DSS) is effective for locating rare groups are parallel to the conditions under which telephone cluster sampling (TCS) is effective: TCS is effective when the target group is geographically clustered, which is tantamount to saying that the group's prevalence varies across geographic areas. This might be taken to imply that TCS and disproportionate stratified sampling are competing procedures and that one or the other should be used where they are applicable. However, this is not necessarily so, because the two procedures work through different mechanisms. In fact, the methods may be complementary.

TCS works by eliminating banks of telephone numbers in which the target group does not appear. There is a common misconception that it also works by undersampling banks of numbers with relatively few group members, but this is not so. The procedure is EPSEM, and it does not oversample banks with high levels of group prevalence or undersample banks with low prevalence. Once empty banks are eliminated, the effectiveness of TCS is unaffected by the target group's distribution across the populated banks. In contrast, disproportionate stratified sampling *does* oversample and undersample populated banks with higher and lower prevalence, and the procedure's effectiveness does not require that any banks be completely empty. In effect, stratified sampling works by over-sampling telephone banks where the target group's prevalence is high, while TCS works by eliminating banks where the group does not occur.

The two procedures are redundant if the available stratifying information allows one to identify telephone banks in which the target group does not occur: In this situation, one will simply allocate zero sample to the empty stratum, and there will be no further gains from TCS. The procedures also are redundant if there is little variation in prevalence among the nonzero banks: In this situation, once TCS eliminates the empty banks, there will be little to gain from dispropor-tionate stratified sampling.

Usually, if there are sufficient variations in prevalence to justify the use of stratification, we can separate higher versus lower prevalence areas (either a priori or through adaptive procedures), but we cannot state with certainty that any given telephone bank is empty of the target group. For example, we know that the Castro district has a higher prevalence than other areas for men who have sex with men, and we know that Beverly Hills has a higher prevalence for extremely affluent households, but we cannot a priori identify banks of 100 telephone numbers in which those groups are guaranteed not to occur. In such situations, it may be use-ful to combine stratification with clustering and oversample the high-prevalence areas while using TCS to eliminate empty banks in the low-prevalence areas.

8.3.3 Network Sampling

Another way to enhance the efficiency of screening for rare groups is *network sampling,* also called *multiplicity sampling.* Much of the early work on network sampling was done by Sirken and his colleagues (Sirken, 1970, 1972; Sirken & Levy, 1974; Levy, 1977). A brief summary on this topic (and other methods for sampling rare groups) is found in Sudman, Sirken, and Cowan (1988) and Blair (1990).

Network sampling for rare groups works as follows. Members of a random sample drawn from the general population are screened for the defining characteristic(s) of the target group and also are asked whether the members of some prespecified social network such as their brothers and sisters have the characteristic(s). If any member of the network falls into the target group, the respondent is asked for contact information, and the researcher attempts to interview those network members. The effect of measuring these social networks, as well as the respondents themselves, is to identify more members of the rare group in the initial screening interviews.

For network sampling to be useful, the following conditions must be met.

- First, the informant must be able to report accurately whether each network member is or is not in the target population. This requires that the defining characteristics of the group are visible (or known) to other members of the network. Reporting errors (producing both false-negative and false-positive target population member identification) are often a serious source of bias in network samples and a drain on the design's efficiency.

- Second, if network members are to be interviewed, network sampling requires that the initial respondents be willing to provide referrals to other network members and, perhaps more important, that they be able to provide adequate contact information such as telephone numbers or e-mail addresses.

- Third, it must be possible to obtain an accurate estimate of network size for weighting purposes. The probability of any given member of the target group being identified is proportional to the number of people who might identify him: For example, if the network is defined as siblings, a rare group member with one sibling has two ways to be identified (he might be drawn in the initial sample or his sibling might be drawn and identify him), while a group member with three siblings has four ways to be identified and an only child has one. In effect, each member of the network functions as a duplicate listing for every other member, which creates a selection bias in favor of people with larger networks. To correct this bias, it is necessary to measure network size and weight by its inverse.

Note that the key issue in this regard is the not number of people that a first-stage respondent might identify (the initial respondent's network size) but rather the number of people that might identify each target group member. Therefore, the initial respondent usually cannot provide useful information about network size unless the network is reflexive; for example, if the network is defined as siblings, and the initial respondent says that he has three siblings, each network member also has three siblings.

Empirically, it has been shown that these conditions are best fulfilled when the network consists of close relatives who are likely to know the most about the member of the rare population and who can report accurately regarding the network size. While it is tempting to define networks more broadly so as to cast a wider net, one pays a price in rapidly increasing reporting error when more distant relatives or other types of networks are used.

This type of network sampling is particularly useful when the purpose of the research is to estimate the prevalence of a rare group rather than contact its members. If all one needs is prevalence data, then network sampling has the potential to expand the effective sample size without imposing the difficulty of obtaining referrals and finding networked respondents. This, in fact, is the purpose for which the method was developed and used in its early days (cf. Sirken, 1970).

Network sampling for rare populations also can be used in a snowballing fashion with multiple networking stages: This type of sampling is called *snowball sampling, chain referral sampling,* or *respondent-driven sampling.* Here, the initial respondent is screened for membership in the rare population of interest: If and only if he is a member of that population, he is asked to identify additional group members, who in turn are asked to identify other group members, and so on until no new members are identified. The logic of this procedure is that if members of the target population know each other, and these social networks are exhaustively pursued when encountered, then, for any given network, it should be possible to give each person in the network a 100% probability of being selected (given that the network is selected) as long as the person knows at least one other member of the network who can identify him. The probability that the network is selected will be a function of its size, measured through the number of identified members, and data should be weighted by the inverse of network size to correct the resulting selection bias in favor of larger networks.

If snowball referrals are incomplete, and the probability that any given network member will be identified through referral falls below 100%, there will be a selection bias in favor of members who know more people in the network and hence are more likely to be identified. Referrals may be incomplete for various reasons: for example, respondents don't take the time to list everyone they know, or they overlook someone, or the researcher stops early.

To be effective, snowballing requires not that members of the rare population are known to people in the general population, as in the first type of network sampling that we described, but that they are known to each other. This condition is most likely to be met for small, closed populations, such as social or political elites or specialized professional groups. Snowballing also has been used to identify groups of gay men (Heckathorn, 1997), although, in such an application, one might question whether the procedure is limited by respondents' willingness to identify other members of their social networks, especially if they know that those members are not "out" and prefer not to be identified.

A drawback of snowballing is that the size of the research task cannot be well specified in advance, because it depends on the number and size of networks encountered, and once the project begins, you must exhaustively map each identified network to maintain control of the sampling probabilities.

8.3.4 Dual-Frame Sampling

Dual-frame sampling for rare populations is a special case of stratified sampling that is useful when there is an efficient but incomplete frame of the target group, such as a membership list. It combines a sample from the efficient but incomplete frame with a sample from the general population to augment coverage. Consider the following example that was introduced in Chapter 2:

CASE STUDY 8.1

A researcher wishes to conduct a telephone survey of 200 people who visited an open-air "art festival" last weekend. These people can be found by screening the general population, but only 5% of the local population is estimated to have attended the festival. Of those who did attend, an estimated 20% registered for a prize drawing, and the registrations are available to the researcher.

(Continued)

(Continued)

Assume, for purposes of example, that festival attendees who registered for the drawing can be contacted and interviewed at a cost of $12 per completed interview (including the costs of noncontacts and nonresponse). Assume that screening for attendees in an RDD sample of the general population will cost $5 per screening interview and $10 per main interview (again including the costs of noncontacts and nonresponse, which in this case are primarily borne at the screening stage).

If the sample is drawn entirely from the list of registrants, 200 interviews can be obtained for $2,400 (200 @ $12 per interview). However, there is substantial room for coverage bias because the frame only covers 20% of the population.

If a sample of 200 attendees is screened from the general population, the coverage problem is eliminated, but the cost is much higher. If 5% of the population attended the festival, it will take 20 screeners to get an attendee. Therefore, the cost per completed main interview will be $110 (20 screeners @ $5 each to get the respondent, plus $10 for the main interview), and the cost of 200 main interviews will be $22,000 (200 @ $110 per).

A dual-frame design will allow full coverage of the population of attendees at a lower cost than general screening. Under this procedure, the attendees are stratified into those who registered and those who did not. Nonregistrants, who account for 80% of attendees, will be screened from the general population at a screening rate of 4% (80% of the 5% of the population who attended). It will take 25 screeners to get a nonregistrant, and the cost per completed main interview will be $135 (25 screeners @ $5 each, plus $10 for the main interview). Registrants, who account for 20% of attendees, will be contacted directly from the registration list, and the cost per interview will be $12, as before. Using the formula shown in Chapter 5 for optimal stratum allocations when costs differ by strata, it may be seen that the optimal procedure in this example is to allocate approximately 45% of the sample to attendees who registered for the drawing and 55% to attendees who did not register. So, for a sample of 200, the researcher should take 90 registrants from this list and screen 110 nonregistrants from the general population, for a total interviewing cost of $15,930 (90 @ $12 per, or $1,080, plus 110 @ $135 per, or $14,850).

Note that in the process of screening the general population for 110 people who attended the festival but did not register for the drawing, we will encounter some people who attended the festival and *did* register (specifically, we should hit 110 * 20/80, or 27 such people). Here, we assume that these people are treated as ineligibles when encountered in the general population frame. It also would be possible to interview these people, and reduce the sample from the registration list accordingly, but in this example, there would be relatively little savings from doing so (27 * $12 = $324, or about 2% of the current expected cost of $15,930), and there is some administrative appeal in having each stratum drawn from one and only one frame.

In general, since dual-frame sampling is a form of stratified sampling, some way of distinguishing the strata will be necessary. This is not a problem if the efficient frame and general frame can be physically cross-checked to identify members of the general frame that are also in the efficient frame (so they can be treated as ineligible in the general sample or reassigned to the efficient sample). If the identifying information in the two frames is not consistent or accurate enough to allow physical cross-checking, then we will need for respondents from the general population to be able to self-report whether they are in the efficient frame. If they cannot do so reliably—for example, if general population respondents in our example can tell us whether they went to the festival but cannot reliably tell whether they registered for the drawing—then errors in these reports will create errors in stratum assignments and a corresponding potential for errors in estimates.

8.3.5 Location Sampling

Rare populations that tend to congregate at particular places can be sampled at those places. For example, recreational groups such as deep-sea fishermen might be contacted at harbors from which they embark. Likewise, researchers interested in HIV risk behaviors have gone to gay bars to obtain samples of gay men. Location sampling is particularly useful in contexts where face-to-face contact and "street credibility" are important in getting members of the rare population to identify themselves, as when gay men are asked about HIV risk behaviors.

In many applications, location sampling by itself may not give satisfactory population coverage: For example, samples obtained at gay bars will omit gays who do not patronize these places, and nonpatrons may differ systematically from patrons. If coverage is a concern, location sampling can be combined with a general probability sample that screens for target group membership and availability at the interview location. This is a form of dual-frame sampling.

Location samples also can be combined with snowballing (as described earlier in this chapter) to reach outside the location frame. However, this is not likely to be a complete solution to coverage problems, because the population members who are not accessible via location sampling may not socialize with the population members who are: For example, gay men who do not patronize gay bars may not socialize with those who do. Also, note that in a location-driven snowball sample, probabilities of selection for members of any given network will depend not on total network size, as in regular snowball sampling, but rather on the number of network members who patronize the selected places.

Ideally, in location sampling for rare groups, some form of probability sampling will be applied at the location, rather than haphazard intercepts. Our earlier discussion of sampling visitors to a place is relevant in this regard.

8.3.6 Online Data Collection for Rare Groups

Earlier in this chapter, we noted problems with online samples of the general population: Response rates are low, and there is substantial exposure to coverage bias because (a) online access varies widely across income, education, and ethnic groups, and (b) there is no complete frame of the online population. However, given the cost challenges of studying rare groups, if data can be gathered at lower cost on the web, then one might consider dual-frame designs in which the web is used for target group members who are accessible online, and telephone (or some other method with broad coverage) is used for those who are not online (Blair & Blair, 2006). The logic of using online data collection for rare groups is that the web should have lower screening costs than other methods because no incremental labor or postage is needed to contact potential respondents.

A key issue in this regard is the potential for coverage bias stemming from the fact that available sampling frames cover only a fraction of the online population. A theoretically clean approach to this issue is to stratify the target population on the basis of "in frame versus not in frame" rather than "online versus not online." However, this approach is of little practical use, because if the "in frame" stratum contains only a small percentage of the total population (such as an online panel with 2 million members out of a U.S. population of more than 300 million), then the optimal allocation to this stratum will be too small to justify the incremental costs of web-based data collection. There also is the practical difficulty of getting telephone respondents to give an accurate indication of whether they appear in any given online frame, so they can be sorted out. Overall, the most practical approach is to stratify on the basis of online versus offline, but this requires a leap of faith that the online frame represents the broader online population.

In this regard, an important feature of dual-frame web-phone designs is that they will allow a comparison of web and phone results. If results from web and phone do not differ, one generally might assume that the effects of coverage bias in the web data are negligible. If the results do differ substantially by mode, that difference might be caused by coverage bias or might reflect legitimate differences between the two strata (e.g., if the survey has a subject matter, such as frequency of online purchases, that relates to presence in the web frame). Either way, if mode differences are observed, some form of weighting adjustments may be used to correct for potential bias.

8.4 SAMPLING ORGANIZATIONAL POPULATIONS

The most significant issue that distinguishes organizational samples from those of individuals or households is the enormous variability in the size of organizations. For example, a researcher trying to get an estimate of the potential demand for a new type of industrial equipment will quickly realize that demand is greatly affected by a few very large firms. As a result, it usually is optimal to stratify organizations by size and oversample the larger organizations, as discussed in Chapter 5. A further simplification is to sample *all* the very large organizations that account for most of the sales and/or variance in a category (see Hansen, Hurwitz, & Madow, 1953).

A second and related issue is how to measure the size of organizations for efficient stratification. Common standards include the value of annual revenues, the value of company assets, and the number of employees. In general, these standards are correlated, but there are differences: For example, a manufacturing company is likely to have a high value of assets relative to the number of employees, while a service company is likely to have a high number of employees relative to assets. The choice of a measure usually will depend on two factors. First, what measures are available? For example, if the sampling frame lists companies along with their annual revenues, it will be easy and inexpensive to stratify using revenues as a measure of size. Second, what measure is likely to have the best correlation with the phenomenon of interest? For example, if the research concerns employment issues, then stratification based on number of employees may be more efficient than stratification based on revenues.

A third sampling issue is determining the appropriate unit to study within organizations (i.e., the appropriate population unit). For businesses, is it a plant, a regional office, a division, or the entire firm? For educational institutions, is it a classroom, an academic department, a school, or a school district? The choice depends primarily on the topic of the study and whether decision authority and/or policies vary within organizational subunits. For example, in a study of educational policies, the defining issue will be the level at which relevant policies are set.

A fourth issue is determining who within the organization will be an appropriate informant and whether multiple informants are needed to provide accurate results. In highly formal organizations, such as many school systems, it may be easy to identify decision authority through job titles and choose respondents in this manner. In many other organizations, things are not so obvious, and it may be necessary to contact selected organizations to identify the right informant(s). This is usually done by telephone, starting with the switchboard or possibly a relevant job title, and being transferred from phone to phone until the right person is reached. Even if a list is available, it is necessary to confirm that you have the right person, because organizational lists can go out of date rapidly, especially for business managers.

8.5 SAMPLING GROUPS SUCH AS INFLUENCE GROUPS OR ELITES

Earlier in this chapter, we discussed how *snowball sampling* might be used to find members of a rare population that are linked in social networks. The same procedure can be used to identify other types of social groups.

Consider, for example, sociometric studies where the topic of interest is communication or influence patterns in small groups. Here, the population unit of interest is the group, but there is usually no list of groups. Rather, a sample is drawn of individuals, and these individuals are asked to identify other people who stand in some relationship to them, who may in turn be asked to identify other members of the group, and so on. Similarly, consider research where the topic of interest is the nature and activities of social or political elites. Here, initial respondents may be selected by their formal roles (e.g., city councilperson), but informal members of the elite are found through snowballing.

If the initial sample is random (as opposed to a list of role titles), then the probability of identifying any given group through snowball sampling depends on the size of the group (because each member provides a chance of identifying the group), so there is a selection bias in favor of larger groups. This bias can be corrected by measuring group size and weighting for its inverse. Also, there may be a selection bias at the individual level in that the person who is known to more people has a higher probability of being mentioned than does the isolate. This bias is least important if the snowball procedure is continued until no new names are mentioned, because an exhaustive listing of the group should ensure that every member is identified as long as there is at least one other group member who can identify him or her. Also, if the group is exhaustively listed, its size can be measured by simply counting the listed members.

8.6 PANEL SAMPLING[5]

A panel is a group of individuals, households, or organizations that provide information for more than one period in time. The simplest panels involve respondents who report before and after an event, such as studies that track voters through an election. More complex panels involve respondents who report weekly on a continuous basis on household expenditures or other behavior. Panels are used for the following purposes:

- *To measure change.* A fundamental advantage of panels is that the sampling variances of measures of change are much smaller for panels than for a series of independent samples, and it is possible to measure changes in individual as opposed to group behavior over time. For example, "scanner panels" monitor participants' grocery purchases over time, and the results can be used to measure general brand switching and changes in behavior resulting from promotions.

- *To measure behaviors that accrue over time.* By measuring behaviors as they occur, panels may be able to provide more accurate data than retrospective measurements, even if change per se is not of interest. For example, panels are used to measure television viewing or radio listening, not to document program switching but simply to gather more accurate data about this ephemeral phenomenon.

- *To provide balanced sampling frames.* As noted in Chapter 2, some companies maintain online panels from which samples can be drawn for one-time surveys. The use of these panels is motivated primarily by convenience, cost, and speed: For example, it is possible to draw a geographically and demographically balanced sample from an online panel and obtain a reasonable number of responses within days.

A researcher who wishes to establish and maintain a panel, especially a long-term panel, faces three principal sampling issues: (1) possible nonresponse bias associated with the initial request to participate, (2) possible nonresponse bias associated with differential panel mortality over time, and (3) possible bias associated with panel aging.

---

5. This section is based on Sudman (1976).

8.6.1 Initial Nonresponse in Panels

Regarding initial nonresponse, no research project achieves full cooperation from selected respondents. However, the problem is larger for panels because of the greater burden placed on respondents. For example, which would you be more likely to accept: a request to participate in a one-time survey about your purchasing habits or a request to maintain a purchasing diary for the next year? Initial response rates for panel studies are usually at least 1/3 lower than for surveys, with the difference depending on the nature of the panel request.

Initial response rates for panel studies also vary across different types of respondents, creating potential bias. For example, Jordan (2004) describes problems that the A. C. Nielsen company has had in recruiting Hispanics to its U.S. consumer panels, which have, among other things, led to criticism that Nielsen's well-known television ratings are culturally biased because they undercount Hispanic audiences. Likewise, Sudman and Wansink (2002) show that people who cooperate with consumer panels are less likely to be in one- or two-person households, more likely to be in households with young children, more likely to have a nonemployed woman, and more likely to report being price conscious: In other words, households that participate in consumer panels are more likely to have stay-at-home mothers with some discretionary time during the day and an interest in the topic of home economy. More generally, willingness to participate in a panel is positively related to free time and interest in the task.

The level of cooperation achieved with a panel request is, of course, not independent of the recruiting methods used and the tasks required of panel members. Interestingly, though, continuing cooperation tends to be similar regardless of the initial response rate. When greater efforts are made to get initial cooperation from respondents, there seems to follow a higher dropout rate on a continuing basis.

8.6.2 Differential Mortality Over Time

As just noted, panels suffer from mortality (dropouts) over time. For periodic, repeated interviews, an additional 5% or 10% loss should be expected from the remaining sample on each subsequent interview. Mortality may result from changes in a respondent's life, such as getting married or having a baby, or simply from fatigue or loss of interest in the task.

Keeping mortality to a minimum is not an automatic process but one that requires considerable effort and experience in the techniques of maintaining panel cooperation. Even though most panels find it important to compensate participants with money or prizes, a continuing program of communication with panelists is equally essential to establish and maintain the high level of morale that reduces panel turnover.

Despite one's best efforts, some level of mortality will occur in a panel. If this mortality is evenly spread across different types of panel participants, it will not threaten the representativeness of the panel. Unfortunately, it usually is not evenly spread across participants. Just as people who are busier or less interested are less likely to accept the initial request to participate, they are more likely to drop out over time. As a result, differential mortality over time tends to exacerbate any nonresponse biases found in the initial panel sample.

8.6.3 Panel Aging

The third problem encountered in panel sampling is loss in representativeness due to panel aging. Imagine, for example, a consumer panel formed 50 years ago. Even if the sample for this panel was randomly drawn, and the initial response rate was 100%, and nobody dropped out, the panel would not be representative of today's general population. We would have panel mortality in the truest sense of the world, as many of the initial panel members would have died over the years, and the survivors would all be old. There would be no panel members in their 20s, 30s, 40s, or even 50s. Their shopping baskets would be low on children's cereals, baby diapers, chips, and soft drinks and perhaps heavy on high fiber cereals and denture adhesive.

8.6.4 Implications for Panel Sampling

The basic point to remember in maintaining a long-term continuing sample is that panels are dynamic and should not be treated as a sample drawn for a one-time survey. The population is changing continuously because of new household formations (or new business startups), dissolution of old households (or businesses), and household (or business) moves. A panel, if it is to remain representative of this changing population, must reflect these changes.

In this regard, panelists should be followed when they move. This may be conceived as a dynamic system that is frozen for just an instant to allow a sample to be drawn from it and then released, and the subsequent motion of the sample represents the motion of the population. If one made the mistake of sticking to a fixed sample frame (e.g., by dropping households that move and replacing them with households that move into the same dwellings), it would be difficult to locate and include dwelling units that were built after the sample frame was designed, and it would be difficult to allow for shifts in population from place to place. Also, dropping households that move will lead to mortality bias because certain types of families (e.g., young, small households) are more likely to move than others.[6]

Accounting for moves is not enough. Some method must be designed for continually rejuvenating a long-term panel by bringing into it the proper number of new households and dropping dissolved households. Dissolved households are easy to handle. The only necessity is to drop them when they are observed. An example is when one member of a couple dies and the other moves in with relatives or to an assisted living facility: If this person has been a panel member, she is dropped at this time, and there is no need to replace her in the panel with a new household. Regarding new household formations, panel members may be periodically asked whether there has been any change in the number of adults or children living in the home and if anyone has moved away to set up a new household. Family members who move away to set up new households are recruited with probabilities inversely proportional to the number of persons who will constitute the new household (this is done so that all new households have the same probability of being added, regardless of the size of the new household). Thus, in the case of marriages, half the split-offs are recruited. Empirical evidence has indicated that this recruiting method brings new young households into a panel at the proper rate.

Even after allowing such evolution in a panel, the panel is likely to lose representativeness over time as a function of aging and differential mortality. To maintain representativeness, replacement panel members must be recruited disproportionately from geographic and demographic categories that become underrepresented. So, for example, if 18- to 24-year-old unmarried men have disproportionately high dropout rates, replacements should be disproportionately recruited from this group. If Hispanics are becoming a larger portion of the general population and are underrepresented in the panel, they should be disproportionately recruited to bring the panel in line with the broader population.

---

6. For some studies, a panel may be limited to residents of a specified geographic area, such as a city, county, or state. In this case, if a household moves from the area, it becomes ineligible and is dropped from the panel.

Given that continuing response rates in a panel are likely to be well under 50% after allowing for initial nonresponse and subsequent mortality, and given that disproportionate, stratum-driven recruitment will be needed to maintain panel representativeness over time, one might ask whether it is worthwhile to use probability sampling to recruit panel members. Why spend top dollar on probability methods if they are undermined by low response: Instead, why not use looser methods such as quotas to control panel composition and reduce cost? The answer is that probability samples are preferable because, even if they are not perfect, they are the best samples available. They are theoretically measurable and they minimize potential biases associated with convenience sampling or volunteerism.

Having said that, we should acknowledge that quota-based panels are the norm in the field of market research. For example, all of the large online panels except for the GfK KnowledgePanel are recruited through nonrandom methods and controlled through demographic balancing. The argument in favor of these panels is that their repetitive use makes it possible to benchmark their performance over time, so that one can come to know and accommodate any biases. This is a reasonable argument.

8.6.5 Other Issues in Panel Sampling

In the case of panels that are used primarily as sampling frames, a sampling question that arises is how to manage disproportionate response across geographic and demographic groups (and consequent nonresponse bias) in individual studies. Two methods may be used: *disproportionate outgo* and *back-end weighting.* In disproportionate outgo, groups with a history of lower response rates are oversampled as needed to balance the resulting data. In back-end weighting, a proportionate sample is drawn, and any resulting discrepancies in sample composition are controlled through weighting. Disproportionate outgo is somewhat more complicated at the sampling stage but allows one to use the data without weighting, which can be an advantage in a panel context where one might wish to compare results from parallel studies over time and such comparisons are most easily done with natural (unweighted) data.

Also, in situations where one wants to track changes in a population over time but does not wish to face the issues associated with a fixed panel, an alternative procedure that might be used is a rotating panel, or rotating surveys with partially overlapping samples. For example, to study the process by which people buy home appliances, a well-known company has used a rotating design in which respondents are surveyed once, then a second time 6 months later, then a third and last time 6 months after that, and in any given month, 1/3 of the total sample is participating for the first time, 1/3 for the second time, and 1/3 for the third time. This design produces response rates similar to surveys while still allowing the company to study how purchase intentions flow into purchases of home appliances over a 1-year period. A discussion of rotating designs may be found in Kish (1965, 1987).

8.7 SAMPLING IN INTERNATIONAL CONTEXTS

In general, this book has discussed survey sampling in a U.S. context. Here we consider some points of difference across countries. Of course, the basics of sampling do not change—that is, inaccuracy can stem from sampling error or sample bias, sampling error is controlled through sample size, stratification and/or clustering may improve efficiency, sample bias is controlled through sampling process, and so on.

The principal differences seen across nations from a sampling perspective relate to frame availability, sample design issues related to frames and data collection modes, and response rates.

Sampling frames that are available for the general population can be quite different from one country to another. For example, European countries typically have publicly available registers of residents that can be used for sampling. This can improve sampling coverage for the general population, although it may not be of value in sampling subgroups within the population. On the other hand, information for sample design that can be found in censuses in some countries may be completely unavailable or unreliable in developing countries with infrequent or poorly executed censuses.

Within the United States, high female participation in the workforce and relatively high labor costs for interviewers have made it very expensive to do in-home interviewing, while high telephone ownership means that telephone surveys can be done with little coverage bias (although nonresponse is a significant problem). This has led to extensive use of telephone surveys and thus extensive use of sampling techniques that address the challenges of telephone surveys, such as random-digit dialing. In developing nations, telephone ownership may be lower or skewed toward cellphones, making telephone surveys less attractive, while the economics of in-home interviewing may be much more favorable. This leads to greater use of in-home surveys and thus greater use of techniques such as cluster sampling with geographically defined areas.

Similarly, the coverage problems faced by online surveys are more severe in developing nations. Exhibit 8.2 shows that while Internet access has grown in developing as well as developed nations, it lags far behind in the developing world.

Also, shopping mall surveys are common in the United States for purposes of market research. Mall-based shopping is less common in other, more densely populated countries, where people are more likely to shop on commercial streets. It is still possible to sample and interview people in public locations, but the working environment for interviewers is different, and the ways in which respondents are selected and screened may change accordingly.

A final sampling difference across nations relates to response rates. Response rates have been dropping in the United States and can present major concerns for potential nonresponse bias. In many developing nations, this is less of an issue. There can be major challenges in accessing secure properties, but if interviewers are able to reach households, they are less likely to encounter nonresponse.

Exhibit 8.2 Coverage Problems for Online Surveys Are More Severe in Developing Nations

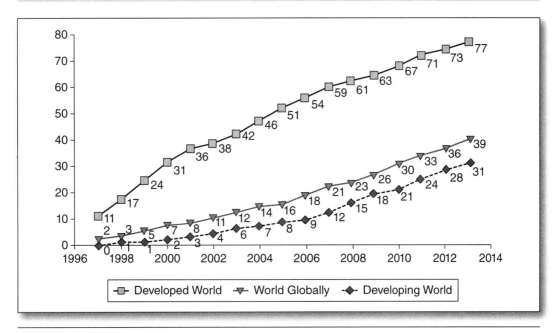

Source: Courtesy of Jeff Ogden (W163) with CC-BY license on Wikimedia Commons.

8.8 "BIG DATA" AND SURVEY SAMPLING

In recent years, increased computing capabilities have led to increased ability to store, analyze, and cross-reference data and a corresponding use of *big data* or *data science*. While there is no standard definition of *big data,* in general it is data that reside in a database or combination of databases that may contain millions of records and require specialized software to manage and analyze. Some of these databases have existed for years, such as government databases of federal program participants or, in the private sector, medical records databases. More recently, researchers have assembled large databases from sources such as Google search data, social media websites, and websites with product reviews. Many of these newer databases are generated automatically by user activities.

In some phases of standard surveys, big data may supplement the usual survey sampling and operations. A big data set may

- provide additional information about a target population to aid survey design or analyses,
- help compensate for item nonresponse,
- provide information about unit nonrespondents for analysis and weighting,
- be merged with a survey data set to enrich analysis possibilities.

This type of use for big data is simply an extension of the procedures that surveys commonly use. A more radical use of big data sets is as a fundamental, sometimes defining, resource for data collection. We will discuss each type of use in turn.

8.8.1 Big Data as a Survey Complement

We will illustrate the possible use of big data as a survey complement in the context of government surveys. Many large and complex surveys are conducted by the U.S. federal government and its contractors. As large as many of these samples are, and as lengthy as the interviews can be, the surveys could make use of additional information, especially at the individual case level, if it was easily and cheaply available. These data could be used in the ways just listed to improve the quality of the surveys.

In some cases, data that a survey is intended to collect may already reside in government databases. For example, it is typical for government surveys to ask questions about individual or household income. Such questions are sensitive to many respondents and consistently have item nonresponse that exceeds most other variables. Also, the answers to such questions can have significant response error. However, much of the desired information is already available in Internal Revenue Service (IRS) databases. The IRS data are not perfect but are likely to be at least as good as answers to survey questions. If it were possible to access and merge individual financial information from IRS records—it won't be, for legal reasons, but if it were—then questions could be eliminated from the survey, thus shortening the questionnaire or making space for other items while simultaneously reducing potential bias from item nonresponse or response errors.

There are substantial barriers to using government records in this way, including technical difficulties in merging administrative records with survey data, and regulatory or ethical obstacles that must be addressed before such records can be used at the individual level. There are also issues on the survey side in collecting identifiers that are specific enough to merge such data sets. The general idea, though, is that administrative records might contain a variety of information that could be appended to survey responses to enrich the data or simplify data collection, in much the same way that an online panel can automatically add previously collected demographic information to data obtained from any panel member.

Administrative records also might help in sample design. For example, if an addressed-based sample is selected from the U.S. Postal Service Master Address File (MAF), IRS data corresponding to the same people at the same addresses might be used to stratify the sample on financial variables.

Similarly, to the extent this sample has nonrespondents (as any survey will), IRS or other administrative records might provide some information about the nonrespondents that is useful in assessing the types of people who responded and hence in estimating nonresponse bias and constructing weights to adjust for nonresponse.

8.8.2 Big Data as a Survey Replacement

The second category of big data applications give big data a central role in data collection and possibly replace surveys (or their sampling stage) altogether. For example, consider a company that wishes to measure consumer attitudes toward its products. A traditional approach is to draw a sample of consumers and conduct a survey in which such questions are asked. A big data approach is to scrape websites with product reviews, blogs, and other websites with user-generated content to capture and code comments about the company's products. Some sampling of websites might be done to narrow the data collection task, and the collected data might be sampled to reduce the coding task, or the full data might be used. The obvious appeal, at least on a first look, is the possibility of using the entire data set and foregoing sampling altogether.

Under some conditions, this approach could be very cost-effective. There may be, however, some problems that have to be resolved. For example, if the researcher is interested in a sample of individual persons, then people who make more comments will have proportionally higher inclusion probabilities. This is the common frame problem of duplication. We can try to clean the data of duplicates, but this becomes cumbersome as the data set becomes enormous, and duplicates will be difficult to identify unless the same person has made the exact same comments under the exact same name.

More important, although the comments may contain a key variable of interest, there is likely to be information of interest that is not included. For example, the company might wish to measure attitudes among users and nonusers of its products, heavy users versus light users, and younger people versus older people, and the dataset may not contain the relevant information.

Most important, the people who post comments are essentially a sample of volunteers. Who are these people? For example, are fans of the products overrepresented? Are people with extreme attitudes (positive or negative) overrepresented, in the same way that online political comments may overrepresent partisans relative to the "silent majority"?

These issues reveal a basic difference between the "data first" approach sometimes associated with big data and a traditional survey design approach as reflected throughout this book. The survey design approach begins with the survey purpose, followed by defining the relevant population and making decisions about the method of data collection and sampling. This approach does *not* begin with the features of data that happen to be available. It is tempting to capture comments about the company's products made by people on the web, because those data are essentially free, but that advantage comes at the cost of changing the population definition from "consumers" to "people who make comments about these products on the web."

Essentially, big data can be mistaken for the entire population when it is, in fact, a sample that has gone unrecognized. The question is whether the process that has given rise to the data makes it the *right population* or at least a proxy without obvious biases.

Once we think of big data in this way, it becomes clear that just as big data may be useful as a survey complement, so surveys may be useful as a complement to big data. In the above example, online comments might be taken as the primary data source, and a survey might be conducted to assess the nature of any biases in those data relative to the consumer population of interest. The survey might measure attitudes of interest, whether respondents had posted comments online, and the number and location of such posts. Such information would allow us to weight the online data for "nonresponse" (i.e., nonposting) and duplications; more generally, it would allow us to improve model-based estimates drawn from the online data. The analogy is using data from a sample of nonrespondents to evaluate and improve survey estimates. Like any such enterprise, the size and/or frequency of the survey would be less than if the survey was used as a primary data source.

Another issue that sometimes arises with big data is the fact that every analysis of data patterns finds statistical significance because the number of observations is so large. For example, we might observe that people who post comments about a company's products on Tuesday are more likely to be negative than people who post on Saturday—or people who post between 9:00 and 10:00 a.m. are more likely to be negative than people who post between 10:00 and 11:00 a.m.—or people who post between 9:00 and 9:05 a.m. are more likely to be negative than people who post between 9:05 and 9:10 a.m. Such results may reveal a meaningful phenomenon if you can explain them. The concern, though, is that an abundance of significant findings with extremely large samples can lead the researcher to see patterns where none really exist.

8.9 INCORPORATING SMARTPHONES, SOCIAL MEDIA, AND TECHNOLOGICAL CHANGES

Survey sampling and data collection, like all aspects of society, are influenced by computing and communications technologies. We are currently witnessing an unprecedented wave of new devices (smartphones, tablet computers), software (mobile apps), services (web-based social media), and technical capabilities

(fast processors, cloud computing). These developments have rapidly trans-
formed how people connect with friends, peers, and strangers (e.g., Facebook,
Google +, LinkedIn), communicate generally (blogs, Twitter), share information
(YouTube), and interact (Second Life). They also are affecting survey practice in
ways that range from minor tweaks to radical changes.

As with big data, these resources can be used in the context of standard
survey methods—for example, to supplement a standard data collection mode
to improve coverage or reduce costs. It is also feasible that a technology or service may replace one or more standard survey methods by providing new
frames, new data capture methods, or access to special populations that tradi-
tionally have been exceedingly difficult to identify and survey, as well as creating
special populations of interest in themselves (e.g., Facebook members).

8.9.1 Smartphones and Surveys

Cellphones in general and smartphones in particular have affected survey
research because of their prevalence and their rapidly expanding features. For
example, surveys no longer have to depend on contacting sample members in
their residences but may potentially access them anywhere. This has a variety of
implications, including a shift in optimal calling times to maximize response
rates (Brick et al., 2007) and a need to verify that the respondent is not engaged
in some activity such as driving a car that would make it inappropriate to proceed with a survey at that time.

A significant implication of cellphone use is that the telephone sampling
frame now contains a mixture of landline numbers corresponding to households
and cellphone numbers corresponding to individuals. If the desired population
unit is individuals, it is necessary to deal with clustering in the landline frame
and sample within households. If the desired population unit is households, it is
necessary to determine whether the cellphone holder is the appropriate informant for their household, deal with potential duplication in self-reported informants, and deal with the possibility that the cellphone holder is an ineligible
minor.

Increasingly, cellphones are smartphones that permit survey participation
requests to be sent by text message or e-mail. As part of this sort of use, it may
be possible to screen a sample to identify target subpopulation members. The
device also gives respondents the option to download an app so that they can
answer the survey questions on the phone's screen. Follow-up contacts or refusal

conversion can be administered in the same way as the initial contact. In addition, smartphones have the capacity to add visual features to surveys or collect location information using GPS. These capabilities can clearly benefit some survey objectives. On the other hand, the researcher can lose some control over the quality of the realized sample (e.g., ensuring that minors are not inadvertently included in a survey).

To learn more about the implications of smartphones for surveys, Peytchev and Hill (2011) provided smartphones to a small probability sample of adults after an initial in-person interview and subsequently conducted a number of methodological experiments over the course of a 19-week longitudinal study. Their results are limited in a number of ways, including the sample size ($n = 92$), but raise important questions about how factors such as the screen display of questions, visuals, and response options, as well as using the keyboard to enter answers, can all potentially affect response behaviors. From a sampling perspective, the use of these devices may differ across population members, producing unintended changes in the sample composition.

At this time, smartphones are owned by only about 35% of adults in the United States (Smith, 2011), although coverage is growing rapidly. This means that a general population survey must use another mode(s) along with the smartphone to achieve reasonable coverage of the general population.

8.9.2 Social Media and Surveys

Social media currently relate to survey sampling in four ways. First, they may be used as a vehicle for establishing contact with respondents who are missing other contact information or who decline to participate. For example, longitudinal surveys almost always have some amount of attrition due to losing contact with panel members, and Facebook and other social media can be useful in reestablishing contact with panel dropouts.

Second, social media may be used as a vehicle for recruiting respondents. For example, the personal data that are part of social media may be very helpful in lowering the cost of recruiting a target population with particular characteristics such as educational background, type of employment, or leisure activities. Social media also might be used for respondent-based sampling, where one respondent leads to another. Of course, using social media to recruit respondents has the effect of using social media as the sampling frame for a broader population, and one must consider the possible coverage bias that may result.

Third, the personal data found on social media may be useful for stratifying the sample or simply enriching the data set.

Fourth, in some cases, the population of interest may be defined by social media usage. Tessitore and Macri (2011) considered methods to use Facebook for sampling when the target population is partly defined by Facebook membership. They describe severe difficulties in applying standard probability sampling and concluded that quota sampling or some type of convenience sample was necessary.

As one might expect, the effectiveness of using social media for locating or recruiting respondents varies substantially across population subgroups and across nations. For example, within the United States, social networking site use drops significantly across age groups, as shown in Exhibit 8.3.

Two potential ethical issues should be recognized in sampling from social media databases. One is the possible inclusion of minors. When minors are

Exhibit 8.3   Percent of Internet Users in Each Age Group Who Use Social Networking Sites

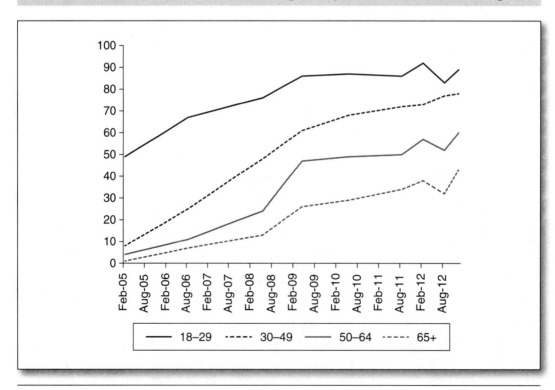

Source: Data from Pew Research Center "Social Networking Use." Pew Research Center, Washington, D.C. (May 1, 2013) http://www.pewresearch.org/data-trend/media-and-technology/social-networking-use/, accessed on 9/23/14.

surveyed, special procedures and safeguards are required by university institutional review boards (IRBs), including parental approval for the minor to participate in the research. In most surveys, people under the age of consent are excluded from the survey population, but if samples are compiled by opt-in or other voluntary procedures or recruited from social media sites, it is possible for minors to be inadvertently included. The fact that the researcher is unaware of minors being selected does not obviate the researcher's responsibility not to survey persons under the age of consent without parental approval.

Also, an unintended consequence of sampling from social media databases is the possible inclusion of information about respondents that is not relevant to the research. Once personally identifiable information is collected, the researcher is responsible for safeguarding it. That obligation can become difficult or impossible if the sample and data are stored on a server that the researcher does not control. When using free or inexpensive commercial resources, such as cloud storage and processing, the researcher can, without having specifically considered the shift, move her research data, sample, and respondent identifiers into an unsuitable research environment.

8.9.3 A General Framework for Incorporating New Technologies

Technological developments beyond smartphones and social media are likely to have implications for survey sampling. Here we present a general framework for responding to such developments.

In the opening chapter of *Envisioning the Survey Interview of the Future*, Conrad and Schober (2008) provide an excellent summary of many issues, potential benefits, and cautions generally applicable to using new technologies for survey interviewing. Conrad and Schober recognize that the same error sources—from coverage, selection, nonresponse, and measurement—will be of concern, but how each source is affected will require research and experience with the new methods. Some of the potential decisions, benefits, and risks they list include the following:

- How prevalent is the technology?
- What are the "costs" of *not* adopting a new technology (e.g., on respondent perceptions and response)?
- What can one assume about how well people can use a new technical tool (e.g., answering questions on a smartphone screen)?

- Will technologies have positive or negative effects on population groups with varying cultures and languages?
- What are the pros and cons of using the full capabilities of new technologies—for example, to link (potentially in real time) the survey interview to other information that is available about the respondent? This includes ethical issues such as the need for informed consent to employ some types of available information or technical capabilities.

Conrad and Schober's (2008) thorough presentation (as well as the remainder of their book) is informative, important, and engaging. Their framework leads to the following suggestions.

Start by reviewing available literature on how the technology at issue has performed for uses similar to yours. In general, if the literature on the technology is sparse, weak, or nonexistent, the risk of extreme or unanticipated effects is greater.

In considering the likely positive and negative effects on various sources of error, keep in mind that those effects are likely to differ depending on whether the proposed technology will be used to supplement more traditional methods versus relying solely on the new tool. Also ask whether there are design changes that may alleviate negative effects. If, for example, you know that a new method will reduce cost but also yield a lower response rate, perhaps you can "move" the negative effect. It may be feasible to shift the balance of sample size between modes or compensate with additional follow-ups—such as reworking smartphone nonresponses with more callbacks or using a different mode—while retaining most of the cost advantages.

What if lower response and poorer coverage both disproportionately affect a particular demographic subgroup? If that group is important overall or for separate analysis, lower cost may be a false savings.

The bottom line is to consider the main threats to your survey's reliability and validity, as well as how the technology will affect them. If there is insufficient information to make this assessment, then some type of pilot study, even a very small trial, may be wise. Often, a small amount of real data is far more informative than a large amount of speculation or conjecture.

8.10 CHAPTER SUMMARY

This chapter discussed issues in sampling special populations. We considered (1) online populations, (2) visitors to a place, (3) rare populations, (4) organizational populations, (5) groups such as social influence groups and elites, and (6) panel sampling. We also considered sampling aspects of "big data" and smartphones, social media, and other technological changes.

Regarding online populations, we noted three principal sampling problems: potential coverage bias stemming from the fact that many people are not online, potential coverage bias stemming from the incomplete coverage of available frames, and potential nonresponse bias stemming from low response rates. Because of these issues, online data collection is best suited to situations in which the population of interest has a high level of online access, a reasonably complete list of the population is available, and the topic of the research is of interest to the population. Online data collection also may be used in dual-frame sampling of rare populations, as discussed later in the chapter.

Regarding visitors to a place, we noted that nonprobability sampling is common in this context, but careful samples can be drawn. Cluster sampling may be used to obtain a probability sample of places, and probability samples of visitors within places may be sampled via systematic sampling of people or time (with clustering by entrances and time periods if appropriate). Issues that arise in this type of sampling include when to do the intercepts, what to do if you don't have an estimate of population size, how to adjust the sample size for nonresponse, what to do if your estimates of population size or response rate are incorrect, what to do if the number of entrances and exits is large, how to treat children and groups, what to do if visits are not the desired population unit, and whether to weight the data for time on site.

Regarding rare populations, we described various methods that might be used to improve screening efficiency and reduce the cost of studying such groups. These methods are (1) telephone cluster sampling, which may be useful when the group has heavy geographic clustering and is very rare; (2) disproportionate stratified sampling, which is useful when the group's prevalence varies substantially from one place to another; (3) network sampling, which is useful when the defining characteristics of the rare population would be known to others; (4) dual-frame sampling, which is useful when you have an efficient but incomplete list of the rare population; (5) location sampling, which is useful when the rare population tends to congregate in certain places; and (6) online sampling, which may be useful for very rare populations or if one has access to a productive sampling frame.

Regarding organizational populations, we noted four principal sampling issues. First, organizations usually vary enormously in size, and therefore it is appropriate to stratify samples on the basis of size. Second, one must choose an appropriate measure of size. Third, decisions must be made regarding the organizational unit that is appropriate for research purposes. Fourth, one must determine who speaks for the organization—that is, who is the appropriate informant and whether multiple informants are needed.

Regarding groups such as social influence groups and elites, we noted the applicability of snowball sampling in identifying and mapping these groups.

Regarding panels, we noted three sampling issues: potential nonresponse bias associated with the initial request to participate, potential nonresponse bias associated with differential mortality over time, and potential loss in representativeness associated with panel aging. In general, panel response is biased in favor of people with more time and/or more interest, and these biases tend to become greater over time. To maintain representativeness over time, a well-designed panel will track household moves, household dissolutions, and new household formations: In addition, it usually will be necessary to stratify the panel by geographic and demographic groups and disproportionately recruit groups as needed to maintain panel balance.

Regarding sampling and "big data," we noted that cross-referencing databases may hold great promise for reducing interview length and cost, enriching data, stratifying samples, and assessing possible nonresponse bias. However, there is danger in assuming that a database will provide accurate results just because it is large. A "data first" mentality runs the risk of changing the implicit population that is studied.

Finally, regarding smartphones, social media, and other technological developments, we noted the specific benefits and problems associated with smartphones and social media, and we presented a general framework for evaluating whether and how to incorporate new technologies into your research. Key points are to (1) check the literature and learn from others, (2) consider whether you will be using the new technology to complement proven methods or using it to replace methods, (3) think about how you might mitigate negative features of the technology, (4) think about how the positives and negatives of the technology will affect not just your broad population but also subgroups of special interest, and (5) if you don't have enough information to know how the technology will work, consider a pilot study.

Exercise 8.1

Imagine that you are on a team of students that wishes to conduct a survey of student opinions regarding various issues on your campus. The team's plan is to conduct intercept surveys with at least 50 students. How would you obtain this sample? What location(s) would you use? When would you do the research? How would you select respondents?

Exercise 8.2

A public health researcher wishes to conduct a U.S. national telephone survey of households that are (a) headed by a woman living without an adult partner, (b) with at least one child present younger than 14 years, and (c) a household income under $25,000 per annum. How would you design the sample for this survey? Would you expect any of the methods described in Section 8.3 to be useful?

Exercise 8.3

A health scientist at a university wishes to conduct a panel study of dietary practices, exercise practices, and weight changes among students. The plan is to conduct an initial survey with entering freshman, with online follow-up questionnaires administered monthly to all participants for the following 3 years (including summers). What sampling plan would you propose for this study? How would you draw the initial sample? How would you maintain the panel? Would you propose any changes to the intended data collection procedures?

9

Evaluating Samples

In this final chapter, we turn to the question of how to describe and evaluate samples and how good the sample needs to be. You will learn the following:

- What information should be provided in a sample report
- Factors that influence how good the sample must be
- General advice for obtaining better, even if imperfect, samples

9.1 THE SAMPLE REPORT

To evaluate a sample, you need information about it. This information is normally contained within a more general *methodology report* that should be prepared for any survey. The methodology report documents the design and procedures of the survey for future reference. This documentation serves various purposes, such as allowing the researcher to answer questions about the survey without having to rely on memory and allowing other researchers to replicate the survey or better understand its results.

In addition to information related to the sample, the methodology report will contain information such as interviewer training materials, any pretesting methods and results, when the data were collected, the method(s) of administration, the number and timing of any follow-ups or callbacks, and any methods that were used to monitor or validate the interviews.

Relevant information about the sample includes the following.

- *Sampling design.* The methods report often begins with a discussion of the sampling design. This section provides a framework for the remainder of the report as well as a background for later discussion of sampling frames, weighting, estimation, and other issues. It also begins to tell the reader whether the design was efficient in light of the study's primary objectives.

This section should, at a minimum, include the conceptual and operational definitions of the survey's target population and a general description of the main objectives and features of the sampling method. Was stratification and/or clustering employed? If stratification was used, was it proportional, disproportional, or some combination of the two? If disproportional stratification was used, was the main reason to provide sufficient cases for separate subgroup analysis, to compare subgroups, to oversample high variance or high cost strata, or what? Within strata, were elements selected with equal probabilities or not? The definitions of any strata or clusters should, of course, be provided as well.

- *Sampling error.* Sampling error is an incomplete measure of the uncertainty around survey estimates, because total survey error also stems from any sample bias and measurement error that may be present. Even so, a methodology report should address the issue of sampling errors and, if at all possible, provide sampling errors for all or key variables or provide a generalized table that can be used for many of the study variables.

- *Frame problems.* The primary sampling frame issue for the methodology report is undercoverage of the population, because presumably any other frame problems such as ineligibles, duplication, or clustering were handled in the sampling, data collection, or analysis stages. The kinds of statements that one can make about population coverage are often fairly general but may still be informative; for example, "The membership list was 8 months old. Therefore, there were some omissions of new members, but the percentage cannot be specified." Such a statement would be particularly useful if the data show differences between long-term and newer members. Even though the user of the survey results would not be able to specify the exact impact of the frame omissions on results, at least something is known of its direction if not its magnitude.

The importance of including such statements depends on two things: the percentage of undercoverage and its likely relationship to our study variables. Ideally, we would like to have exact numbers that allow us to specify the direction and the magnitude of coverage bias, but even if all we know is the nature of undercoverage, it is better than nothing at all. If there are any reasons to expect specific biases stemming from undercoverage—or from any other factor—they should be explicitly mentioned. This may be helpful by providing at least a general notion of which analyses may be most affected. As Sudman (1976) noted about discussions of sample design biases, far from detracting from the value of the survey, these types of details make it more useful by giving an indication of the study's limitations. On the other hand, we should not overlook positive aspects of our research when writing the methodological report. For example, it may be that we incorporated a full random-digit dialing (RDD) design for which there is no frame undercoverage. Such design strengths should be mentioned here and elsewhere in the report.

- *Response rates.* Response rates are a useful piece of information in evaluating results drawn from probability samples. How much confidence would you have in a result if you knew that the survey had a 2% response rate? A 50% response rate? Certainly, we would intuitively trust the higher rate to lend more support to the finding. But beyond intuition, the higher response rate is important because we would be less concerned that the nonrespondents, had they been interviewed, could have changed the result. Response rates also reveal information about the extent to which the survey followed best practices.

The terms *response, refusal, cooperation,* and *completion rates,* among others, are used by different researchers to mean quite different things. In Chapter 3, we described how to calculate a response rate and a cooperation rate, but because these terms are not always used in the same way by different researchers, it is useful to show exactly how the rates for the particular study were computed and what rules govern the sample dispositions that go into those rates. Also, if there was considerable variation in response rates by stratum or location, such as lower response in central cities or urban areas, that information can complement the overall response rate. As noted by Blair and Zinkhan (2006), a high response rate does not necessarily indicate a good sample. Nonprobability samples may substitute potential selection or coverage bias for potential nonresponse bias. A classic example is a sample of volunteers, where the response rate is 100% but the sample is not random.

- *Special procedures and follow-ups.* Any special procedures that were used as part of the data collection effort, such as refusal conversion or follow-up samples of nonrespondents, should be described. The description should explain the procedure used and how successful (or not) the effort was. In addition, if a large proportion of the cases (say, 15% or more) resulted from these efforts, it is useful to report whether these respondents differed on key variables (at statistically significant levels) from the other sample respondents. The number of callbacks or follow-ups and the general rule for how they were scheduled should also be mentioned, as well as the percentage of interviews monitored or verified.

9.2 HOW GOOD MUST THE SAMPLE BE?

After all is done and said—after we have done our best to design, draw, and execute an appropriate sample, and after we have documented our procedures—how do we know if we have done well enough? How good must the sample be?

We will address this question in two parts. First, we will discuss concepts of representation. We want our samples to be representative of the broader population, but what does that mean, and what flexibility (if any) does it give us? Second and finally, we will consider how requirements for sample quality vary across research contexts.

9.2.1 Concepts of Representation and Error

We select a sample to learn particular facts about a specified population. We are interested in the sample itself only to the extent that it represents the population in terms of the kind of information that is wanted and major analyses that are planned. For example, the intent of the *Literary Digest* poll discussed in Chapter 1 was to represent voters' preferences among presidential candidates, and it clearly failed in that goal. The failure was due at least in part to overrepresentation of upper-income households, a demographic group that turned out to favor the Republican candidate more than households with lower incomes. The *Literary Digest* sample may have been suitable for other purposes—such as market research regarding luxury goods—but it was not well suited to predicting the results of a general election.

The early adopters of quota sampling wanted to ensure that the sample they selected represented the general population distributions on gender and income, presumably on the assumption that the information of interest correlated with those population characteristics. And again, the resulting samples may have better represented the population for some purposes than for others.

So, exactly how should a sample selected for a survey reflect the population from which it was taken? In 1979 and 1980, William Kruskal and Frederick Mosteller, two of the major figures in modern statistics, published a series of four articles in which they examined how the term *representative sampling* was used by different people for various purposes, both general and scientific. Kruskal and Mosteller's intent was, in part, to "improve the clarity of discourse in statistics." Their papers, in describing some of the ways a sample can be said to represent a population, can help illustrate what we may expect of a sample given the survey goals.

Kruskal and Mosteller (1979a, 1979b, 1979c, 1980) list four possible meanings of representative sampling:

- Miniature of the population
- Coverage of the population
- Representative sampling as good enough for a particular purpose
- Representative sampling as permitting good estimation

One of the ways that a sample can be a miniature of the population is if "the important characteristics of the population are contained, in their proper proportions, in the sample" (Kruskal & Mosteller, 1979c, p. 250). Specifying what these "important characteristics" are may not be easy for any given survey, but quota sampling aims for representation along these lines. Depending on how many characteristics one wants to control for and what those characteristics are, this approach can become quite complicated, but its objectives are clear.

Coverage of the population has to do with reflecting the population's heterogeneity and can take stronger or weaker forms. A weak form might limit the objective to giving all "parts of the population ... a chance of being sampled" (Kruskal & Mosteller, 1979c, p. 254). A strong form could require actually "getting the sample from as many parts of the population as possible." The weak form focuses on the method of sampling, the strong on the achieved composition of the sample. In both cases, sample coverage is less stringent than a sample being a miniature of the population because neither requires that these "parts" appear in the sample in the same proportions as in the population. The *Literary Digest* poll may well have had coverage of all of the income parts of the voter population without achieving anything close to the correct population's percentage distribution.

One example of "representation being good enough for a particular purpose" given by Kruskal and Mosteller (1979c) concerns a medical question: "If physicians thought that all patients with a particular kind of burn [always] developed a particular symptom, but a sample showed that a number did not, that would be good enough to settle the particular issue" (p. 259).

Finally, Kruskal and Mosteller (1979c) note that selecting samples that permit "satisfactory estimation of population characteristics ... is a fundamental idea of statistical inference" (p. 259). Survey sampling theory is primarily concerned with this notion of representativeness, and we have discussed throughout this book how it may be achieved. But we want to avoid mistakenly focusing on one idea of representation when our research needs call for or can make do with another.

The development of survey sampling in the United States, against a backdrop of alternative notions of how a population can be "represented" by a sample, has resulted in a discipline of multiple dimensions—substantive, statistical, and operational. Substantive aspects of a survey—including its purpose, the types of data to be collected, and the availability and nature of sampling frames—affect sample design and selection. Efficient sampling methods require some understanding of the underlying statistical theory, but primarily survey sampling is, as O'Muircheartaigh (2005) described it, "the province of the [survey] practitioner ... faced with the problem of obtaining sufficient information about a population without having the resources to measure all the elements in the population." That practitioner needs both "an adequate level of technical expertise to appreciate the implications of design decisions" on precision, as well as "an understanding of the interdependence of sample design and survey operations." And ultimately, the practitioner must put meaning to the idea of "sufficient information about a population."

9.2.2 Requirements for Sample Quality Across Research Contexts

It isn't always possible to get as good a sample as one would like because of limits on time, funding, or access. For example, a graduate student in education may only be able to conduct research in schools that are within driving distance and willing to provide access. Fortunately, in most situations, samples need not be perfect to be usable. It is important to recognize the burden that your research objectives impose on the sample. Relevant points include the following.

Imperfect Samples May Be Useful for Exploration or Screening

As Bob Dylan observed, "You don't need a weatherman to know which way the wind blows." If research is done to see which way the wind blows—that is, if the research is exploratory in nature, done to get some sense of a phenomenon or to identify issues that might be worth more formal study—then informal convenience samples may be adequate for the purpose. Even biased samples may be useful if the direction of bias is predictable; for example, if members of the Parent-Teacher Association don't think a school improvement project is worth the amount that it would cost, it probably should be dropped from further consideration.

Convenience samples also may be useful when the population is homogeneous on the variable being studied. For example, if a cleaning products manufacturer wishes to test new scents for a dish detergent, and the buying population is known to be relatively homogeneous in terms of scent preferences, a convenience sample of mall shoppers will provide adequate comparisons between products at a much lower cost than a probability sampling for in-home testing.

Imperfect Samples May Be Useful for Testing Relationships

The key purpose of a research project might be to make univariate estimates for certain variables or to estimate relationships between variables. For example, one might do a public health study to estimate the percentage of schoolchildren in the state of California who have had vaccinations for certain diseases such as measles. In this case, the key goal is to make univariate estimates regarding vaccination rates. Alternately, a study might be done to estimate the relationships between variables such as parents' income and education and the likelihood of children being vaccinated. If the focus of research is on relationships rather than univariate estimates, the burden on the sample is not as great. In general, if one draws a biased sample with respect to one variable, estimates of relationships involving that variable will have smaller bias than the univariate estimates because the sample is likely to have commensurate, self-adjusting biases on the related variables.

Exhibit 9.1 illustrates this point. First, in its left-hand columns, the exhibit shows what we will stipulate to be an unbiased sample distribution for an X and Y variable, along with means for each variable and the correlation between variables. Next, the exhibit shows a sample that is biased via disproportionate representation of the "high X" group, along with the resulting means and correlation. Notice that the means (univariate statistics) are clearly affected by the sample bias, but the correlation (a measure of relationship) remains virtually unchanged.

It is important to note that the resistance of relational measures to sampling bias is only guaranteed if the sample covers the full range of the related variables, and the bias stems from over- and underrepresentation at different levels. Problems may arise if the relationship is only observed across a limited range of the related variables, and the bias stems from omission of relevant data.

Exhibit 9.1   Effects of Sample Bias on Estimates of Relationships

	Unbiased Sample		Biased via Disproportionate Sampling		Biased via Omission	
	X	Y	X	Y	X	Y
	1	1	1	1	1	1
	1	2	1	2	1	2
	1	3	1	3	1	3
	2	2	2	2	2	2
	2	3	2	3	2	3
	2	4	2	4	2	4
	3	3	3	3		
	3	4	3	4		
	3	5	3	5		
			3	3		
			3	4		
			3	5		
Mean	2.00	3.00	2.25	3.25	1.50	2.50
Correlation	0.71		0.71		0.52	

In this case, the measured relationship may be attenuated by range or biased for local conditions. For example, the right-hand side of Exhibit 9.1 shows the *X* and *Y* distribution biased by omission of the "high *X*" group," and this form of bias is seen to affect the correlation as well as the means. Likewise, a measured relationship may be misleading if the sample is restricted to a limited range on variables that moderate the relationship.

The implication is that measures of relationships should be resistant to sample bias as long as the sample is diverse but not necessarily if the sample is restricted. For purposes of generalization and resistance to sample bias, diversity in the sample is highly desirable. This returns to Kruskal and Mosteller's (1979a, 1979b, 1979c) notion of representativeness as reflecting the full heterogeneity of the population.

Imperfect Samples Are Usable in Academic Research

The generalizability of academic research is fairly robust with respect to variations in sample quality, and academic research can tolerate imperfect samples. Part of this is because academic research tends to study relationships, which are resistant to sampling bias. More important, academic research has three paths to generalization and is not wholly dependent on sample quality for this purpose.

The first and foremost path to generalization in academic research is through theory (*theoretical generalization*). Academic research typically states and tests hypotheses. Like Babe Ruth pointing to the bleachers before he hit a home run, researchers call the relationship before they see it. Therefore, we don't think the relationship is general because we saw it in a good sample, but rather, we thought we would see it in the sample because it is general. To put it another way, the research is confirmatory, not inferential. Any sample will do for this purpose.

The second path to generalization is through sampling or modeling process (*probabilistic or model-based generalization*). As in any research, we feel better about the generalization of academic research if sample quality is good.

The third path to generalization is through replication (*empirical generalization*). In academic research, if a finding is important, other researchers will elaborate on it and try to define moderators, boundary conditions, and so forth. In the process, if the finding is a fluke of the sample or otherwise not robust, it will tend to fall by the wayside.

Given these three paths to generalization, along with the fact that relational results are resistant to sample bias, we can afford to be lenient about sample quality in academic research. In a sense, academics bracket sample quality front and back. They preempt it through theory, and they remediate it through replication.

The Heaviest Burden on Sample Quality

The heaviest burden on a sample comes when the key research objective is to estimate univariate characteristics of a population, such as means or proportions, with some level of precision. This is common in policy research, health research (such as epidemiology studies), political polling, and market research. For example, in a study concerning public health policy, we might wish to estimate the proportion of preschool children who have received certain vaccinations. In a political poll, we might wish to estimate the proportion of voters who support a particular candidate. In a market research study, we might wish to estimate the proportion of potential buyers who have interest in a product and the average amount that they are likely to spend. In these situations, we need specific univariate estimates, and our ability to generalize the result is wholly dependent on the quality of the sample: We can't rely on theory, and we can't rely on replication. Here, it is very important to get a good sample with full and fair coverage of the population.

One major situation where this "heavy burden" applies is in fulfilling the mandate of many large, ongoing government surveys (such as the National Health Interview Survey, National Crime Victimization Survey, National Assessment of Educational Progress, Current Population Survey, etc.) to produce public use files (PUFs) that can be used for other purposes. These data sets are constructed specifically to make the survey data (stripped of individual identifiers) available to academics, businesses, analysts, or government staff for a variety of uses, and high sample quality is needed to accommodate all of those purposes.

General Advice

We close, then, with general advice.

Regardless of the situation, do the best you can, and recognize the limitations of your sample. Use probability sampling to the extent possible; for example, even if the participating schools in an education study are defined by distance and access, it may be possible to randomly select classrooms or students. Try to get variety in the sample; for example, even if an education study must be done within driving distance, try to get more than one school, and try to get a mixture of urban/suburban/rural, upper income/middle income/low income, or whatever seems relevant to the research. Don't just settle for the easy observations; try to get the reluctant participants and, even if time and funds are limited, allocate some of your resources for follow-up. And at the end, know enough to recognize the limitations of the sample. Don't make inferences that go beyond what the sample will bear, and provide enough information about the sample to allow others to interpret the results properly.

While our recommendation is always to use good sampling practice, don't give up if perfection is not possible. Do the best you can, acknowledge the limitations of your sample, and recognize that the sample may be usable even if it is not perfect.

9.3 CHAPTER SUMMARY

The sample report, part of the general methodology report, documents the sample design and procedures so users can replicate the survey or better understand its results. Relevant information includes the following:

- Sample design, with conceptual and operational definitions of the target population and a description of the objectives and features of the sampling method, including any use of stratification or clustering
- Sampling errors for all key variables
- Description of the sampling frame and any known problems
- Response rates, how they were calculated, and any important differences among population subgroups
- Special procedures and follow-ups, including the number of callbacks or follow-ups, how they were scheduled, any special procedures such as refusal conversions or follow-ups of nonrespondents, and the percentage of interviews monitored or verified

The sample report allows us to evaluate the sample, but it leaves open the following question: How good must the sample be?

One way to answer this question is to ask how representative the sample is, considering different notions of representativeness. Kruskal and Mosteller (1979a, 1979b, 1979c, 1980) list four possible meanings of representative sampling: (1) a miniature of the population that reflects all subgroups in proportion; (2) coverage of all population groups, although not necessarily in proportion; (3) good enough for a particular purpose, including biased samples that allow us to reject certain possibilities; and (4) permitting good estimation, including model-based estimates.

It isn't always possible to get as good a sample as one would like because of limits on time, funding, or access. Fortunately, in most situations, samples need not be perfect to be usable. Imperfect samples may be useful for exploration or screening, for testing relationships (which are robust to sample bias as long as the sample covers the full range of the related variables), and for academic research, which has three paths to generalization (theoretical through hypotheses, probabilistic through sampling, and empirical through replication). The heaviest burden on a sample comes when the key research objective is to estimate univariate characteristics of a population, such as means or proportions, with some level of precision. Here, it is very important to get a good sample with full and fair coverage of the population.

Regardless of the situation, do the best you can, and recognize the limitations of your sample. Use probability sampling to the extent possible. Try to get variety in the sample. Don't just settle for the easy observations; try to get the reluctant participants and, even if time and funds are limited, allocate some of your resources for follow-up. At the end, know enough to recognize the limitations of the sample. Don't make inferences that go beyond what the sample will bear, and provide enough information about the sample to allow others to interpret the results properly.

Most important, don't give up if perfection is not possible. Do the best you can, acknowledge the limitations of your sample, and recognize that the sample may be usable even if it is not perfect.

EXERCISES AND DISCUSSION QUESTIONS

Exercise 9.1

Imagine the following situation. A friend of yours is running for a place on the local school board. You agree to help her by surveying local voters to learn which issues are most important to them and what they would like the school board to do. How will you obtain a sample for this survey?

REFERENCES

American Association for Public Opinion Research (AAPOR) Cell Phone Task Force. (2010). *New considerations for survey researchers when planning and conducting RDD telephone surveys in the U.S. with respondents reached via cell phone numbers.* Lenexa, KS: Author.

American Association for Public Opinion Research. (2011). *Standard definitions: Final dispositions of case codes and outcome rates for surveys* (7th ed.). Lenexa, KS: Author.

Baker, R., Blumberg, S. J., Brick, J. M., Couper, M. P., Courtright, M., Dennis, J. M., . . . Zahs, D. (2010). Research synthesis: AAPOR report on online panels. *Public Opinion Quarterly, 74,* 711–781.

Barber, M. J., Mann, C. B., Monson, J. Q., & Patterson, K. D. (2014). Online polls and registration-based sampling: A new method for pre-election polling. *Political Analysis, 22*(3), 321–335.

Battaglia, M., Hoaglin, D., & Frankel, M. (2009). Practical considerations in raking survey data. *Survey Practice, 2*(5).

Bethelhem, J. (2009). *The rise of survey sampling.* The Hague, the Netherlands: Statistics Netherlands.

Blair, E. (1983). Sampling issues in trade area maps drawn from shopper surveys. *Journal of Marketing, 47,* 98–106.

Blair, E., & Blair, J. (2006). Dual frame web-telephone sampling for rare groups. *Journal of Official Statistics, 22*(2), 211–220.

Blair, E., & Zinkhan, G. M. (2006). Nonresponse and generalizability in academic research. *Journal of the Academy of Marketing Science, 34*(1), 4–7.

Blair, J. (1990). Improving data quality in network samples of rare populations. In G. E. Liepins & V. R. Uppuluri (Eds.), *Data quality control.* New York: Marcel Dekker.

Blair, J. (1999). A probability sample of gay urban males: The use of two-phase adaptive sampling. *Journal of Sex Research, 36,* 25–38.

Blair, J., & Czaja, R. (1982). Locating a special population using random digit dialing. *Public Opinion Quarterly, 46,* 585–590.

Blair, J., Czaja, R., & Blair, E. (2013). *Designing surveys* (3rd ed.). Los Angeles, CA: Sage.

Blumberg, S. J., & Luke, J. V. (2012). *Wireless substitution: Early release of estimates from the National Health Interview Survey, January–June 2012.* Atlanta, GA: Centers for

Disease Control and Prevention. http://www.cdc.gov/nchs/data/nhis/earlyrelease/wireless201212.PDF

Boyle, J., Fleeman, A., Kennedy, C., Lewis, F., & Weiss, A. (2012). Sampling cell phone only households: A comparison of demographic and behavioral characteristics from ABS and cell phone samples. *Survey Practice*, *5*(1).

Brewer, K. R. W. (1999). Design-based or prediction-based inference? Stratified random vs. stratified balanced sampling. *International Statistical Review*, *67*, 35–47.

Brick, J. M. (2011). The future of survey sampling. *Public Opinion Quarterly*, *75*(5), 872–888.

Brick, J. M., Andrews, W., Brick, P., King, H., Mathiowetz, N., & Stokes, L. (2012). Methods for improving response rates in two-phase mail surveys. *Survey Practice*, *5*. http://surveypractice.org/index.php/SurveyPractice/article/view/17

Chowdhury, S., Khare, M., & Wolter, K. (2007). *Weight trimming in the National Immunization Survey (NIS)*. Alexandria, VA: American Statistical Association.

Cillizza, C. (2014). *The New York Times rocked the polling world over the weekend: Here's why*. http://www.washingtonpost.com/blogs/the-fix/wp/2014/07/31/the-new-york-times-rocked-the-polling-world-over-the-weekend-heres-why

Cohn, N. (2014). *Explaining online panels and the 2014 midterms*. http://www.nytimes.com/2014/07/28/upshot/explaining-online-panels-and-the-2014-midterms.html?_r=0

Conrad, F. G., & Schober, M. F. (Eds.). (2008). *Envisioning the survey interview of the future*. New York: Wiley-Interscience.

Council of American Survey Research Organizations. (1982). *On the definition of response rates: A special report of the CASRO task force on completion rates*. Port Jefferson, NY: Author.

Couper, M. (2000). Web surveys: A review of issues and approaches. *Public Opinion Quarterly*, *64*(4), 464–494.

Couper, M. P., Peytchev, A., Strecher, V. J., Rothert, K., & Anderson, J. (2007). Following up nonrespondents to an online weight management intervention: Randomized trial comparing mail versus telephone. *Journal of Medical Internet Research*, *9*(2), e16.

Eckman, S., & O'Muircheartaigh, C. (2011). The performance of the half-open interval missed housing unit procedure. *Survey Research Methods*, *5*(3), 125–131.

Elliott, M. R. (2008). Model averaging methods for weight trimming. *Journal of Official Statistics*, *24*(4), 517–540.

Ericson, W. A. (1965). Optimum stratified sampling using prior information. *Journal of the American Statistical Association*, *60*, 750–777.

Gile, K. J., & Handcock, M. S. (2010). Modeling social networks from sampled data. *Annals of Applied Statistics*, *4*(1), 5–25.

Goodnough, A. (2002, May 2). Post 9/11 pain found to linger in young minds. *New York Times*, p. A1.

Green, D. P., & Gerber, A. S. (2006). Can registration-based sampling improve the accuracy of midterm election forecasts? *Public Opinion Quarterly*, *70*(2), 197–223.

Groves, R., & Couper, M. (1998). *Nonresponse in household interview surveys*. New York: John Wiley.

Guterbock, T., Diop, A., Ellis, J., Le, T. K., & Holmes, J. L. (2008, May). *Who needs RDD? Combining directory listings with cellphone exchanges for an alternative telephone sampling frame*. Paper presented at the AAPOR Conference, New Orleans, LA.

Hansen, M. H., Dalenius, T., & Tepping, B. J. (1985). The development of sample surveys in finite populations. In A. C. Atkinson & S. E. Feinberg (Eds.), *A celebration of statistics* (pp. 326–354). New York: Springer Verlag.

Hansen, M. H., Hurwitz, W. N., & Madow, W. G. (1953). *Survey sample methods and theory* (2 vols.). New York: John Wiley.

Heckathorn, D. (1997). Respondent driven sampling: A new approach to the study of hidden populations. *Social Problems, 44*(2), 174–199.

Hidiroglou, M. A., Drew, J. D., & Gray, G. B. (1993). A framework for measuring and reducing nonresponse in surveys. *Survey Methodology, 19*(1), 81–94.

Iannacchione, V. G. (2011). The changing role of address-based sampling in survey research. *Public Opinion Quarterly, 75*(3), 556–575.

Jewish Daily Forward. (2013, February 8). http://forward.com/articles/170248/how-we-got-it-wrong

Jordan, M. (2004, October 11). Nielsen's search for Hispanics is a delicate job. *Wall Street Journal,* pp. B1–B6.

Kalton, G. (1983). Models in the practice of survey sampling. *International Statistical Review, 51,* 175–188.

Kalton, G. (2001). *Practical methods for sampling rare and mobile populations*. Alexandria, VA: American Statistical Association.

Kalton, G. (2002). Models in the practice of survey sampling revisited. *Journal of Official Statistics, 18*(2), 129–154.

Kish, L. (1949). A procedure for objective respondent selection within the household. *Journal of the American Statistical Association, 44*(247), 380–387.

Kish, L. (1965). *Survey sampling*. New York: John Wiley.

Kish, L. (1987). *Statistical design for research*. New York: John Wiley.

Knaub, J. R., Jr. (2008, June). *Cutoff vs. design-based sampling and inference for establishment surveys*. InterStat. http://interstat.statjournals.net/YEAR/2008/abstracts/0806005.php?Name=806005

Kruskal, W., & Mosteller, F. (1979a). Representative sampling I: Nonscientific literature. *International Statistical Review, 47,* 13–24.

Kruskal, W., & Mosteller, F. (1979b). Representative sampling II: Scientific literature, excluding statistics. *International Statistical Review, 47,* 111–127.

Kruskal, W., & Mosteller, F. (1979c). Representative sampling III: The current statistical literature. *International Statistical Review, 47,* 245–265.

Kruskal, W., & Mosteller, F. (1980). Representative sampling IV: The history of the concept in statistics 1895–1939. *International Statistical Review, 48,* 169–195.

Lavrakas, P. J., Bauman, S. L., & Merkle, D. M. (1993). *The last birthday method: Within unit coverage problems.* Alexandria, VA: American Statistical Association.

Lavrakas, P., Stasny, E., & Harpruder, B. (2000). *A further investigation of the last-birthday respondent selection method and within unit coverage.* Alexandria, VA: American Statistical Association.

Lee, D. S. (2009). Training, wages, and sample selection: Estimating sharp bounds on treatment effects. *Review of Economic Studies, 76,* 1071–1102.

Levy, P. (1977). Optimum allocation in stratified random network sampling for estimating the prevalence of attributes in rare populations. *Journal of the American Statistical Association, 72,* 758–763.

Lind, K., Link, M., & Oldendick, R. (2000). *A comparison of the accuracy of the last birthday versus the next birthday methods for random selection of household respondents.* Alexandria, VA: American Statistical Association.

Michael, R. T., & O'Muircheartaigh, C. A. (2008). Design priorities and disciplinary perspectives: The case of the U.S. National Children's Study. *Journal of the Royal Statistical Society, Series A, 171*(Pt. 2), 465–480.

Mitofsky, W., Bloom, J., Lenski, J., Dingman, S., & Agiesta, J. (2005, May). *A test of a combined RDD/registration-based sampling model in Oregon's 2004 national election pool survey: lessons from a dual frame RBS/RDD sample.* Paper presented at the Annual Conference of the American Association for Public Opinion Research, Miami Beach, FL.

Neyman, J. (1934). On the two different aspects of the representative method: The method of stratified sampling and the method of purposive selection. *Journal of the Royal Statistical Society, 97*(4), 558–625.

Nowell, C., & Stanley, L. R. (1991). Length-biased sampling in mall intercept surveys. *Journal of Marketing Research, 28,* 475–479.

O'Muircheartaigh, C. (2005). *Balancing statistical theory, sampling concepts, and practicality in the teaching of survey sampling.* The Hague, the Netherlands: International Statistical Institute. http://isi.cbs.nl/iamamember/CD6-Sydney2005/ISI2005_Papers/1456.pdf

O'Rourke, D., & Blair, J. (1983). Improving random respondent selection in telephone surveys. *Journal of Marketing Research, 20,* 428–432.

Peytchev, A., & Hill, C. A. (2011). Experiments in mobile web survey design: Similarities to other methods and unique considerations. *Social Science Computer Review, 28*(3), 319–335.

Politz, A., & Simmons, W. (1949). An attempt to get the not-at-homes into the sample without callbacks. *Journal of the American Statistical Association, 44,* 9–31.

Rizzo, L., Brick, J. M., & Park, I. (2004). A minimally intrusive method for sampling persons in random digit dial surveys. *Public Opinion Quarterly, 68*(2), 267–274.

Roth, S., Han, B. D., & Montaquila, J. M. (2013). The ABS frame: Quality and considerations. *Survey Practice, 6*(4).

Sarndal, C.-E., Swensson, B., & Wretman, J. (1992). *Model-assisted survey sampling.* Berlin, Germany: Springer-Verlag.

Schlaifer, R. (1959). *Probability and statistics for business decisions.* New York: McGraw-Hill.

Shook-Sa, B. E. (2013). Extending the coverage of address-based sampling frames beyond the USPS computerized delivery sequence file. *Public Opinion Quarterly, 77*(4), 994–1005.

Sirken, M. (1970). Household surveys with multiplicity. *Journal of the American Statistical Association, 65*(329), 257.

Sirken, M. (1972). Stratified sample surveys with multiplicity. *Journal of the American Statistical Association, 67*(337), 224.

Sirken, M., & Levy, P. (1974). Multiplicity estimation of proportions based on ratios of random variables. *Journal of the American Statistical Association, 69*(345), 68.

Smith, T. (2011). *The general social survey.* Ann Arbor: Institute for Social Research, University of Michigan.

Sudman, S. (1967). *Reducing the cost of surveys.* Chicago: Aldine.

Sudman, S. (1976). *Applied sampling.* New York: Academic Press.

Sudman, S. (1980). Improving the quality of shopping center sampling. *Journal of Marketing Research, 17,* 423–431.

Sudman, S. (1985). Efficient screening methods for the sampling of geographically clustered special populations. *Journal of Marketing Research, 22*(1), 20–29.

Sudman, S., & Blair, E. (1998). *Marketing research: A problem solving approach.* New York: McGraw-Hill.

Sudman, S., & Blair, E. (1999). Sampling in the twenty-first century. *Journal of the Academy of Marketing Science, 27,* 269–277.

Sudman, S., Sirken, M., & Cowan, C. (1988). Sampling rare and elusive populations. *Science, 240,* 991–996.

Sudman, S., & Wansink, B. (2002). *Consumer panels* (2nd ed.). Mason, OH: South-Western Educational Publishing.

Tessitore, E., & Macri, C. (2011, February). *Facebook sampling methods: Some methodological proposals.* Paper presented at NTTS: New Techniques and Technologies for Statistics, Brussels, Belgium.

Troldahl, V. C., & Carter, R. E., Jr. (1964). Random selection of respondents within households in phone surveys. *Journal of Marketing Research, 1*(2), 71–76.

U.S. Catholics in poll see a church out of touch. (2013, March 5). *New York Times,* p. 1.

U.S. Census Bureau. (2012). *Statistical abstract, Table 73: Group quarters population by type of group quarter and selected characteristics: 2009.* Washington, DC: Government Printing Office.

Waksberg, J. (1978). Sampling methods for random digit dialing. *Journal of the American Statistical Association, 73*(361), 40–46.

Waksberg, J. (1983). A note on "Locating a special population using random digit dialing." *Public Opinion Quarterly, 47,* 576–578.

AUTHOR INDEX

SUBJECT INDEX

Address-based sampling (ABS), 47–48, 52, 209
   See also In-home surveys; Mail surveys;
      Omitted population elements;
      Registration-based sampling (RBS)
American Association for Public Opinion
    Research (AAPOR), 46, 47, 86, 175
Area probability sampling, 6
   cost of, 6, 8
   in-home interviewing and, 7, 8
   shift to, 6–7
   See also Sampling
Availability bias, 78–79, 80, 161

Back-end weighting, 205
Bias:
   availability bias and, 78–79, 80, 161
   coverage bias and, 10, 19, 20, 23 (exhibit),
      36, 49, 52
   nonprobability samples and, 18
   nonresponse bias and, 10, 19, 20–21,
      23 (exhibit), 47
   population coverage, maximization of, 10
   probability samples and, 18–19
   resource availability and, 10
   sample size and, 10–11
   sampling bias, research error and,
      9–10, 20, 23 (exhibit), 54
   selection bias and, 10, 18–19, 20,
      23 (exhibit)
   telephone surveys and, 7
   See also Error; Nonresponse bias
Big data, 208
   address-based sampling and, 209
   complement to surveys and, 208–209, 211
   cost-effectiveness of, 210
   data first approach and, 210

   duplicate population listing and, 210, 211
   government databases and, 209
   inclusion probabilities and, 210
   nonresponse bias and, 209, 211
   omitted population elements and, 210
   populations of interest and, 211
   replacement for surveys and, 209–211
   statistical significance, implicit
      patterns and, 211
   surveys as complement to, 211
   traditional survey design approach
      and, 210
Bootstrapping procedure, 174–175, 177

Cell Phone Task Force, 46
Cellphone survey methods,
    45–47, 46 (exhibit), 212
Census, 5, 8
Chain referral sampling, 194, 195
Cloud computing, 212
Cluster sampling, 11, 12, 113, 129, 130 (exhibit)
   applications of, 129–133, 133 (exhibit)
   cluster configurations/populations and,
      142–144, 143 (table)
   clustering units and, 136
   cost-effectiveness of, 129, 131, 132, 141, 153
   cost/sampling variance, trade-off between
      and, 138–139, 139 (table), 154
   design effect/deff and, 136–137, 139 (table),
      153–154
   equal probability sampling and,
      144–145, 146, 147, 148
   fixed costs and, 132, 138, 140
   household clusters and, 141–142, 212
   implicit stratification and,
      149, 152 (exhibit), 152

⑤SAGE research**methods**

The essential online tool for researchers from the world's leading methods publisher

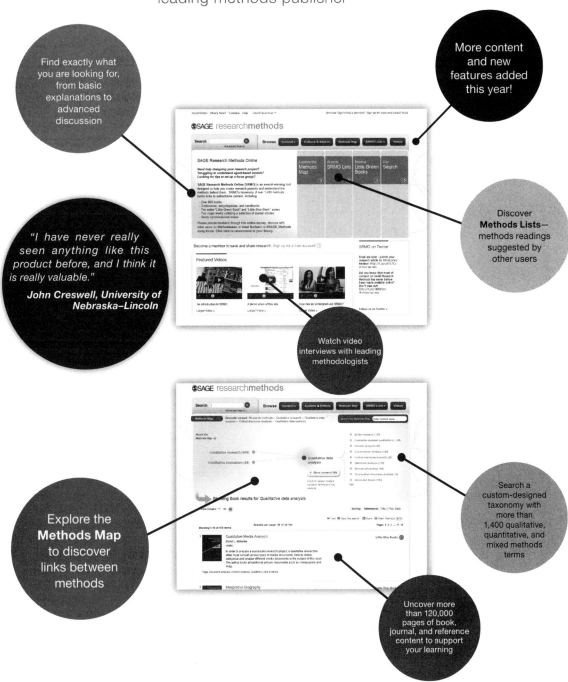

Find exactly what you are looking for, from basic explanations to advanced discussion

More content and new features added this year!

"I have never really seen anything like this product before, and I think it is really valuable."

John Creswell, University of Nebraska–Lincoln

Discover **Methods Lists—** methods readings suggested by other users

Watch video interviews with leading methodologists

Explore the **Methods Map** to discover links between methods

Search a custom-designed taxonomy with more than 1,400 qualitative, quantitative, and mixed methods terms

Uncover more than 120,000 pages of book, journal, and reference content to support your learning

Find out more at
www.sageresearchmethods.com